Under God?
Religious Faith and Liberal Democracy

The proper role of religious faith in the public life of a liberal democracy is one of the most important and controversial issues in the United States today. In this new book, Michael J. Perry argues that political reliance on religious faith violates neither the Establishment Clause of the United States Constitution nor, more broadly, the morality of liberal democracy. Nonetheless, Perry argues, religious believers sometimes have good reasons to be wary about relying on religious beliefs in making political decisions. Along the way, Perry thoughtfully addresses three subjects at the center of fierce contemporary political debate: school vouchers, same-sex marriage, and abortion.

Michael J. Perry has held the University Distinguished Chair in Law at Wake Forest University since 1997. Before that, he held the Howard J. Trienens Chair in Law at Northwestern University, where he taught for fifteen years. Perry is the author of eight books, including *Love and Power: The Role of Religion and Morality in American Politics* (1991) and *The Idea of Human Rights: Four Inquiries* (1998).

For Dean Robert K. Walsh and the faculty
of the Wake Forest University School of Law,
where, from 1997 to 2003, I was privileged to teach.

And for Errol Rohr,
dear friend and brother,
godfather to my children.

Under God?
Religious Faith and Liberal Democracy

MICHAEL J. PERRY
Wake Forest University
School of Law

CAMBRIDGE
UNIVERSITY PRESS

PUBLISHED BY THE PRESS SYNDICATE OF THE UNIVERSITY OF CAMBRIDGE
The Pitt Building, Trumpington Street, Cambridge, United Kingdom

CAMBRIDGE UNIVERSITY PRESS
The Edinburgh Building, Cambridge CB2 2RU, UK
40 West 20th Street, New York, NY 10011-4211, USA
477 Williamstown Road, Port Melbourne, VIC 3207, Australia
Ruiz de Alarcón 13, 28014 Madrid, Spain
Dock House, The Waterfront, Cape Town 8001, South Africa

http: // www.cambridge.org

First published 2003

Printed in the United States of America

Typeface New Baskerville 10.5/13 pt.   *System* LATEX 2ε   [TB]

A catalog record for this book is available from the British Library.

Library of Congress Cataloging in Publication data
Perry, Michael J.
Under God? : religious faith and liberal democracy / Michael J. Perry.
p.   cm.
Includes bibliographical references and index.
ISBN 0-521-82539-3 – ISBN 0-521-53217-5 (pb.)
1. Religion and politics – United States.   2. Church and state – United States.
3. United States – Religion.   I. Title.
BL2525 .P467   2003
322'.1'0973 – dc21   2002034810

ISBN 0 521 82539 3 hardback
ISBN 0 521 53217 5 paperback

Contents

Introduction
The Controversy over Religion in Politics

As politically alert Americans are well aware, the proper role of religious faith in the public life of the nation is one of the most controversial issues in the United States today. The controversy erupted
anew when, on August 27, 2000, Senator Joseph Lieberman of
Connecticut – at the time, the Democratic candidate for vice president of the United States – addressed the congregation of the Fellowship Chapel, one of Detroit's largest African-American churches. In
his speech, Senator Lieberman called for a larger role for religious
faith in American politics. "As a people," said Lieberman, "we need
to reaffirm our faith and renew the dedication of our nation and ourselves to God and God's purpose." The next day, on the front page,
under the headline "Lieberman Seeks Greater Role for Religion in
Public Life," the *New York Times* reported that Lieberman "bluntly
made the case for allowing faith into politics." The *Times* then quoted
some key passages from Senator Lieberman's speech:

"I want to talk to you this morning about another barrier that may fall ... as a
result of my nomination," he said. "I hope it will enable people, all people who
are moved, to feel more free to talk about their faith and about their religion.
And I hope that it will reinforce the belief that I feel as strongly as anything else,
that there must be a place for faith in America's public life." He added that "we
know that the Constitution wisely separates church from state, but remember:
the Constitution guarantees freedom *of* religion, not freedom *from* religion."
Without biblical traditions from the Ten Commandments to "the compassion
and love and inspiration of Jesus of Nazareth," he said, "it could never have
been written, and wouldn't have been written, in our Declaration of Independence, 'We hold these truths to be self-evident, that all men are created
equal.' "[1]

Senator Lieberman, as is well known, is an Orthodox Jew, but
many Christians applauded what Lieberman said. Indeed, Lieberman
had an ally in no less a Christian than the Roman Catholic pontiff,

vii

John Paul II. Almost three years before Lieberman addressed the congregation of the Fellowship Chapel, John Paul II had spoken in much the same spirit, and said much the same thing, on the occasion of the presentation by Lindy Boggs of her credentials as U.S. ambassador to the Vatican:[2]

> It would truly be a sad thing if the religious and moral convictions upon which the American experiment was founded could now somehow be considered a danger to free society, such that those who would bring these convictions to bear upon your nation's public life would be denied a voice in debating and resolving issues of public policy. The original separation of church and state in the United States was certainly not an effort to ban all religious conviction from the public sphere, a kind of banishment of God from civil society. Indeed, the vast majority of Americans, regardless of their religious persuasion, are convinced that religious conviction and religiously informed moral argument have a vital role in public life.[3]

Reaction to Lieberman's speech was swift and, from some quarters, harsh. Perhaps the most noteworthy criticism – most noteworthy because of who said it – came from the Anti-Defamation League, which in its own description is "the world's largest organization fighting anti-Semitism through programs and services that counteract hatred, prejudice and bigotry." In a letter dated August 28, 2000, the ADL national chairman, Howard P. Berkowitz, and the group's national director, Abraham H. Foxman, asked Senator Lieberman, the first Jew nominated for national office by a major political party, "to refrain from overt expressions of religious values and beliefs." Berkowitz and Foxman stated:

> Candidates should feel comfortable explaining their religious convictions to voters. At the same time, however, we believe there is a point at which an emphasis on religion in a political campaign becomes inappropriate and even unsettling in a religiously diverse society such as ours. . . . Language such as [that which you used yesterday in speaking to the congregation of the Fellowship Chapel] risks alienating the American people. . . . We feel very strongly, and we hope you would agree, that appealing to voters along religious lines . . . is contrary to the American ideal.[4]

For a few weeks after Senator Lieberman's speech, many editorial writers, op-ed columnists, and political pundits weighed in on the issue.[5] The commentary, however, was generally predictable and uninspired. The furor soon died down; as the presidential election neared, other issues, issues of more immediate practical concern – such as health care for poor children and prescription drug benefits for the elderly – understandably dominated political debate.[6] But it wasn't long before the controversy over religion in politics erupted again: Soon after moving into the White House, George Bush proposed (as during the campaign he had promised he would) that the federal government spend money to support the efforts of nongovernmental organizations, even those that are "faith-based," to ameliorate various pressing social problems, such as poverty, homelessness, drug abuse, and unemployment. Bush's proposal ignited a firestorm of controversy, with many critics insisting that government aid to faith-based social service providers would violate the constitutionally mandated separation of church and state.

Because the proper role of religion in politics is a complex issue, one cannot adequately address it without carefully disentangling, and addressing, all the various questions that the issue comprises. Such an effort, which I undertake in this book, is well beyond the scope of an editorial or op-ed piece, much less a sound bite or bumper sticker. Although I am principally concerned in this book with religion in the politics of the United States, much of what I say here is applicable to other, kindred liberal democracies.

The questions I address in this book have engaged me since the mid-1980s; I have addressed many of them before, principally in two books: *Love and Power: The Role of Religion and Morality in American Politics* (1991) and *Religion in Politics: Constitutional and Moral Perspectives* (1997). I revisit the questions here, because my views have continued to develop and even, in some important respects, to change. Although some of what I say in this book is continuous with, and amplifies, my previous writings on religion in politics, much of what I say here represents a break, sometimes a sharp break, with my previous work.

By way of introduction, and to provide the reader with an overview, I want to sketch the agenda of each of the six chapters in this book. (In doing so, I oversimplify a bit; I must defer a more precise delineation of the several issues and various positions to the chapters that follow.) Let me begin by dividing those to whom my arguments in this book are addressed into three groups. The *agnostics* are those who have no firm convictions about the proper role of religion in politics. (That one is agnostic about the proper role of religion in politics does not entail that one is an agnostic in the more conventional sense of the term – that is, agnostic about the existence of God. One can be agnostic about the proper role of religion in politics without being agnostic about the existence of God, just as one can be agnostic about the existence of God without being agnostic about the proper role of religion in politics.) The *inclusionists* and the *exclusionists*, by contrast, do have firm convictions about the proper role of religion in politics. While the inclusionists believe that religious faith may be included in the public life of the nation, the exclusionists believe that religious faith should be excluded, as much as possible, from it. The inclusionists affirm, and the exclusionists deny, that religion may play a significant role in politics. It bears emphasis that the distinction between inclusionists and exclusionists does not track the distinction between religious believers and religious nonbelievers: Although some religious believers are inclusionists, some others are exclusionists; and although some religious nonbelievers are exclusionists, some others are inclusionists.

While I hope that the arguments I make in every chapter of this book will be of interest to all three groups, my arguments in Part One – Chapters 1–3 – are addressed mainly to the agnostics and the exclusionists. I begin, in Chapter 1, by articulating a general understanding of what it means to say, as American constitutional law does, that government may not "establish" religion – a general understanding, that is, of what the "nonestablishment norm" (as I prefer to call it) does and does not forbid government to do. I then turn to the question of whether the nonestablishment norm leaves any room for government to spend money in support of religiously affiliated schools. Government aid to religiously affiliated schools, in the form of vouchers that parents may use to make tuition payments to such schools, is a flash point in contemporary American politics. In my judgment, the nonestablishment norm *does* leave room for government to spend money in support of religiously affiliated schools. Moreover, although I focus, in Chapter 1, on government aid to religiously affiliated schools (in the form of vouchers), the logic of my argument extends to government aid to "faith-based" social service providers. Such aid is another flash point in contemporary American politics. The argument I make in Chapter 1, in support of the proposition that government does not *necessarily* violate the nonestablishment norm by including religiously affiliated schools in a program of aid to nonpublic schools, also supports the further proposition that government does not necessarily violate the norm by including faith-based social service providers in a program of aid to nongovernmental social service providers.

In Chapter 2, I address a second large question about the meaning of the imperative that government not "establish" religion: Does government violate the nonestablishment norm by outlawing conduct, or otherwise disfavoring it, on the basis of a religiously grounded belief that the conduct is immoral – a religiously grounded belief, for example, that same-sex unions are immoral? This question is obviously relevant to citizens of the United States, because the nonestablishment norm is an important part of the fundamental law – the constitutional law – of the United States. In Chapter 3, I move beyond the nonestablishment norm to address a question that, though closely related to the question I address in Chapter 2, is relevant not just to citizens of the United States but to those of any liberal democracy, even one whose fundamental law does not forbid government to establish religion: Does government contravene the morality of liberal democracy by outlawing (or otherwise disfavoring) conduct on the basis of religiously grounded moral belief? Even if government does not violate the nonestablishment norm by outlawing conduct on the basis of religiously grounded moral belief, it may nonetheless be the case that government betrays the morality of liberal democracy by doing so. I conclude in Chapters 2 and 3, however, that by outlawing conduct on the basis of religiously grounded moral belief, government runs afoul *neither* of the nonestablishment norm *nor* even of the morality of liberal democracy. (In Chapter 2, I clarify what I mean by a "religiously grounded" moral belief and by making a political choice "on the basis of" a belief.)

I said that my arguments in Part One are addressed mainly to the agnostics and the exclusionists. In Part Two – Chapters 4–6 – my arguments are addressed mainly to the agnostics and the inclusionists; they are addressed especially to those who, because they are both inclusionists and religious believers, are not at all shy about bringing their religion to bear on their politics. Although I defended an exclusionist position in my two previous books on religion in politics,[7] in this book – in particular, in Chapters 2 and 3 – I defend an inclusionist position. Perhaps I am better situated than many who have always been exclusionists or inclusionists to understand sympathetically – from the inside, as it were – the concerns of *both* sides. Whereas in

Part One I speak as an inclusionist to agnostics and exclusionists, in Part Two I speak to agnostics and inclusionists from the perspective of one who, though no longer an exclusionist, nonetheless shares some exclusionist concerns.

In Chapter 4, I argue that some religious believers – Christians – have good reason to be wary about relying on one kind of religiously grounded morality – biblically grounded morality – in deciding whether to oppose laws or other public policies that grant official recognition to same-sex unions. In Chapter 4, I speak (mainly) to Christians generally, and I speak to them about the Bible, which is authoritative for Christians generally; in Chapter 5, by contrast, I speak (mainly) to Roman Catholics, and I speak to them about the magisterium of the Roman Catholic Church, which is authoritative for Roman Catholics. It is sometimes observed that for Roman Catholics, it is not the Bible that is supremely authoritative but the "magisterium" of the Church: the bishops and, ultimately, the Pope.[8] (It would be misleading to reply that for Roman Catholics, as for other Christians, the Bible is supremely authoritative, because is it the Bible *as interpreted by the magisterium of the Church* that is authoritative for Roman Catholics.) Whereas in Chapter 4, I contend against uncritical political reliance on what one imagines the Bible to say about the morality of same-sex unions, in Chapter 5, I contend against uncritical political reliance on what the magisterium of the Church says about the morality of same-sex unions; in particular, I argue that Catholic citizens and legislators have good reason to make independent judgments about some moral controversies – including the controversy over the morality of same-sex unions – rather than simply yield to whatever happens to be the official position of the magisterium on the contested matter. I have chosen to address, among all Christians, Roman Catholics in particular, because Roman Catholicism, which is the religious tradition that has been formative for me, is such a formidable presence in American politics. There are now more than sixty-two million Catholics in the United States; in the context of American politics, "moral arguments within Catholicism about [homosexuality] will be very significant."[9]

For many religious believers and others, the contemporary American debate about religion in politics is animated and shaped, in part, by two large controversies that are at once moral and political in character: the controversies over same-sex unions and abortion.

Addressing the issue of religion in politics without addressing those two controversies would be like staging *Hamlet* without the prince. As I've just indicated, in Chapter 4 I discuss same-sex unions as a political issue for Christians, and in Chapter 5 I use the controversy over the morality of same-sex unions to frame my argument about the responsibility of Catholic citizens and legislators. In Chapter 6, still speaking mainly to religious believers who hold (as I do) that political reliance on religiously grounded morality is neither illegitimate in a liberal democracy nor unconstitutional in the United States, I turn to the moral/political controversy that, in the last generation, has been the most difficult and divisive of all: abortion. Indeed, "many consider [abortion] to be the most divisive American issue since slavery...."[10] To an even greater extent than the controversy over same-sex unions, the abortion controversy looms large in the background, it looms large as a subtext, of the debate about the proper role of religion in the politics of the United States. More than any other American political controversy in the second half of the twentieth century, the abortion controversy has been a principal, if sometimes unspoken, occasion of the debate about religion in politics.[11] My overarching aim in Chapter 6 is to address the abortion controversy in a way that is true to each of two propositions. The first proposition, which I defend in Chapters 2 and 3, is that a citizen's religious faith has a legitimate, important role to play in her politics. The second proposition, which is at least as well illustrated by the moral/political controversy over abortion as by any other such controversy in our time, is that "political issues deal with complex problems of justice, every solution for which contains morally ambiguous elements."[12]

That neither the American constitutional ideal of nonestablishment nor the morality of liberal democracy calls for marginalizing the role of religious faith in, much less excluding it from, American politics does not mean that religious participation in politics is unproblematic. To bring one's religion to bear as one participates in politics – to rely on religiously grounded moral belief in the course of deliberating about or making political choices – is not necessarily to do so in an appropriate way. In my brief conclusion to this book, I point to the challenge of relating religion to politics in an appropriate way, given that the United States may now be the most religiously diverse nation on earth.[13]

Introduction

ACKNOWLEDGMENTS

For helpful comments on one or more chapters in this book, I am grateful to many friends, colleagues, and students, too numerous to mention. I owe a special debt of gratitude, for extensive, helpful comments and discussions, to Chris Eberle and Steve Smith. Eberle's book, *Religious Conviction in Liberal Politics* (Cambridge University Press, 2002), is a superb contribution to the discourse about religion in politics.

Although I have from the beginning conceived of the chapters in this book as intimately related parts of a single, overarching inquiry, each chapter, in an earlier version, has been published separately over the past two years. Chapter 1 (in an earlier version) was my contribution to a conference, on the moral and legal aspects of the "school choice" controversy, sponsored by and held at the Boston College Center for Religion and American Public Life on March 9–10, 2001. Chapter 1 also served as the basis of a lecture I was privileged to deliver – the Roger Aaron Lecture – at the Rockefeller Center of Dartmouth College on April 30, 2001. An earlier version of Chapter 1 was published in the book that grew out of the Boston College conference: Alan Wolfe, ed., *School Choice: The Moral Debate* (2003). I am grateful to Princeton University Press for permission to republish here material that appeared in that earlier version.

Chapter 2 was my contribution to the conference on Religion in the Public Square at the Marshall-Wythe School of Law, College of William and Mary, on March 24, 2000, and was published (in an earlier version) at 42 William & Mary Law Review 663 (2001). I was honored to present Chapter 2 in three venues in addition to the William and Mary conference: on March 1, 2000, as the Calvin W. Corman Lecture at the Rutgers University (Camden) School of Law; on March 2, 2000, as a lecture at Lafayette College (Easton, Pennsylvania); and on November 3, 2000, as an address to the conference on Law, Religion, and the Public Good at the St. John's University School of Law.

Chapter 3 was one of my two contributions to the symposium on Religiously Grounded Morality: Its Proper Role in American Law and Public Policy? at the Wake Forest University School of Law on October 20–21, 2000, and was published (in an earlier version) at 36 Wake Forest Law Review 217 (2001). I am grateful to the *DePaul Law Review* and to Oxford University Press for permission to use here material that originally appeared elsewhere: Michael J. Perry, "Liberal Democracy and Religious Morality," 48 DePaul L. Rev. 1 (1998) (the 1998 Church/State Lecture, Center for Church/State Studies, DePaul University); and Michael J. Perry, *Religion in Politics: Constitutional and Moral Perspectives* (1997).

Chapter 4 was the second of my two contributions to the symposium on Religiously Grounded Morality: Its Proper Role in American Law and Public Policy? at the Wake Forest University School of Law on October 20–21, 2000, and was published (in an earlier version) at 36 Wake Forest Law Review 449 (2001). Chapter 4 was also published (in a still earlier version) in a collection of essays: R. Bruce Douglass and Joshua Mitchell, eds., *A Nation Under God? Essays on the Fate of Religion in American Public Life* (2000). I am grateful to Rowman and Littlefield for permission to republish here material that appeared in *A Nation Under God?*

Chapter 5 was the basis of a lecture I was privileged to deliver at the University of Dayton School of Law on February 8, 2001, and was published (in an earlier version) at 26 University of Dayton Law Review 293 (2001). Chapter 5 was also published (in a still earlier version) elsewhere: Michael J. Perry, "American Catholics and American Politics," 55 CTSA Proceedings 55 (2000). I am grateful to the Catholic Theological Society of America for permission to republish here material that appeared in "American Catholics and American Politics."

Chapter 6 was the basis of a lecture I was privileged to deliver – the Philip J. McElroy Lecture – at the University of Detroit Mercy School of Law on April 5, 2001, and was published (in an earlier version) at 79 University of Detroit Mercy Law Review 1 (2001).

Part I

Mainly for the Agnostics
and the Exclusionists

What Does the Establishment Clause Forbid?

Reflections on the Constitutionality of School Vouchers

INTRODUCTION

[This chapter was completed before the Supreme Court, on June 27, 2002, decided the Cleveland school voucher case: *Zelman v. Simmons-Harris*.[1] The Court ruled, by a vote of five to four, that the Cleveland school voucher program does not violate the Establishment Clause of the United States Constitution. As one can infer from my argument in this chapter, I think that the Court's ruling was correct.[2]]

Both during his campaign for the presidency of the United States and after moving into the White House, George Bush made two proposals that fanned the flames of the ongoing controversy over the proper role of religion in the nation's public life. Expressing alarm at the persistently sorry state of many of the nation's public elementary and secondary schools, Bush proposed a program of school vouchers in which even religiously affiliated schools would be eligible to participate.[3] More famously, he proposed making it easier for "faith-based" social service providers[4] to gain access to federal financial support.[5] In response to Bush's (and similar) proposals, many have insisted, and many others have denied, that government aid to religiously affiliated entities, such as elementary and secondary schools and social service providers, would violate the constitutionally mandated separation of church and state. In this chapter, I inquire whether the constitutional imperative that government not "establish" religion leaves any room for government to spend money in support of religiously affiliated schools. I begin by elaborating a general understanding of what the Establishment Clause – or, as I prefer to call it, the "nonestablishment norm" – does and does not forbid government to do.

I focus in this chapter on just one sort of government aid to religiously affiliated schools: school vouchers. However, the logic of my argument in this chapter extends beyond school vouchers to other forms of government aid to religiously affiliated schools; indeed, it extends even to government aid to faith-based social service providers. There is, in my judgment, no constitutionally relevant distinction – no distinction relevant to the nonestablishment norm – between school vouchers and other forms of government aid to religiously affiliated schools; nor is there any constitutionally relevant distinction between government aid to religiously affiliated schools and government aid to faith-based social service providers. If, as I argue here, including religiously affiliated schools in a program of school vouchers does not necessarily violate the nonestablishment norm, then, by a parity of reasoning, including them in other programs of government aid to nonpublic elementary and secondary schools does not necessarily violate the nonestablishment norm; and if including religiously affiliated schools in programs of government aid to nonpublic schools does not necessarily violate the nonestablishment norm, then including faith-based social service providers in programs of government aid to nongovernmental social service providers does not necessarily violate the nonestablishment norm. Of course, the reader must decide for herself whether the logic of my argument about the constitutionality of school vouchers extends as far as I claim; she must also decide whether, even if the logic of my argument does extend as far as I claim, the argument is persuasive.

A word of caution may be useful. I address, in this chapter, the question of the constitutionality of school vouchers – and, by implication, the constitutionality both of other forms of government aid to religiously affiliated schools and of government aid to faith-based social service providers. I do *not* address the different question of whether, as a matter of sound public policy, government should adopt a program of school vouchers; nor do I address, even by implication, the question of whether government should adopt any other program of aid to religiously affiliated schools or any program of aid to faith-based social service providers. Because proposals to adopt such programs have been so controversial, it bears emphasis, here at the outset, that the fact that a government program may be, all things considered, bad public policy does not entail that the program is unconstitutional, any more than the fact that the program is a good idea entails that the program is constitutional. Nor does the fact that a government program is constitutional entail that the program is, all things considered, good public policy, any more than the fact that the program is unconstitutional entails that the program is otherwise bad public policy. If, for example, the state program of school vouchers that I describe in this chapter does not violate the nonestablishment norm, this does not not entail that, as a matter of sound public policy, any state should adopt the program. There is no inconsistency in concluding *both* that government is constitutionally free to adopt a voucher program like the one I describe here *and* that, as a matter of sound public policy, no government should do so.[6] We disserve careful analysis of difficult issues by conflating, or confusing, the question of the constitutionality of a government program with the different question of whether, apart from the question of its constitutionality, the program is sound public policy.[7] My concern here is constitutionality, not sound public policy.[8]

THE NONESTABLISHMENT NORM

The First Amendment to the Constitution of the United States famously insists that "Congress shall make no law respecting an establishment of religion, or prohibiting the free exercise thereof; or abridging the freedom of speech, or of the press; or the right of the people peaceably to assemble, and to petition the Government for a redress of grievances." Yet, according to the authoritative case law – law that is constitutional bedrock in the United States[9] – it is not just Congress but all three branches of the national government that may not prohibit the free exercise of religion, abridge the freedom of speech, and so forth. Moreover, it is not just the (whole) national government but the government of every state that may not do what the First Amendment forbids. I have suggested elsewhere that there is a path from the text of the First Amendment, which speaks just of Congress, to the authoritative case law.[10] But even if there were no such path, it would nonetheless be constitutional bedrock in the United States that neither the national government nor state government may either prohibit the free exercise of religion or establish religion (or abridge "the freedom of speech, or of the press; or the right of the people peaceably to assemble, and to petition the Government for a redress of grievances").[11] For Americans at the beginning of the twenty-first century, the serious practical question is no longer whether the free exercise norm and the nonestablishment norm apply to the whole of

American government, including state government. They *do* so apply. And there is no going back. The sovereignty of the free exercise and nonestablishment norms over every branch and level of American government – in particular, their sovereignty over state government as well as the national government – is now, as I said, constitutional bedrock in the United States. For Americans today, the serious practical inquiry is about what it means to say that government (state as well as national) may neither prohibit the free exercise of religion nor establish religion. I have addressed elsewhere what it means to say that government may not prohibit the free exercise of religion.[12] However, it is not the free exercise norm that bears on the principal question I address in this chapter – the constitutionality of school vouchers – but the other constituent of the American constitutional law of religious freedom: the nonestablishment norm. In the United States, what does it mean to say that government may not establish religion? What does the nonestablishment norm forbid government to do?

From 1947, when the U.S. Supreme Court first applied the nonestablishment norm to the states,[13] to the present, the justices of the Court have been sharply divided about what it means to say that government may not establish religion.[14] They have been divided both about what the nonestablishment norm means as a general matter and, especially, about what the norm means, about what its implications are, for government aid to religiously affiliated schools. The division among the present justices is as great as it has ever been: The four most relevant recent cases decided by the Court (in 1995, 1997, 2000, and 2002) were decided by votes of five to four or six to three.[15] In any event, I mean to give, in the paragraph that follows, not the Supreme Court's answer to the question of what, as a general matter, the nonestablishment norm forbids government to do, but the most sensible answer.

The idea of an "established" church is a familiar one.[16] For Americans, the best-known and most relevant example is the Church of England, which, from before the time of the American founding to the present, has been the established church in England[17] (though, of course, the Church of England was much more established in the past than it is today).[18] In the United States, however, unlike the situation in England, there may be no established church: The nonestablishment norm forbids government to enact any law or pursue any policy that treats a church (or more than one church) as the official church of the political community; government may not bestow legal favor or privilege on a church – that is, on a church *as such* – in relation to another church or in relation to no church at all. More precisely: *Government may not take any action that favors a church in relation to another church, or in relation to no church at all, on the basis of the view that the favored church is, as a church – as a community of faith – better along one or another dimension of value (truer, for example, or more efficacious spiritually, or more authentically American).* The nonestablishment norm deprives government of jurisdiction to make judgments about which church (or churches), if any, is, as such, better than another church or than no church. The norm requires government to be agnostic about which church – which community of faith – is better; government must act without regard to whether any church is in fact better.[19] (As Justice Brennan once put it: "It may be true that individuals cannot be 'neutral' on the question of religion. But the judgment of the Establishment Clause is that neutrality by the organs of *government* on questions of religion is both possible and imperative.")[20] In particular, government may not privilege, in law or policy, membership in a church – in the Fifth Avenue Baptist Church, for example, or in the Roman Catholic Church, or in the Christian Church generally;[21] nor may it privilege a worship practice – a prayer, liturgical rite, or religious observance – of a church.[22]

THE CONSTITUTIONALITY OF SCHOOL VOUCHERS

Just as I gave, in the preceding paragraph, not the Supreme Court's answer to the question of what, as a general matter, the nonestablishment norm forbids government to do, but (what I believe to be) the most sensible answer, I now want to give the most sensible answer to the question of what the nonestablishment norm means, what its implications are, for government aid to religiously affiliated schools – in particular, for government aid in the form of school vouchers.

Assume that a state legislature, with the support of the governor, has responded to a growing, insistent demand for greater "school choice" in two main ways. First, the legislature has made state funds available to local school districts for the purpose of establishing charter schools.[23] Second, the legislature has funded a statewide voucher program designed to enable poor families to send their children either (a) to a public school (a public elementary or secondary school) to which such a family would not otherwise be entitled to send its children – that is, a public school outside the school district in which the family lives – or (b) to a nonpublic school.[24] Assume further that the state's new voucher program includes, *inter alia*, the following three features:

1. Only poor families – families that meet a strict standard of financial need – may participate in the voucher program.[25]
2. Any nonpublic school may participate in the program, even one that is religiously affiliated, if it (a) meets certain strict requirements concerning curriculum, teacher certification, student performance, and the like and (b) does not engage in discrimination or other conduct that violates the public policy of the state or endorse or otherwise promote such behavior.[26]
3. If a voucher is to be used for a nonpublic school, the amount of the voucher may not exceed, in any school year, the average per-pupil expenditure in the preceding school year by the school district in which the family lives.[27]

It is the second feature of the state's voucher program that concerns me here: Does the nonestablishment norm forbid the state to permit religiously affiliated schools to participate in the voucher program; that is, does the nonestablishment norm require the state to exclude from the program schools that are religiously affiliated? Or, instead, does the nonestablishment norm permit the state to include schools in the program without regard to whether or not they are religiously affiliated?

The state does not violate the nonestablishment norm by permitting religiously affiliated schools to participate in its voucher program; that is, the state does not *necessarily* violate the nonestablishment norm by doing do. The reason is simple. By including schools in its voucher program without regard to whether or not they are religiously affiliated, the state is not necessarily taking any action that favors one or more churches in relation to one or more other churches, or in relation to no church at all, on the basis of the view that the favored church(or churches) is, as a church, truer, or more efficacious spiritually, or more authentically American, or otherwise better; nor, in particular, has the state privileged either membership in, or a worship practice of, one or more churches. So long as (but only so long

8

as) each of two criteria are satisfied, the state may include religiously affiliated schools in its voucher program (or other aid program). The first criterion speaks to the design of the voucher program, the second to the basis of the political choice to adopt the program.

First. The eligibility requirements for school participation in the program are religiously neutral; school participation in the program does not depend on whether or not the school is religiously affiliated.

If this criterion is *not* satisfied, it is fair for the courts to presume that the political choice to adopt the program is based on the belief that the favored church (or churches) is, as a church, truer, or more efficacious spiritually, or more authentically American, or otherwise better than one or more other churches or than no church at all. But even if this criterion *is* satisfied (as in the real world it surely will be), it still may be the case that the political choice to adopt the program is based on – that the program would not have been adopted but for – that belief.[28] In that sense, the program may be a subterfuge: a covert establishment of religion.[29] Hence, the need for this second criterion, which comes into play only if the voucher program satisfies the first criterion:

Second. The state's adoption of the voucher program, though it may operate in some jurisdictions to favor one or more churches (namely, those that in those jurisdictions sponsor many eligible primary or secondary schools) in relation to one or more other churches (those that do not sponsor many or even any such schools), is not based on the belief that the favored church (or churches) is, as a church, better (truer, etc.) than one or more other churches or than no church at all.[30]

It bears mention that four justices of the present Supreme Court have recently espoused a position substantially like the one articulated in the preceding paragraph: Chief Justice Rehnquist and Justices Scalia, Kennedy, and Thomas.[31] The other five justices require that additional criteria be satisfied if a government aid program is to survive review under the nonestablishment norm.[32] According to one of the principal additional criteria, if government money is to end up in the pocket of a religiously affiliated school, it must do so not because government gave the money directly to the school, upon certification that an eligible child has enrolled there, but only because the person(s) to whom government gave the money chose to use it to pay expenses incurred in sending the child to that particular school.[33] This direct/indirect distinction seems to me entirely formalistic: I cannot fathom why it should make a constitutional difference that voucher money goes directly to a parent, who then gives it to the school, rather than directly to the school, upon certification that an eligible child has enrolled there. If a voucher program would be constitutional in the former case, then it should be constitutional in the latter case, too – and if unconstitutional in the latter case, then in the former case, too.[34] But because five justices, including Justice O'Connor, see the matter differently,[35] no state should adopt a voucher program that does not include the requirement that the voucher money go directly to the parents. According to the Ohio Pilot Project at issue in the Cleveland school voucher case, "[e]ach scholarship for children attending a private school is payable to the parents of the student entitled to the scholarship.... Scholarship checks are mailed to the school selected by the parents, where the parents are required to endorse the checks over to the school in order to pay tuition."[36] Therefore, Justice O'Connor was able to join Chief Justice Rehnquist and Justices Scalia, Kennedy, and Thomas in ruling that the Ohio Pilot Project did not violate the nonestablishment norm.

The story of the evolution of the Supreme Court's nonestablishment jurisprudence – in particular, its evolution in the context of constitutional controversies over government aid to religiously affiliated entities, especially schools – is an important one. But because the story has been well told elsewhere, there is no need to rehearse it here.[37] One feature of the story bears brief mention, however: Anti-Catholicism has animated not only Protestant opposition to Catholic schools but also judicial opposition (in the name of the nonestablishment norm) to government aid to such schools, even when the aid program could not plausibly be said to establish religion.[38] The anti-Catholicism is now largely spent, but not the position – still defended by some Supreme Court justices[39] and some scholars[40] and others[41] – that government aid to religiously affiliated primary and secondary schools can and often does violate the nonestablishment norm, even though (a) participation by such schools in the aid program would be pursuant to eligibility requirements that are religiously neutral and (b) government's decision to include such schools in the aid program is not based on the belief that one or more churches are, as such, better than one or more other churches or than no church at all.[42] That position took root in the soil of anti-Catholicism, as the historian John McGreevy and the legal scholars Thomas Berg and Douglas Laycock have each explained.[43] Laycock notes, near the end of his discussion, that

[r]espectable anti-Catholicism faded in the 1950s and all but collapsed in the 1960s in the wake of the Kennedy presidency and Vatican II. But even at the time of *Lemon* [*v. Kurtzman*, 403 U.S. 602 (1971)], some justices were influenced by residual anti-Catholicism and by a deep suspicion of Catholic schools. This appears most clearly in Justice Douglas's citation of an anti-Catholic hate tract in his concurring opinion in *Lemon* [403 U.S. 602, 635 n. 20 (1971)] and in Justice Black's dissenting opinion in *Board of Education v. Allen* [392 U.S. 236, 251–52 (1968)]. The Court's opinion in *Lemon* is more subtle and arguably open to more charitable interpretations, but it relied on what it considered to be inherent risks in religious schools despite the absence of a record in *Lemon* itself and despite contrary fact-finding by the district court in the companion case.[44]

The position identified in the preceding paragraph is tantamount to the position that the nonestablishment norm sometimes (often) requires the state to discriminate against religiously affiliated schools vis-à-vis nonpublic schools that are not religiously affiliated.[45] As Akhil Amar has observed, it is the position of the three justices who dissented in *Mitchell v. Helms*[46] – Justice Souter, who wrote the dissenting opinion, and Justices Stevens and Ginsburg, who joined it – that (in Amar's words)

the government may not, pursuant to a genuinely secular law, give computers on a completely evenhanded basis to all public schools and private schools. To put it yet another way: The Constitution requires that if the government decides to give computers to private schools, it may give them to the Secular School and the Indifferent Institute but must withhold them from various religious schools. If a given private school eligible for certain computers later decides to add prayer to its curriculum, while otherwise continuing to teach all the basics, that school must forfeit the computers. The Constitution requires this discrimination, depriving religious schools, and only religious schools, of a benefit that all other schools receive.[47]

Amar's response to this position is correct: "The Constitution, however, requires no such thing, at least if the test is the best reading of its words, history, and structure, as opposed to the many outlandish (and contradictory) things that have been said about it in the *United States Reports*."[48]

The *Mitchell* dissenters' construal of the nonestablishment norm is indeed troubling – not only as a matter of the Constitution's "words, history, and structure," but also as a matter of what we may call, for want of a better term, political morality. We can all agree that the state should not discriminate in favor of religiously affiliated schools (because there is no good reason for it to do so). That is, we can all agree that the state should not privilege, in law or policy, either (a) some religiously affiliated schools in relation to some other religiously affiliated schools or (b) some or all religiously affiliated schools in relation to nonpublic schools that are not religiously affiliated. But that the state should not discriminate *in favor of* religiously affiliated schools does not entail that the state must discriminate *against* such schools. That it is wrong for government to discriminate *in favor of* an activity does not mean that it is right for government to discriminate *against* the activity – any more than that it is wrong for government to discriminate against an activity means that it is right for government to discriminate in favor of the activity. There is no good reason for concluding that the state should discriminate against religiously affiliated schools.

Nor is there any good reason for concluding that the nonestablishment norm should be construed to require the state to discriminate against religiously affiliated schools.[49] In particular, the fact that some persons object to their taxes being spent in a way that has the effect of supporting religiously affiliated schools (even though their taxes are not being spent in a way that discriminates in favor of such schools) no more justifies according constitutional status to their objection, however conscientious it may be, than the fact that some persons object to their taxes being spent in a way that has the effect of supporting – indeed, that is designed to support – military activities, for example, or capital punishment, or abortion (and so on), justifies according constitutional status to *their* objection. "As citizens we are taxed to support all manner of policies and programs with which we disagree. Tax dollars pay for weapons of mass destruction that some believe are evil. Taxes pay for abortions and the execution of capital offenders, that some believe are acts of murder. Taxes pay the salaries of public officials whose policies we despise and oppose at every opportunity. Why is religion different?"[50] Religion does not seem to be different in any relevant way. (Michael McConnell has observed that "[r]eligious differences in this country have never generated the civil discord experienced in political conflicts over such issues as the Vietnam War, racial segregation, the Red Scare, unionization, or slavery.")[51] To assert, at this point, that the nonestablishment norm accords constitutional status to the objection of some to their taxes being spent in a way that has the effect of supporting religiously affiliated schools, is to beg the question here, which is *whether* the nonestablishment norm should be so construed. My argument here is that the nonestablishment norm should *not* be so construed.[52] Moreover, the claim that permitting religiously affiliated schools to participate in a school voucher program "would compel some taxpayers to support religious schooling with which they disagree"[53] is false: "As long as the voucher amounts do not exceed the value of the secular components of religious schooling, taxpayers in reality will be subsidizing K-12 education, not religion. Given the combination of low tuition and relatively high academic achievement that characterizes the average religious school, it seems clear that the public would almost always get its secular money's worth."[54]

Now, none of this is to deny that one's objection to taxes being spent, whether one's own taxes or someone else's, to fund a state program that "establishes" religion – an aid program whose eligibility criteria are religiously partial rather than religiously neutral, or that is based on a belief that one or more churches are, as such, better than one or more other churches or than no church at all – does have constitutional status, in this sense: The nonestablishment norm forbids the state to have such a program. But the nonestablishment norm does not forbid a state to have an aid program whose eligibility requirements are religiously neutral and that is not based on any such belief. And, therefore, one is not constitutionally entitled, under the nonestablishment norm, to have taxes *not* spent in a way that has the effect of supporting religiously affiliated schools. Thus, the claim pressed by Dean Kathleen Sullivan of Stanford Law School, the Baptist Joint Committee on Public Affairs, the American Civil Liberties Union, and others – that one's objection to taxes being spent in aid of religious activities has constitutional status[55] – is simply mistaken. Moreover, and unsurprisingly, this mistaken claim has no warrant in American constitutional history. As Justice Thomas explained in his concurring opinion in *Rosenberger v. Rectors and Visitors of University of Virginia*:

[T]he history cited by the dissent cannot support the conclusion that the Establishment Clause "categorically condemn[s] state programs directly aiding religious activity" when that aid is part of a neutral program available to a wide array of beneficiaries. Even if Madison believed that the principle of non-establishment of religion precluded governmental financial support for religion *per se* (in the sense of government benefits specifically targeting religion), there is no indication that at the time of the framing he took the dissent's extreme view that the government must discriminate against religious adherents by excluding them from more generally available financial subsidies. . . . The dissent identifies no evidence that the Framers intended to disable religious entities from participating on neutral terms in evenhanded government programs. The evidence that does exist points in the opposite direction. . . .[56]

MAY GOVERNMENT DISCRIMINATE AGAINST RELIGIOUSLY AFFILIATED SCHOOLS?

Again, one is not constitutionally entitled, under the nonestablishment norm, to have taxes *not* spent in a way that has the effect of supporting religiously affiliated schools, because the nonestablishment norm does not require a state to exclude such schools from an aid program whose eligibility requirements are religiously neutral and that is not based on a belief that one or more churches are, as such, better than one or more other churches or than no church at all. That is, the nonestabishment norm does not require a state to discriminate against religiously affiliated schools. Indeed, not only is it inaccurate to say that, under the nonestablishment norm, the state, in its voucher program or other program of government aid, must discriminate against religiously affiliated schools; it is also open to serious question whether the state *may* discriminate against such schools.

Some states do choose to discriminate against religiously affiliated schools. Indeed, in some states this choice has been enshrined in the state constitution, so that as a matter of *state* constitutional law, the state must discriminate against religiously affiliated schools.[57] But, of course, the United States Constitution trumps a state constitution: If the U.S. Constitution forbids a state to discriminate against religiously affiliated schools, no state may do so, even if its own constitution requires it to do so; if the U.S. constitution forbids a state to discriminate against religiously affiliated schools, a state constititional provision, insofar as it requires the state to discriminate against such schools, is itself, under the U.S. Constitution, unconstitutional. Assume for the sake of discussion that the Supreme Court has ruled that a state is not required by the nonestablishment norm to discriminate against religiously affiliated schools. Does it then follow that a state is not constitutionally free to discriminate against religiously affiliated schools? More precisely: Does it then follow that the U.S. Constitution forbids a state to exclude religiously affiliated schools from a program of aid to nonpublic schools – a program that, were it to include religiously affiliated schools, would not violate the nonestablishment norm? The answer, in my judgment, is that if a state is not constitutionally required to discriminate against religiously affiliated schools, neither is it constitutionally free to discriminate against religiously affiliated schools by excluding them from such an aid program. The strongest argument in support of that answer is a simple one, and it is based on the American constitutional doctrine of freedom of expression.

Here is a bare sketch of the argument: In adopting a program of aid to nonpublic schools, a state is not constitutionally free to discriminate against (by excluding) a nonpublic school because it espouses a particular view, whether partisan or agnostic, on a certain issue. That is, a state is not constitutionally free to do so *unless the school's espousing the view is a state of affairs from which a state must dissociate itself and therefore may not support.* An example of such a state of affairs: a school's espousing white supremacy. Why must a state dissociate itself from a school's espousing white supremacy; why is a state required to do so, both constitutionally and morally? A state is *constitutionally* required to do so, because for a school to espouse white supremacy is for it to reject a fundamental aspect of the constitutional morality of the society, according to which no person is to be deemed inferior to another by virtue of skin color; a state may not cooperate with, it must dissociate itself from, such a view.[58] A state is *morally* required – that is, as a matter of human rights it is required – to dissociate itself from a school's espousing white supremacy, because for a school to espouse white supremacy is for it to reject the very idea of human rights, according to which each and every person is sacred and no person is less sacred than another by virtue of skin color.[59] Now, that a state must dissociate itself from a state of affairs – here, a group's espousing a particular ideology – does not entail that the state may outlaw the state of affairs. Perhaps a constitutional provision – for example, the First Amendment's protection of freedom of expression – forbids the state to do so. (With some exceptions not relevant here, the right to freedom of expression surely does forbid the state to outlaw a group's espousing a particular ideology.) But that a state must dissociate itself from a state of affairs *does* entail that a state must not subsidize or otherwise support the state of affairs.[60]

However, there is no reason to think that a state is either constitutionally or even morally (i.e., as a matter of human rights) required to dissociate itself from a school's espousing the view that God exists, or that Jesus is Lord, or that the Roman Catholic Church is the one true church – any more than it is required to dissociate itself from a school's espousing the view that God does not exist, or that Jesus is not Lord, or that Roman Catholicism is a false religion, or the view that we do not and perhaps cannot know if God exists, or if Jesus is Lord, or if the Roman Catholic Church is the one true church. In espousing any of these views, a school is not rejecting a fundamental aspect of the constitutional morality of the society; nor is it rejecting the idea of human rights. Because a state is neither constitutionally nor even morally required to dissociate itself from a school's espousing any of these views, no state, in adopting a program of aid to nonpublic schools, may discriminate against (by excluding) a nonpublic school because it espouses any of these views.[61]

Are there other arguments that support the claim that a state may not discriminate against religiously affiliated schools?[62] One possibility: an argument based on the constitutional mandate that government not prohibit the free exercise of religion. The free exercise norm is, whatever else it may be, an antidiscrimination norm. According to my understanding of the norm (or perhaps I should say, according to my understanding of the Supreme Court's understanding),[63] which I have elaborated elsewhere, if a state's exclusion of religiously affiliated schools from its voucher program (or other program of government aid) is based on hostility to one or more churches, then the exclusion – the discrimination – violates the free exercise norm.[64] It is undeniable – history is clear – that many state policies against extending aid to religiously affiliated schools were originally and conspicuously adopted on the basis of hostility to Roman Catholicism.[65] But today it seems likely that the maintenance of such policies is based less, if at all, on anti-Catholicism than on one or more other factors, the principal one of which is an inaccurate understanding of what the nonestablishment norm forbids – an inaccurate understanding abetted by many decisions of the U.S. Supreme Court.[66]

Assume, however, that the Supreme Court changes course and rules that no state is required by the nonestablishment norm to exclude religiously affiliated schools from its voucher program (or other program of aid to nonpublic schools) – and that a state nonetheless persists in excluding such schools from its voucher (or other aid) program. Does that make the free exercise argument more promising? Not necessarily. The fact remains that a state legislature might well have reasons other than hostility to one or more churches for continuing to exclude religiously affiliated schools from its voucher program. First, the legislature might disagree with the Court's change of course; it might believe that, contrary to the Court's new ruling, the nonestablishment norm, correctly understood, requires the exclusion of religiously affiliated schools. Second, there might be a provision in the state's own constitution that requires the exclusion of religiously affiliated schools; or, at least, the legislature might believe that the provision requires their exclusion. Third, the legislature might believe that, whether or not the federal nonestablishment norm or any state constitutional provision requires their exclusion, it is wiser, all things considered, to exclude religiously affiliated schools from the state's voucher program than to include them. One could claim that each and every one of those legislative beliefs – about what the nonestablishment norm requires, about what the state constitutional provision requires, and about what good public policy requires – is embedded in hostility to one or more churches[67] and that, therefore, excluding religiously affiliated schools on the basis of one or more of the beliefs violates the free exercise norm. But surely it would be difficult, at best, to sustain such a claim. The free exercise argument is, at best, problematic.

But even if the free exercise argument were not problematic, the argument based on freedom of expression would be preferable, for this reason: Unlike the free exercise argument, the freedom of expression argument does not invite judges to inquire into the subterranean attitudes of legislators or other policymakers toward one or more religions or religion generally; it does not require litigants or, if they are to accept the argument, judges to impute religious hostility (prejudice, bigotry) to those who defend exclusion of religiously affiliated schools from state voucher programs.[68] Rather, the freedom of expression argument requires only that litigants claim and judges conclude that in excluding religiously affiliated schools, the state has drawn a line that it may not draw; it has employed a criterion of selection – here, a criterion of exclusion – that it may not employ.[69] In that sense, the freedom of expression argument is focused on legislative "outputs";

the free exercise argument, by contrast, is focused on legislative "inputs." Unlike the free exercise argument, therefore, the freedom of expression argument avoids what Steve Smith has aptly called "the discourse of disrespect." That constitutional doctrine minimizes the need for reliance on the discourse of disrespect is, as Smith has powerfully argued, an important virtue.[70]

CONCLUSION

It is not true that a state must exclude religiously affiliated schools from its voucher program: The nonestablishment norm, correctly understood, does not forbid a state to include such schools.[71] In this respect, a state is constitutionally free to take the path that other liberal democracies have taken. "The United States is one of the few modern democracies that does not provide publicly supported options for parents who prefer to have their children educated in schools that reflect their religious values."[72]

As I suggested at the beginning of this chapter, the logic of my argument extends beyond school vouchers to other forms of government aid to religiously affiliated schools and even to government aid to faith-based social service providers. There is, in my judgment, no constitutionally relevant distinction – no distinction relevant to the nonestablishment norm – between school vouchers and other forms of government aid to religiously affiliated schools; nor is there any constitutionally relevant distinction between government aid to religiously affiliated schools and government aid to faith-based social service providers. If, as I have argued here, including religiously affiliated schools in a program of school vouchers does not necessarily violate the nonestablishment norm, then, by a parity of reasoning, including them in other programs of government aid to nonpublic elementary and secondary schools does not necessarily violate the nonestablishment norm; and if including religiously affiliated schools in programs of government aid to nonpublic schools does not necessarily violate the nonestablishment norm, then including faith-based social service providers in programs of government aid to nongovernmental social service providers does not necessarily violate the nonestablishment norm.

I said that it is not true – it is false – that a state must exclude religiously affiliated schools from its voucher program. May a state nonetheless choose to exclude religiously affiliated schools from its voucher program or other program of aid to nonpublic schools? In my judgment, in providing aid to nonpublic schools, no state may discriminate – no state is constitutionally free to discriminate – against religiously affiliated schools. It is not only false that a state *must* discriminate against such schools; it is also false that a state *may* discriminate against them. By a parity of reasoning, in providing aid to nongovernmental social service providers, government may not discriminate against faith-based social service providers. Again, this is not to deny that there are some ideologies – a racist ideology is the clearest example – from which government should and indeed must dissociate itself, even if the ideologies are religious in character.

Why Political Reliance on Religiously Grounded Morality Does Not Violate the Establishment Clause

I say, sir, that the purity of the Christian church, the purity of our holy religion, and the preservation of our free institutions, require that Church and State shall be separated; that the preacher on the Sabbath day shall find his text in the Bible; shall preach "Jesus Christ and him crucified," shall preach from the Holy Scriptures, and not attempt to control the political organizations and political parties of the day.

Senator Stephen A. Douglas[1]

PRELIMINARIES

In this chapter, as in the preceding one, I address a question about the meaning of the constitutional imperative that government not "establish" religion. The question I address in this chapter is: Do legislators or other policymakers violate the nonestablishment norm by outlawing particular conduct, or otherwise disfavoring it, on the basis of a religiously grounded belief that the conduct is immoral — a religiously grounded belief, for example, that same-sex unions are immoral?[2] (Government can disfavor conduct without banning it. For example, for a legislature to decline to extend to homosexual unions any of the benefits it grants to heterosexual marriages is not for the legislature to outlaw same-sex unions, but it is for the legislature to disfavor them.) This question is relevant to citizens of the United States, because the nonestablishment norm is an important part of the fundamental law — the constitutional law — of the United States. In the next chapter, I move beyond the nonestablishment norm to address a question that, though closely related to the question I address in this chapter, is relevant not just to citizens of the United States but to those of any liberal democracy, even one whose fundamental law does not forbid government to establish religion: Do legislators or other policymakers contravene the morality of liberal democracy by outlawing (or otherwise disfavoring) conduct on the

basis of religiously grounded moral belief? Even if government officials do not violate the nonestablishment norm by outlawing conduct
on the basis of religiously grounded moral belief, it may nonetheless be the case that they betray the morality of liberal democracy by
doing so. That we are constitutionally free to do something – utter
racial epithets, for example – does not entail that as a moral matter
we should do it. In my judgment, however, which I defend partly in
this chapter and partly in the next, government, by outlawing conduct on the basis of religiously grounded moral belief, runs afoul
neither of the nonestablishment norm *nor* of the morality of liberal
democracy.

As I noted in the Introduction to this book, the proper role of
religion in politics is one of the most controversial issues in the United
States today. Indeed, the issue of religion in politics is controversial
in the United States not just today, but perennially. We citizens of
the United States are perennially divided about the proper role of
religiously grounded morality in our politics. This is due in substantial
part, no doubt, to the fact that we are perennially divided in our
judgments about a host of important moral issues – and about a host
of connected political issues. If we were united in our judgments about
these moral/political issues, we would have less reason to argue with
one another about the extent to which religiously grounded morality
should figure in our politics. But we are not united; we are perennially
divided.

The moral issues and connected political issues that divide us
change over time, of course. Here are four prominent contemporary
examples:

- Some believe that homosexual sexual conduct is always immoral
  and oppose the legal recognition of same-sex unions; others believe that there is no morally relevant difference between heterosexual marriage and same-sex marriage and support legal
  recognition.
- Some believe that physician-assisted suicide is always immoral
  and oppose de-criminalization of the practice; others believe that
  physician-assisted suicide is sometimes a morally acceptable option
  and support de-criminalization.
- Some believe that the death penalty is always immoral and support
  abolition of the death penalty; others believe that the death penalty
  is sometimes morally appropriate and oppose abolition.

- Some believe that most abortions are immoral and support re-criminalization of most abortions;[3] others believe that abortion is often a morally acceptable option and oppose re-criminalization.

These examples of political controversy rooted in moral controversy are not meant to suggest that one who believes that particular conduct is immoral will always want the law to ban the conduct. One who believes that (particular) conduct is immoral may have good reasons to want the law *not* to ban the conduct.[4] (Similarly, one who believes that particular conduct – e.g., physician-assisted suicide – is sometimes a morally acceptable option may have good reasons to want the law to ban the conduct.)[5] Nonetheless, with respect to conduct believed by many to be immoral, the claim that the conduct is immoral is typically an important part of the argument that the law ought to ban, or otherwise disfavor, the conduct.[6]

Because I am concerned, in this and the next chapter, with the proper role of religiously grounded morality in the politics and law of the United States and of other, kindred liberal democracies, let me clarify the idea of a moral belief – for example, the belief that homosexual sexual conduct is always immoral – that is (a) *religiously* (b) *grounded*.

(a) A moral belief is "religiously" grounded, in whole or in part, if it is rooted, in whole or in part, in one or more of three ideas:

- The idea of a God-inspired text (or texts), such as the Bible, believed to teach moral truth – if not all moral truth, at least all the moral truth that one needs to be saved.
- The idea of a God-anointed figure (or figures), such as the Pope, believed to teach moral truth.
- The idea of a God-created and God-maintained order – including, in particular, a God-fashioned human nature – believed to be a fundamental criterion of moral truth.

(b) The religious grounding *vel non* of a moral belief is person-relative: A moral belief that is religiously grounded for one person may not be for another. Two persons may both believe that homosexual sexual conduct is always immoral but each for a different reason – one, solely for a religious reason, the other, solely for a nonreligious (secular) reason. In the strong sense in which I mean it here, a person's moral belief is religiously "grounded" if and only if she accepts the moral belief because she accepts one or more religious premises that support the belief – for example, the premise that the Bible teaches that the conduct is immoral – and if she would not accept the belief if she did not accept the supporting religious premise or premises. Thus, a person's moral belief is not religiously grounded, in this strong sense, if she would accept the belief even if she did not accept any supporting religious premise – that is, if she would accept it solely because she accepts one or more nonreligious (secular) premises that support the belief.

One more clarification: In the strong sense in which I mean it here, to make a political choice (e.g., to enact a law) "on the basis of" a belief – to base the choice on the belief – is to make a political choice that one would not make in the absence of the belief. (To make a political choice partly, not solely, "on the basis of" a belief is still to make a political choice that one would not make in the absence of the belief.) To rely on a belief in making a political choice is not necessarily to base the choice on the belief: One may be relying on the belief as principal or merely as additional support for a choice that one would make, on the basis of some other ground, even in the absence of the belief. The claim that one may not base a political choice on a belief of a certain kind – for example, a religiously grounded belief – is therefore weaker, in the sense of less restrictive, than the claim that one may not rely on the belief at all, that one may not put any weight whatsoever on the belief, in making a political choice. If the weaker (less restrictive) claim cannot be sustained, then a fortiori the stronger (more restrictive) claim cannot be sustained either. If, as I conclude in this chapter, the weaker claim cannot be sustained – the claim that, under the nonestablishment norm, government, and particularly legislators and other policymakers, may not disfavor conduct on the basis of a religiously grounded belief that the conduct is immoral – then it is unncessary to focus on the stronger nonestablishment claim that in disfavoring the conduct government may not rely on the belief at all.

THE ISSUE

Now, imagine a legislator who must decide whether to vote to outlaw, or otherwise disfavor, particular conduct – abortion, for example, or same-sex unions. She is a very conscientious legislator, and she wonders what weight, if any, she and her fellow legislators may put on the religiously grounded belief that the conduct is immoral; in particular, she wonders whether the nonestablishment norm forbids them to disfavor conduct on the basis of religiously grounded moral belief. The paragraphs that follow are meant to address that question. Moreover, they are are meant to present the best answer to the question, not to predict the answer the U.S. Supreme Court would give – though, as it happens, there is no reason to doubt that in an appropriate case the Court (a majority of it, at least) would give the best answer.[7]

THE ARGUMENT

Recall, from the preceding chapter, what the nonestablishment norm forbids government to do: Government may not enact any law or pursue any policy that treats a church (or more than one church) as the official church of the political community; government may not bestow legal favor or privilege on a church – that is, on a church *as such* – in relation to another church or in relation to no church at all. More precisely: *Government may not take any action that favors a church in relation to another church, or in relation to no church at all, on the basis of the view that the favored church is, as a church – as a community of faith – better along one or another dimension of value (truer, for example, or more efficacious spiritually, or more authentically American).* The nonestablishment norm deprives government of jurisdiction to make judgments about which church (or churches), if any, is, as such, better than another church or than no church. The norm requires government to be agnostic about which church – which community of faith – is better; government must act without regard to whether any church is in fact better.[8] In particular, government may not privilege, in law or policy, membership in a church – in the Fifth Avenue Baptist Church, for example, or in the Roman Catholic Church, or in the Christian Church generally;[9] nor may it privilege a worship practice – a prayer, liturgical rite, or religious observance – of a church.

In forbidding government to bestow legal favor on a church (or on more than one church) as such – in forbidding it, in particular, to privilege either membership in or a worship practice of a church – the nonestablishment norm does not forbid a legislature (or other policymaker) to disfavor conduct on the basis of religiously grounded moral belief: That a legislature has voted to disfavor same-sex unions, for example, on the basis of a religiously grounded belief that same-sex unions are immoral in no way entails that the legislature has privileged either membership in or a worship practice of a church or that it has otherwise bestowed legal favor on a church.

Now, one may want to insist that the nonestablishment norm does more than just forbid government to bestow legal favor on a church. In particular, one may want to insist that the norm also forbids government to disfavor conduct on the basis of a religiously grounded moral belief. But does the nonestablishment norm go that far? As I noted in the preceding chapter, it is constitutional bedrock for us Americans that government may not establish religion (or prohibit the free exercise thereof). Although the nonestablishment norm that is constitutional bedrock for us forbids government to bestow legal favor on a church – for example, by privileging membership in the church – it does not go so far as to forbid government to make a political choice, including a political choice disfavoring conduct, on the basis of a moral belief *just in virtue of the fact that the moral belief is, for those making the choice, religiously grounded.* No such rule is – no such rule has ever become – part of our constitutional bedrock.[10] Nor does authoritative constitutional case law contain any such rule, as Justice Scalia has emphasized: "Our cases in no way imply that the Establishment Clause forbids legislators merely to act upon their religious convictions. We surely would not strike down a law providing money to feed the hungry or shelter the homeless if it could be demonstrated that, but for the religious beliefs of the legislators, the funds would not have been approved. . . . [P]olitical activism by the religiously motivated is part of our heritage."[11]

However, to say that the rule that government may not disfavor conduct on the basis of religiously grounded moral belief is neither part of our constitutional bedrock nor even contained in authoritative case law is not to say that the rule should not become part of our constitutional law; it is not to say that the Supreme Court should not constitutionalize the rule. In my judgment, however, the rule should *not* become part of our constitutional law; it should *not* become part of the content of the nonestablishment norm.

Consider, first, the practical impediments to construing the nonestablishment norm to disable government – to disable legislators and other policymakers – from outlawing or otherwise disfavoring conduct on the basis of a religiously grounded belief that the conduct is immoral. Remember: The nonestablishment norm, however construed, is, like the free exercise norm, a constitutional norm and, as such, is supposed to be judicially enforceable and enforced.

- For virtually every moral belief on which a legislature might be tempted to rely in disfavoring conduct – for example, the belief that abortion, or homosexual sexual conduct, is immoral – it is the case that although for some persons the belief is religiously grounded (grounded on a religious premise or premises), for some others the belief is not religiously grounded but, instead, is grounded wholly on a secular (nonreligious) premise (or premises). For still others, the belief is supported both by a religious premise and, independently, by a secular premise. How, then, is a court to decide whether a law banning abortion (for example) would have been enacted even in the absence of the religious premise? Indeed, one or more legislators may well be uncertain whether they would have supported the law in the absence of the religious premise. They may be uncertain, for example, whether they would credit the supporting secular premise if they did not already credit the supporting religious premise.
- In the unlikely event that there is a confident answer to such a counterfactual inquiry, is it prudent to fashion a nonestablishment requirement the judicial enforcement of which could easily lead to the following state of affairs?: One state's antiabortion law is adjudged unconstitutional by a court because in the court's opinion the law probably would not have been enacted in the absence of the religious premise, but another state's virtually identical antiabortion law is adjudged constitutional by a different court because in the court's opinion the law probably would have been enacted in the absence of the religious premise.
- Moreover, is it prudent to fashion a nonestablishment requirement the likely principal yield of which is that legislatures would engage in strategic behavior (in particular, they would trumpet secular premises) aimed at making it appear that the antiabortion law would have been enacted even in the absence of the religious premise?

The judiciary could steer around such obstacles – it could opt for a "second-best" solution – by construing the nonestablishment norm to require, not that the law in question would have been enacted even in the absence of a religious premise, but only that the moral belief on which the legislature based the law, a moral belief that for many persons is religiously grounded, have an independent secular ground – that it be a moral belief that for *some* persons is *not* religiously grounded.[12] But *that* requirement is so weak as to be inconsequential: What moral belief on which a legislature in the United States is likely to rely, in banning or otherwise disfavoring conduct, lacks a secular ground? Consider, for example, both the belief that abortion is immoral and the belief that same-sex unions are immoral: Neither belief lacks a secular ground. Although many who believe that abortion is immoral do so only on the basis of a religious premise (or premises), others do so on the basis of a secular premise as well as on the basis of a religious premise; indeed, some do so only on the basis of a secular premise. The same holds true for many who believe that same-sex unions are immoral. Indeed, both some who affirm that abortion is immoral and some who affirm that same-sex unions are immoral are not religious believers.

One might respond to this difficulty by saying that the nonestablishment requirement (i.e., the "second-best" requirement) should be not merely that the moral belief on which the legislature based the law have an independent secular ground, but that the independent secular ground be *plausible*. If this plausibility requirement were applied by the courts in a deferential fashion, the issue would be whether a legislature (or other policymaker) could reasonably credit the independent secular ground as, at least, plausible. If applied in a nondeferential fashion, the issue would be whether the court itself credited the independent secular ground as, at least, plausible. If the courts were to apply the plausibility requirement in a deferential fashion, as arguably they should,[13] the requirement would be as inconsequential as the notorious rationality (or "rational basis") requirement has been in the context of socioeconomic regulation.[14] As constitutional lawyers doubtless would be quick to agree, a deferential plausibility requirement – a plausibility requirement applied deferentially – would be little more than a formality; such a requirement would be so weak, so toothless, as to be tantamount to no requirement at all.

Let's assume, then, for the sake of discussion, that if the courts were to apply the plausibility requirement at all, they would apply it in a nondeferential fashion: A court would ask if in *the court's own judgment*, the independent secular ground is, at least, plausible. The problem with that inquiry – the problem, that is, with a plausibility requirement applied nondeferentially – is evident: The secular bases of widely controversial moral beliefs are typically both contestable and contested. Authorizing nondeferential judicial inquiry into the "plausibility" of the secular basis of a widely controversial moral belief comes perilously close to having judges act as the supreme arbiters of controversial moral beliefs. Such a judicial role is scarcely a desirable state of affairs in a democracy. This is not to deny that in a constitutional democracy, a court should be prepared to substitute its *constitutional* judgment for the *constitutional* judgment of a legislature or other part of government. Nor is it to deny that some constitutional provisions rule out, as a basis of political choice, some moral judgments, whether or not those judgments are religiously based. (For example, the Fourteenth Amendment to the United States Constitution rules out, as a basis of political choice, the judgment that it is immoral for a "white" person to marry a person who is not white.[15] In my judgment – though not (yet) in the Supreme Court's – it also rules out, as a basis of political choice, the judgment that same-sex unions are always immoral.[16] For government to disfavor conduct on the basis of any racist belief – or, I think, on the basis of any heterosexist belief[17] – would be for it to violate the Fourteenth Amendment.[18]) My point is simply that we should be wary about fashioning a constitutional requirement the judicial enforcement of which practically invites judges to substitute their moral judgments for the moral judgments of others, including legislators and other policymakers.[19]

Let's assume, however, for the sake of discussion, that in the preceding paragraph I have overstated – exaggerated – the difficulties of a plausibility requirement.[20] There is yet another important reason to be wary about construing the nonestablishment norm to forbid government to disfavor conduct on the basis of a moral belief that, though religiously grounded, lacks a plausible, independent secular ground. (A fortiori, it is a reason to be wary about construing the nonestablishment norm even more radically, to forbid government to disfavor conduct on the basis of a religiously grounded moral belief *whether or not* the belief also has a plausible, independent secular ground.) Unlike the other reasons, this reason for wariness is not about practical impediments or the proper judicial role. It is about maintaining impartiality between religious grounds and secular grounds for moral belief; it is also about the equal citizenship of religious believers. In that sense, this reason is about first principles and is therefore the most fundamental reason of all to reject a construal of the nonestablishment norm according to which government may not disfavor conduct on the basis of a moral belief that, though religiously grounded, lacks plausible, independent secular grounding.

There are, as I have argued elsewhere, three basic categories of moral inquiry: (1) What entities – in particular, what human beings – ought we to care about? (2) What is truly good for those we should care about – and what is bad for them? (3) And how should we resolve conflicts between goods – in particular, between what is good for some we should care about and what is good for others we should care about?[21] (Andrew Koppelman asserts that the nonestablishment norm forbids government to "formulate official answers to religious questions. . . ."[22] But the three basic inquiries I have just articulated are not "religious" questions. They are "moral" questions – albeit moral questions to which some persons give religiously grounded answers.) For many religious believers in the United States, no response to one or more of these three fundamental moral questions is as plausible, *if plausible at all*, as a religiously grounded response. For example: For many religious believers, no secular warrant for the claim that we should care about each and every person – that each and every person is inviolable – is plausible; only a religious warrant is plausible.[23] Therefore, to construe the nonestablishment norm to forbid government to disfavor conduct on the basis of a moral belief that, though religiously grounded, lacks, or may lack, plausible secular grounding makes no sense at all to such believers, for whom the only plausible response to one or more of the three fundamental moral questions, or at least the most plausible response, is a religiously grounded response.

But others, including some religious believers, may wonder what sense it makes, if any, to read the nonestablishment norm to forbid government to privilege one or more churches while leaving a legislative majority free to disfavor conduct on the basis of a moral belief that has only a religious ground – a ground that, almost certainly, only some churches accept. Is this distinction – between, on the one side, government's privileging one or more churches and, on the other, government's disfavoring conduct on the basis of a moral belief that has only a religious ground – merely formalistic: Is it a distinction without a difference? Does the distinction bear the weight I am putting on it here? A fair question – to which the answer is yes, the distinction *does* bear the weight. It *does* make sense to read the nonestablishment norm as I do. Let me explain.

Government can get along very well without privileging one or more churches – without privileging, for example, either membership in or a worship practice of one or more churches. There is simply no practical need for it to do so; indeed, there is a practical need for it *not* to do so. (Or so many of us Americans believe.)[24] But legislators cannot get along without relying on moral beliefs – because they must often resolve controverises that are fundamentally and unavoidably moral in character. One may respond – especially one who rejects religious belief – that legislators *can* get along without relying on moral beliefs *that lack plausible secular grounding*. From the perspective of many religious believers in the United States, however, to forbid legislators to disfavor conduct on the basis of a moral belief that has a religious ground unless the belief also has a plausible, independent secular ground (i.e., for the judiciary to strike down the political choice if it lacks plausible, independent secular grounding) would be to import into the Constitution a controversial conception of the proper relation between morality and religion, according to which morality – at least, morality "in the public square" – can and should stand independent of religion. For some Americans – especially for some who are not religious believers – that conception of the proper relation between morality and religion is attractive. But for the large majority of Americans who are religious believers,[25] their most fundamental moral judgments are inextricably rooted in their religious faith; moreover, they are skeptical that those judgments can stand – can be warranted – independent of religious faith, whether their own religious faith or some other religious faith. For such Americans, to construe the nonestablishment norm to forbid legislators to base a political choice on a religiously grounded moral belief unless the belief also has plausible, independent secular grounding would not only not make sense; it would also unfairly deprivilege religious faith, relative to secular belief, as a ground of moral judgment – and unfairly deprivilege too, therefore, those moral judgments that, in their view, cannot stand independent of religious faith. Such a construal – while understandably appealing to some who reject religious faith – is widely and deeply controversial. Such a construal is, in a word, sectarian and has no claim on the large majority of Americans for whom religious faith and moral judgment are often inextricably related.

From the perspective of those for whom their religious faith and their fundamental moral judgments are inextricably connected, constitutional scholars such as Andrew Koppelman[26] and Kathleen Sullivan[27] (and, in an earlier incarnation, myself)[28] are trying to conscript the nonestablishment norm to serve their own conception of the proper relation between morality and religion – a contestable and widely contested conception that should not be accorded constitutional status in a country most of whose citizens believe that their most fundamental moral judgments cannot stand independent of their religious faith. Indeed, it is far from obvious why *any* conception of the proper relation between morality (in the public square) and religion – including a conception according to which morality should stand independent of religion – should be accorded constitutional status in a society in which the question of the proper relation between morality and religion is so disputed. So, let me emphasize: That there should *not* be a rule that government may not disfavor conduct on the basis of a religiously grounded belief unless the belief also has plausible secular grounding, does not entail that there *should be* a rule that government may not disfavor conduct on the basis of a secularly grounded belief unless the belief also has religious grounding. *Neither rule should be part of our constitutional law.* It comes as no surprise that there has never been a movement to constitutionalize anything like the latter rule; but Koppelman, Sullivan, and some others would have the Supreme Court constitutionalize something like the former rule.

In the course of e-mail discussions as I was revising an earlier version of this chapter, Andrew Koppelman pressed the question "why it's appropriate for the state to be determining the authoritative sources of theological guidance...."[29] (According to Koppelman, for government to disfavor conduct on the basis of the belief that the conduct is immoral is, in the absence of a plausible, independent secular ground for that belief, "indistinguishable from, and amounts to, a state determination of the authoritative sources of theological guidance.")[30] But I'm not arguing that government may determine "the authoritative sources of theological guidance" for you, or for me, or indeed for anyone, as we or they struggle to discern the correct answer to one or another controversial moral question. I am arguing only that in deciding whether to disfavor conduct (at least partly) on the basis of the belief that it is immoral, one or more legislators – even a majority of them – may answer the question of whether the conduct is in fact immoral on the ground or grounds in which *they* have the most confidence, in which *they* place the most trust, and then make their political choice accordingly. In particular, they may do so whether or not the ground (or grounds) is religious – and, so, even if it *is* religious. (Of course, this is not to say that the political choice they make – for example, a choice disfavoring racial intermarriage, or same-sex marriage – is necessarily constitutional. The choice may violate a constitutional provision other than the nonestablishment norm.) Koppelman's position, by contrast, is that they may *not* do so if the ground is religious, unless there is a plausible, independent secular ground for the view that the conduct is immoral.[31]

Nothing I've said is meant to deny that religious grounds for moral beliefs are destined to be controversial in a religiously pluralistic society such as the United States. But secular grounds for moral belief are destined to be controversial – "sectarian" – too. As Chris Eberle has argued, "[t]he challenge to the advocate of restraint is that of discovering some relevant difference between religious and secular norms in virtue of which it is reasonable to advocate restraint regarding the former but not the latter. Only by identifying some such relevant difference can the advocate of restraint non-arbitrarily exclude religious but not secular grounds from political deliberation."[32] In the context of this chapter, the question is whether any "relevant difference" warrants a construal of the nonestablishment norm according to which (a) government is free to disfavor conduct on the basis of a moral belief that has a plausible, independent secular ground, no matter how controversial the secular ground may be, and without regard to whether the moral belief also has religious grounding, but (b) government is not free to disfavor conduct on the basis of a moral belief that has a religious ground, no matter how ecumenical (i.e., how widely shared among religious denominations) the religious ground may be, unless the moral belief also has plausible, independent secular grounding. (It would beg the question to invoke the nonestablishment norm in support of that construal of the norm: The question at hand is precisely whether the nonestablishment norm should be so construed. The claim that such a construal of the nonestablishment norm is axiomatic for us Americans is simply mistaken.) One needs a most compelling argument to warrant such a problematic – indeed, sectarian – reading of the nonestablishment norm.

In the absence of such an argument, there is no warrant for construing the nonestablishment norm to mandate discrimination against religiously grounded moral beliefs that lack plausible, independent secular grounding. Indeed, such discrimination is, as a practical matter, discrimination against many religious believers, namely, those whose most fundamental moral beliefs (all or some of them) fit the profile: beliefs that (a) are religiously grounded, but that (b) have no plausible, independent secular grounding. According to the non-establishment norm, thus construed, such believers would have only a kind of second-class citizenship; they would not have a citizenship equal to that of citizens whose most fundamental moral beliefs are secularly grounded.[33] As I said, one needs a compelling argument to warrant this reading of the nonestablishment norm – a reading that compromises the equal citizenship of many religious believers. I am myself aware of no such argument.[34]

Now, one might want to suggest that under my reading of the non-establishment norm, according to which government may disfavor conduct on the basis of a religiously grounded moral belief for which there may be no plausible, independent secular grounding, a legislature could and might do all sorts of terrible things – for example, ban the use of all electrical devices on Sundays (except, perhaps, those necessary to protect life or health) on the basis of a biblically grounded moral belief.[35] But does anyone really believe that any legislative body in the United States – or in any other religiously pluralistic liberal democracy – would want to do such a thing, much less actually do it, even if were there no nonestablishment norm? Is the nonestablishment norm, construed to forbid government to disfavor conduct on the basis of a religiously grounded moral belief (unless there is plausible, independent secular grounding for the belief), really all that stands between us and such an extreme state of affairs? If the "parade of horribles" argument is the last resort of those who would defend the construal of the nonestablishment norm against which I have argued in this chapter, I am content to rest my case.

This is not to deny that one or more legislatures in the United States might want to do some things that many would regard as terrible. But let's not forget that any "terrible" thing a legislature might want to do – for example, ban most pre-viability abortions or refuse to extend the benefit of law to same-sex unions – is almost certainly something for which there is a secular rationale as well as a religious one. The nonestablishment norm, construed to permit government to disfavor conduct on the basis of a religiously grounded moral belief if there is plausible, independent secular grounding for the belief, would be little if any impediment to legislatures' doing such things. This is not to say that there is never a significant constitutional impediment to a legislature's doing such a thing. (I have argued elsewhere that there *is* such an impediment to a state legislature's refusing to extend the benefit of law to same-sex unions.)[36] The point, rather, is that the nonestablishment norm would not be a significant impediment *even if we adopted the construal of the norm against which I have contended here.* At least, the norm would not be a significant impediment; it would be a weak to nonexistent impediment, if the courts were to apply the plausibility requirement – the requirement that the independent secular ground of the moral belief be plausible – deferentially, as arguably they should. As I explained earlier in the chapter, if the courts were to apply the plausibility requirement nondeferentially, they could and would justly be criticized as usurping politics – as arrogating to themselves issues that should be resolved not by electorally unaccountable judges but by the electorally accountable representatives of the people.[37]

The nonestablishment norm does not stand in the way – and, for the reasons I have given here, should not be construed to stand in the way – of legislators' or other policymakers' outlawing or otherwise disfavoring conduct on the basis of a religiously grounded belief that the conduct is immoral, even if it is assumed that the belief lacks a plausible, independent secular ground.[38]

3

Why Political Reliance on Religiously Grounded Morality Is Not Illegitimate in a Liberal Democracy

INTRODUCTION

In this chapter, as in the preceding one, I am concerned with the legitimacy of political reliance on religiously grounded morality. In the preceding chapter, I was concerned with legitimacy in the sense of consistency with the nonestablishment norm; here, I am concerned with legitimacy in the sense of consistency with the morality of liberal democracy. The two main questions I address in this chapter are these:

- Do citizens or their political representatives contravene the morality of liberal democracy by relying on religiously grounded moral belief in public discussions about whether to outlaw or otherwise disfavor conduct (abortion, for example, or same-sex unions)?
- Do legislators or other policymakers contravene the morality of liberal democracy by outlawing or otherwise disfavoring conduct on the basis of religiously grounded moral belief?

Assume that, as I argued in the preceding chapter, government officials do not violate the nonestablishment norm by disfavoring conduct on the basis of religiously grounded moral belief. This leaves open the possibility that government officials nonetheless betray the morality of liberal democracy by doing so. In my judgment, however, which I defend in this chapter, the morality of liberal democracy does not forbid legislators or other policymakers to disfavor conduct on the basis of religiously grounded moral belief. (I clarified, at the beginning of the preceding chapter, what I mean by "religiously grounded" moral belief and by making a political choice "on the basis of" such belief.) Nor does the morality of liberal democracy forbid citizens or their political representatives to rely on religiously grounded moral belief in public discussions about whether to disfavor conduct.

THE MORALITY OF LIBERAL DEMOCRACY

What is the morality – what are the moral commitments – of liberal democracy? The foundational moral commitment of liberal democracy is to the true and full humanity of *every* person – and, therefore, to the inviolability of *every* person[1] – without regard to race, sex, religion, and so on. This commitment is axiomatic for liberal democracy.

[P]erhaps the litmus test of whether the reader is in any sense a liberal or not is Gladstone's foreign-policy speeches. In [one such speech,] taken from the late 1870s, around the time of the Midlothian campaign, [Gladstone] reminded his listeners that "the sanctity of life in the hill villages of Afghanistan among the winter snows, is as inviolable in the eye of almighty God as can be your own ... that the law of mutual love is not limited by the shores of this island, is not limited by the boundaries of Christian civilization; that it passes over the whole surface of the earth, and embraces the meanest along with the greatest in its unmeasured scope." By all means smile at the oratory. But anyone who sneers at the underlying message is not a liberal in any sense of that word worth preserving.[2]

Moreover, this foundational commitment to the inviolability of every person is a principal ground of liberal democracy's further commitment to certain basic human freedoms. As Charles Larmore has put the point: "The familiar constitutional rights of free-expression, property, and political participation, though no doubt serving to promote the goal of democratic self-rule, also have an independent rationale. They draw upon that most fundamental of individual rights, which is the right [of every person] to equal respect."[3] Indeed, these two allied commitments – to the humanity/inviolability of every person and to certain basic human freedoms – are constitutive of liberal democracy; they are what make a democracy a "liberal" democracy. *These two commitments are the heart of the morality of liberal democracy.*

A conference at which I spoke in May 1999 was titled Political Thought After Liberalism.[4] This was, I thought, a puzzling title. We citizens of the United States, and of other liberal democracies, do not now live in a time that is "after liberalism." We Americans are all liberals now. (There is only slight rhetorical excess here: We Americans are, *almost* all of us, liberals now.) That is, we are all not merely democrats (small "d") but *liberal* democrats. We are all committed both to the true and full humanity of every person and, therefore, to certain basic human freedoms (liberties). Indeed, we have come to cherish these freedoms, and to trumpet them to the world, as human rights. In the United States, the moral arguments and the related political arguments about such matters as same-sex unions, physician-assisted suicide, the death penalty, and abortion are not, in the main, arguments between liberals on the one side and nonliberals on the other. Rather, these arguments are, in the main, arguments among liberals. They are arguments among citizens all of whom are committed to the true and full humanity of every person and to the basic human freedoms characteristic of – indeed, constitutive of – early-twenty-first-century liberal democracies.

This is not to deny that there are important differences among liberals.

- Some liberals are religious believers; others are not. Some liberals give a religious justification for their liberalism – for their commitment both to the true and full humanity of every person and to the basic human freedoms constitutive of liberal democracy; others give a nonreligious justification. (It is not the character of the justification that one gives for one's commitment to the true and full humanity of every person that, in part, makes one a liberal; it is the commitment itself.)
- Some liberals are moral conservatives, reluctant to abandon moral orthodoxies in favor of dissenting moral positions (e.g., about homosexuality); others are not conservative, or are less so.
- Some liberals are pessimistic about the capacity of government, especially centralized national government, to accomplish much good in the world, so they are wary about relying on government to make the world a better place, either the world at home or the world abroad; others are not pessimistic, or are less so.

And so on. But notwithstanding these and other important differences, we Americans are (almost) all liberals now. I know that this thought does not go down easily. We live in a time when demagogues, polemicists, and pundits have largely succeeded in turning the word "liberal" into an epithet – a dirty word. Let us reclaim our discourse. We Americans are all liberals now, because we affirm the true and full humanity of every person, without regard to race, sex, religion, and so on, and we also affirm, therefore, certain basic human freedoms (e.g., the freedoms of speech, press, and religion). It is this twofold affirmation that makes a democracy a "liberal" democracy, a political morality a "liberal" political morality, and a person a "liberal." No understanding or interpretation of the term "liberal" is *less* tendentious than this. We're (almost) all liberals now.

But, again, this doesn't mean that we liberals can't or don't disagree among ourselves – sometimes passionately and deeply – about many things. One of the things we disagree about: the legitimacy of political reliance on religiously grounded morality.

RELYING ON RELIGIOUSLY GROUNDED MORAL BELIEF IN PUBLIC POLITICAL ARGUMENT

In the United States, there is no constitutional impediment to religious believers' (citizens, legislators, policymakers)[5] introducing religiously grounded belief that conduct is immoral into public political argument, including argument of the sort with which I am principally concerned here: argument about whether or not to disfavor the conduct. (There are, however, substantial constitutional impediments to government's disallowing the introduction of such belief into public political argument: the constitutional norms that protect the freedoms of speech and press and the free exercise of religion.)[6] But this does not mean that religious believers *may* introduce religiously grounded moral belief into public political argument. That one is constitutionally free to do something – for example, utter a racial epithet – does not entail that one is also morally free to do it. In a liberal democracy, may religious believers introduce religiously grounded moral belief into public political argument; is it morally permissible, in a liberal democracy, for them to do so? This is a not question about political strategy but about political morality – the morality of liberal democracy. "[T]he distinction between principle and prudence should be emphasized. The fundamental question is not whether, as a matter of prudent judgment in a religiously pluralist society, those who hold particular religious views ought to cast their arguments in secular terms. Even an outsider can say that the answer to that question is clearly, 'Yes, most of the time,' for only such a course is likely to be successful overall."[7]

Again, the two constitutive commitments of liberal democracy – the two commitments that make a democracy "liberal" – are (1) the commitment to the true and full humanity of *every* person, without regard to race, sex, religion, and so on, and (2) the allied commitment to certain basic human freedoms. Nothing in the morality of liberal democracy – nothing in either of liberal democracy's two constitutive commitments – supports the claim that it is illegitimate for religious believers to introduce religiously grounded moral belief into public political argument. Introducing such belief into public political argument does not, in and of itself, betray either of liberal democracy's two constitutive commitments.

Nonetheless, some persons want to keep religiously grounded moral belief out of public political argument as much as possible. The American philosopher Richard Rorty, for example, has written approvingly of "privatizing religion – keeping it out of ... 'the public square,' making it seem bad taste to bring religion into discussions of public policy."[8] However, a powerful practical consideration opposes Rorty's position – a powerful practical reason why even nonbelievers should want religious believers, when they participate in public political argument, to articulate the religiously grounded moral belief that moves them to defend the position they do.

Imagine that it is proposed to make, or to maintain, a political choice disfavoring conduct that many citizens believe to be immoral – the political choice, for example, not to extend the benefit of law to same-sex unions. Imagine, too, that a widely accepted religiously grounded belief holds that the conduct is immoral – for example, the biblically grounded belief that homosexual sexual conduct is, always and everywhere, immoral. It is inevitable, in the United States, that some citizens and legislators will support the political choice at least partly on the ground of the religiously (biblically) grounded belief. It is also inevitable that some citizens and legislators, because they accept the religiously grounded belief, will take more seriously than they otherwise would, and perhaps accept, a secular (i.e., nonreligious) belief that supports the political choice – for example, the belief that homosexuality, like alcoholism, is a pathology that ought not to be indulged,[9] or the belief that legalizing same-sex unions would subvert the institution of heterosexual marriage. Because of the role that religiously grounded moral belief inevitably plays in the political process, then, it is important that such beliefs, no less than secular moral beliefs, be presented in public political argument *so that they can be tested there.*

Indeed, sometimes it is appropriate and even important that religiously grounded moral belief be tested, in the to-and-fro of public political argument, on its own terms. Consider, in that regard, scriptural scholar Luke Timothy Johnson's admonition:

> If liberal Christians committed to sexual equality and religious tolerance abandon these texts as useless, they also abandon the field of Christian hermeneutics to those whose fearful and – it must be said – sometimes hate-filled apprehension of Christianity will lead them to exploit and emphasize just those elements of the tradition that have proved harmful to humans. If what Phyllis Trible has perceptively termed "texts of terror" within the Bible are not encountered publicly and engaged intellectually by a hermeneutics that is at once faithful and critical, then they will continue to exercise their potential for harm among those who, without challenge, can claim scriptural authority for their own dark impulses.[10]

It is easy to anticipate the dismissive reply that public political argument is simply too debased to serve as a context for serious critical discussion of religiously grounded moral belief. My response is twofold. First, if public political debate is too debased to serve as a context for serious critical discussion of religiously grounded moral belief, then it is too debased to serve as a context for serious critical discussion of secular moral belief as well – and of much else, too. Second, the issue that engages me here is the proper role of religiously grounded morality, not in a politics too debased for serious critical discussion of moral belief, but in a politics at least *sometimes* and in *some* places – in *some* fora – fit for such discussion. Is it naive to think that American politics fits that profile? It is useful to recall here that public political discussion takes place in op-ed pieces and magazine articles, for example, as well as in television ads and on bumper stickers; indeed, it takes place much more seriously in the former fora than in the latter.

Still, some persons, such as Rorty, want to privatize religion; they want to keep religiously grounded moral belief out of "the public square" as much as possible. Why? Because religiously grounded arguments about controversial political issues can be quite divisive? American history does not suggest that religiously grounded arguments about controversial moral/political issues – racial discrimination, for example, or war – are invariably, or even usually, more divisive than secular arguments about those issues.[11] Some issues are so controversial that arguments about them are inevitably divisive without regard to whether the arguments are religiously grounded.[12]

To be sure, religious discourse in public – whether in public political argument or in other parts of our public culture – is sometimes quite sectarian and therefore divisive. But religiously grounded moral discourse is not necessarily more sectarian than secular moral discourse. It can be much less sectarian. After all, certain basic moral premises common to the Jewish and Christian traditions, in conjunction with the supporting religious premises, still constitute the fundamental moral horizon of most Americans – much more than do Kantian (or neo-Kantian) premises, or Millian premises, or Nietzschean premises (and so forth). According to Jesuit sociologist John Coleman, "the tradition of biblical religion is arguably the most powerful and pervasive symbolic resource" for public ethics in the United States today. "[O]ur tradition of religious ethics seems . . . to enjoy a more obvious public vigor and availability as a resource for renewal in American culture than either the tradition of classic republican theory or the American tradition of public philosophy." Coleman reminds us that "the strongest American voices for a compassionate just community always appealed in public to religious imagery and sentiments, from Winthrop and Sam Adams, Melville and the Lincoln of the second inaugural address, to Walter Rauschenbusch and Reinhold Niebuhr and Frederick Douglass and Martin Luther King." As Coleman explains, "The American religious ethic and rhetoric contain rich, polyvalent symbolic power to command sentiments of emotional depth, when compared to 'secular' language, . . . [which] remains exceedingly 'thin' as a symbol system." Coleman emphasizes that "when used as a public discourse, the language of biblical religion is beyond the control of any particular, denominational theology. It represents a common American cultural patrimony. . . . American public theology or religious ethics . . . cannot be purely sectarian. The biblical language belongs to no one church, denomination, or sect." In Coleman's view,

The genius of public American theology . . . is that it has transcended denominations, been espoused by people as diverse as Abraham Lincoln and Robert Bellah who neither were professional theologians nor belonged to any specific church and, even in the work of specifically trained professional theologians, such as Reinhold Neibuhr, has appealed less to revelational warrant for its authority within public policy discussions than to the ability of biblical insights and symbols to convey a deeper human wisdom. . . . Biblical imagery . . . lies at the heart of the American self-understanding. It is neither parochial nor extrinsic.[13]

Another reason for wanting to fence religiously grounded moral belief out of public political argument focuses on the inability of some believers to achieve a critical distance from their religious belief – the kind of critical distance essential to truly deliberative argument. But in the United States and in other liberal democracies, many believers *are* able to achieve a critical distance from many if not all of their religious beliefs;[14] they are certainly as able to do so as they and others are able to gain a critical distance from other fundamental beliefs.[15] Undeniably, some believers are unable to achieve much if any critical distance from their fundamental religious beliefs. As so much in the twentieth century attests, however, one need not be a religious believer to adhere to one's fundamental beliefs with closed-minded or even fanatical tenacity.

Although no one who has lived through recent American history should believe that religious contributions to the public discussion of controversial moral issues are invariably deliberative rather than dogmatic, there is no reason to believe that religious contributions are never deliberative. Religious discourse about the difficult moral issues that engage and divide us citizens of liberal democratic societies is not necessarily more monologic (or otherwise problematic) than resolutely secular discourse about those issues. Because of the religious illiteracy – and, alas, even prejudice – rampant among many nonreligious intellectuals,[16] we probably need reminding that, at its best, religious discourse in public culture is not less dialogic – not less open-minded, not less deliberative – than is, at its best, secular discourse in public culture. (Nor, at its worst, is religious discourse more monologic – more closed-minded and dogmatic – than is, at its worst, secular discourse.)[17] The Jesuit theologian David Hollenbach has developed this important point:

> Much discussion of the public role of religion in recent political thought presupposes that religion is more likely to fan the flames of discord than contribute to social concord. This is certainly true of some forms of religious belief, but hardly of all. Many religious communities recognize that their traditions are dynamic and that their understandings of God are not identical with the reality of God. Such communities have in the past and can in the future engage in the religious equivalent of intellectual solidarity, often called ecumenical or interreligious dialogue.[18]

A central feature of Hollenbach's work is his argument, which I accept, that the proper role of "public" religious discourse in a society as religiously pluralistic as the United States is a role to be played, in the main, much more in public culture – in particular, "in those components of civil society that are the primary bearers of cultural meaning and value – universities, religious communities, the world of the arts, and serious journalism" – than in public argument specifically about political issues.[19] He writes: "[T]he domains of government and policy-formation are not generally the appropriate ones in which to argue controverted theological and philosophical issues. . . ."[20] But, as Hollenbach goes on to acknowledge, "it is nevertheless neither possible nor desirable to construct an airtight barrier between politics and culture."[21]

There is, then, this additional reason for not discouraging the introduction of religiously grounded moral belief into public political argument: In a society as overwhelmingly religious as the United States,[22] we do present and discuss – and we should present and discuss – religiously grounded moral belief in our public culture. ("[W]e can freely and intelligently exercise our freedom of choice on fundamental matters having to do with our own individual ideals and conceptions of the good only if we have access to an unconstrained discussion in which the merits of competing moral, religious, aesthetic, and philosophical values are given a fair opportunity for hearing.")[23] Rather than try to do the impossible – maintain a wall of separation ("an airtight barrier") between the religiously grounded moral discourse that inevitably and properly takes place in public culture ("universities, religious communities, the world of the arts, and serious journalism") on the one side, and the discourse that takes place in public political argument ("the domains of government and policy-formation") on the other side – we should simply welcome the presentation of religiously grounded moral belief in *all* areas of our public culture, *including* public argument specifically about contested political choices.[24] Indeed, we should not merely welcome but *encourage* the presentation of such belief in public political argument – so that we can test it there.

But we can and should do more than test religiously grounded moral belief in public political argument. We should also, in the course of testing such beliefs, let ourselves be tested by them. In a political community that aspires to be not merely democratic but *deliberatively* democratic, there is surely virtue in allowing ourselves to be tested by positions with which, at the outset, we disagree. About fifteen years ago, in my book *Morality, Politics, and Law*, I wrote:

If one can participate in politics and law – if one can use or resist power – only as a partisan of particular moral/religious convictions about the human, and if politics is and must be in part about the credibility of such convictions, then we who want to participate, whether as theorists or activists or both, must examine our own convictions self-critically. We must be willing to let our convictions be tested in ecumenical dialogue with others who do not share them. We must let ourselves be tested, in ecumenical dialogue, by convictions we do not share. We must, in short, resist the temptations of infallibilism.[25]

Richard Rorty no doubt speaks for many secular intellectuals in suggesting that we act to "privatiz[e] religion – [to] keep[] it out of . . . 'the public square', making it seem bad taste to bring religion into discussions of public policy."[26] But Rorty is wrong. We should make it seem bad taste to sneer when people bring their religious convictions to bear in public discussions of controversial moral/political issues, such as homosexuality and abortion. It is not *that* religious convictions are brought to bear in public political argument that should worry us, but *how* they are sometimes brought to bear (e.g., dogmatically). But we should be no less worried about how fundamental secular convictions are sometimes brought to bear in public political debate.

Rorty and others to the contrary notwithstanding, we Americans – nonbelievers no less than believers – should welcome and even encourage the forthright presentation of religiously grounded moral belief in public political argument. Let me recapitulate the points I have featured here:

- Given the influential role that some religiously grounded moral beliefs play in our politics, it is important that we test such beliefs in public political argument. Moreover, our political culture cannot be truly deliberative unless we let ourselves be tested by religiously grounded moral beliefs. It is important, therefore, that we "public-ize" religion, not privatize it.
- In the United States, religiously grounded moral belief in public political argument is not necessarily more sectarian or divisive than secular moral belief. Nor are those who rely on religiously grounded moral belief in public political argument necessarily less deliberative than those who rely only on secular moral belief.
- It is quixotic, in any event, to attempt to construct an airtight barrier between religiously grounded moral discourse in public culture – which discourse is not merely legitimate but important – and such discourse in public political argument.

OUTLAWING OR OTHERWISE DISFAVORING CONDUCT ON THE BASIS OF RELIGIOUSLY GROUNDED MORAL BELIEF

Recall, from the preceding chapter, the conscientious legislator who must decide whether to vote to outlaw, or otherwise disfavor, particular conduct – abortion, for example, or same-sex unions. She still wonders what weight, if any, she and her fellow legislators may put on what is, for them, a religiously grounded belief, namely, that the conduct is immoral. In the preceding chapter, I addressed, and allayed, her concern that for a legislature to disfavor conduct on the basis of religiously grounded moral belief might violate the nonestablishment norm. But she still has something to worry about: the possibility that by disfavoring conduct on the basis of a religiously grounded moral belief, a legislature, though it does not violate the nonestablishment norm, nonetheless acts contrary to the morality of liberal democracy.

I said that in the United States there is no constitutional impediment to religious believers' introducing religiously grounded belief about the (im)morality of conduct into public argument about whether to disfavor the conduct. Is there, in the United States, any constitutional impediment to religious believers' – in particular, legislators and other policymakers – disfavoring conduct on the basis of religiously grounded belief that the conduct is immoral? In the preceding chapter, I argued that the nonestablishment norm is not an impediment. But that there is no constitutional impediment does not entail that there is no moral impediment. Does the morality of liberal democracy forbid religious believers, especially legislators and other policymakers, to disfavor conduct on the basis of religiously grounded moral belief? This question has broader relevance than the question of whether the nonestablishment norm forbids them to do so: Not every liberal democracy has a constitutional requirement that government not establish religion. Nor need every liberal democracy have such a requirement; as I have explained elsewhere, if a constitution vigorously protects the free exercise of religion, then the fact that it does not forbid government to establish religion does not imperil anyone's human rights.[27]

Just as nothing in the morality of liberal democracy forbids citizens or their political representatives to introduce religiously grounded moral belief into public political argument, nothing in the morality of liberal democracy forbids legislators or other policymakers to disfavor conduct on the basis of religiously grounded belief that the conduct is immoral. Disfavoring conduct on the basis of religiously grounded moral belief does not, in and of itself, betray either of liberal democracy's two constitutive commitments. Nothing either in the commitment to the true and full humanity of every person or in the allied commitment to certain basic human freedoms forbids legislators or other policymakers to disfavor conduct on the basis of a religiously grounded moral belief *just in virtue of the fact that the belief is religiously grounded.* (Recall that, as I explained in the preceding chapter, if the weaker claim cannot be sustained – the claim that, according to the morality of liberal democracy, one may not make a political choice disfavoring conduct on the basis of religiously grounded belief that the conduct is immoral – then it is unncessary to focus on the stronger claim that in making the choice one may not rely on such belief at all.) Nicholas Wolterstorff is right that the morality of liberal democracy, properly understood, forbids no such thing.[28]

[T]he ethic of the citizen in a liberal democracy imposes no restrictions on the reasons people offer in their discussion of political issues in the public square, and likewise imposes none of the reasons they have for their political decisions and actions. If the position adopted, and the manner in which it is acted upon, are compatible with the concept of liberal democracy, and if the discussion concerning the issue is conducted with civility, then citizens are free to offer and act on whatever reasons they find compelling. I regard it as an important implication of the concept of liberal democracy that citizens should have this freedom – that in this regard they should be allowed to act as they see fit. Liberal democracy implies, as I see it, that there should be no censorship in this regard.[29]

We can all agree, of course, that the morality of liberal democracy – not to mention the First Amendment's protection of the freedoms of speech and press and the free exercise of religion – tolerates no formal (i.e., legal) censorship; Wolterstorff is right to insist that the morality of liberal democracy tolerates no informal (moral) censorship either.

Why, then, might one be inclined to conclude that government – in particular, legislators and other policymakers, acting collectively – should not disfavor conduct on the basis of religiously grounded moral belief? Two main reasons – two main arguments – come to mind: the argument from respect and the argument from divisiveness.

The argument from respect can be understood as an argument based on the morality of liberal democracy, which is committed to

46

the true and full humanity of every person and therefore grounds "the right [of every person] to equal respect."[30] According to the argument from respect, for government to outlaw or otherwise disfavor conduct on the basis of religiously grounded moral belief is for government to act on the basis of a moral belief that some persons subject to the ban or regulation reasonably reject, and for government to do *that* is for it to deny to those persons the respect that is their due as persons – or, as John Rawls has put it, as "free and equal" persons.[31] (Although this claim could be directed at political reliance on religiously grounded moral belief, it is typically directed at political reliance on controversial moral belief, whether or not religiously grounded.) This claim frequently appears, in one guise or another, in essays purporting to present the "liberal" position on the issue of morality's proper role in politics. For example, Stephen Macedo has written that "[t]he liberal claim is that it is wrong to seek to coerce people on grounds that they cannot share without converting to one's faith."[32] Notwithstanding the frequency of its appearance, this "liberal" claim is deeply problematic.

Consider William Galston's response to the claim (as he understands the claim):

> [Charles] Larmore (and Ronald Dworkin before him) may well be right that the norm of equal respect for persons is close to the core of contemporary liberalism. But while the (general) concept of equal respect may be relatively uncontroversial, the (specific) conception surely is not. To treat an individual as person rather than object is to offer him an explanation. Fine; but *what kind* of explanation? Larmore seems to suggest that a properly respectful explanation must appeal to beliefs already held by one's interlocutors; hence the need for neutral dialogue. This seems arbitrary and implausible. I would suggest, rather, that we show others respect when we offer them, as explanation, what we take to be our best reasons for acting as we do.[33]

Galston's response needs to be both corrected and amended. First, the correction: Galston misconceives Larmore's position, which is that political "justification must appeal, not simply to the beliefs that the other happens to have, but to the beliefs he has on the assumption (perhaps counterfactual) that he affirms the norm of equal respect [for persons]."[34] Larmore has recently affirmed this aspect of his position: "The terms of political association are to be judged by reference to what citizens would accept, were they reasonable *and committed to the principle of equal respect for persons.*"[35]

Now, two crucial but friendly amendments to Galston's response: First, it is never for one to show respect for another for him to offer to her – for example, for a Nazi to offer to a Jew – an explanation to the effect that "You are not truly or fully human," even if the Nazi sincerely takes that to be his best reason for acting as he does. Second, respect counsels not only that we offer others, as explanation, what we take to be our best reasons for acting as we do, but also that we try to discern and then communicate to them whatever reason or reasons *they* might have for supporting – or, at least, for being less hostile to – the law or policy at issue. Chris Eberle has developed and defended this important point. As Eberle emphasizes, however, respect requires that we try to discern and then communicate such reasons. It does *not* require that if we fail in the effort, we restrain ourselves from acting as – from supporting the law or policy that – we otherwise would.[36]

Robert Audi has been one of the most important contributors to the literature about the proper role of religion in politics.[37] In his variation on the "liberal" position, Audi writes: "If you are fully rational and I cannot convince you of my view by arguments framed in the concepts we share as rational beings, then even if mine is the majority view I should not coerce you."[38] But *why*? I concur in Gerald Dworkin's observation: "There is a gap between a premise which requires the state to show equal concern and respect for all its citizens and a conclusion which rules out as legitimate grounds for coercion the fact that a majority believes that conduct is immoral, wicked, or wrong. That gap has yet to be closed."[39] Indeed, it is doubtful that the gap *can* be closed. It is altogether obscure why we do not show others the respect that is their due, first, "when we offer them, as explanation, what we take to be our best reasons for acting as we do" (so long as our reasons do not assert, presuppose, or entail the inferior humanity of those to whom the explanation is offered) and, second, when we try (even if in the end we fail) to discern and communicate other reasons that might win their consent, or at least diminish their hostility, to the law or policy at issue.[40]

The argument from divisiveness provides a second main reason why one might be inclined to conclude that government should not outlaw or otherwise disfavor conduct on the basis of religiously grounded moral belief: The social costs – costs mainly in the form of divisiveness and ensuing social instability – are too high. Let me put the argument from divisiveness, as we may call it, in context: In the United States and in kindred liberal democracies, freedom of religion enjoys vigorous constitutional protection; therefore, the set of moral beliefs on which government may base a political choice is limited. For example, government may not base a political choice on the belief that Roman Catholicism is a morally corrupt religion. In thinking about the argument from divisiveness, then, let's focus not on moral beliefs on which government constitutionally may *not* base a political choice – least of all a coercive political choice – but on moral beliefs on which it constitutionally *may* base a political choice.

It is implausible that in a liberal democracy such as the United States, basing a political choice on a constitutionally optional but nonetheless controversial moral belief – such as the belief that same-sex unions are immoral – will usually be *more* divisive if there is only a religious ground for the belief than if there is a secular ground (whether or not there is also a religious ground). As American history makes clear, some issues are so controversial that any political resolution of the issue is destined to be quite divisive without regard to whether the basis of the resolution is solely religious or solely secular or partly religious and partly secular.[41] Even if it be granted that some imaginable instances of political reliance on religiously grounded moral belief might, along with other factors, precipitate social instability, the fact remains that "[c]onditions in modern democracies may be so far from the conditions that gave rise to the religious wars of the sixteenth century that we no longer need worry about religious divisiveness as a source of substantial social conflict."[42] John Courtney Murray warned against "project[ing] into the future of the Republic the nightmares, real or fancied, of the past."[43] As Murray's comment suggests, a rapprochement between religion and politics forged in the crucible of a time or place very different from our own is not necessarily the best arrangement for our time and place. "[W]hat principles of restraint, if any, are appropriate may depend on time and place, on a sense of the present makeup of a society, of its history, and of its likely evolution."[44]

In my judgment, neither the argument from respect nor the argument from divisiveness bears the weight of the proposition that government should not disfavor conduct on the basis of religiously grounded moral belief. (Not that there are no other arguments in support of that proposition, but the argument from respect and the argument from divisiveness are the two main arguments.)[45] Neither argument bears the weight even of the weaker proposition that government should not disfavor conduct on the basis of religiously grounded moral belief if there is no plausible, independent secular grounding for the belief.

I said that nothing in the morality of liberal democracy forbids legislators or other policymakers to disfavor conduct on the basis of a religiously grounded moral belief just in virtue of the fact that the belief is religiously grounded. But an even stronger claim commands our assent: One particular religiously grounded belief – one fundamental religiously grounded moral claim – is not only a legitimate ground of political choice in a liberal democracy but a most fitting ground.

"Moral" argument, as I have explained elsewhere,[46] is often – and most fundamentally – about this:

> Which human beings ought we to care about – which ones, that is, besides those we already happen to care about, those we already happen to be emotionally or sentimentally attached to: ourselves, our families, our tribes, and so on? Which human beings ought to be the beneficiaries of our respect; the welfare, the well-being, of which human beings ought to be the object of our concern? Which human beings are inviolable; which are subjects of justice? All human beings, or just some?

As I noted earlier in this chapter, one of the two constitutive commitments of liberal democracy – one of the two commitments that make a democracy "liberal" – is the commitment to the true and full humanity of *every* person, without regard to race, sex, religion, and so on.[47] (The second constitutive commitment, grounded in part on the first, is to certain basic human freedoms.) This commitment is responsive to the "which human beings ought we to care about" inquiry: It is axiomatic, for liberal democracy, that every person (without regard to race, etc.) is a subject of justice – that every person is inviolable. Of course, the proposition that every person is inviolable is embraced by many who do not count themselves religious believers, but, as I have explained elsewhere,[48] it is obscure *on what basis* one who is not a religious believer, one who is an agnostic or even an atheist, can claim (indeed, can believe) that every person is inviolable: *Why* is it the case – *in virtue of what* is it the case – that every person is "not to be violated; not liable or allowed to suffer violence; to be kept sacredly free from profanation, infraction, or assault"?[49] As Jeff McMahon has emphasized, "[u]nderstanding the basis of our alleged inviolability is crucial both for determining whether it is plausible to regard ourselves as inviolable, and for fixing the boundaries of the class of inviolable beings."[50] In any event, that every person is inviolable is, for many religious believers, a religiously embedded tenet. And, in a liberal democracy, it is altogether fitting – it is altogether "liberal" – for religious believers to make political choices, including *coercive* choices – choices to ban or require conduct – on the ground of what is, for them, a religious claim: that each and every person is sacred, that all persons are subjects of justice.[51]

CONCLUSION

In the preceding chapter, I concluded that the nonestablishment norm does not stand in the way – nor should it be construed to stand in the way – of legislators or other policymakers outlawing or otherwise disfavoring conduct on the basis of a religiously grounded belief that the conduct is immoral (even if it is assumed that the belief lacks plausible, independent sexular grounding). In this chapter, I have concluded that the morality of liberal democracy counsels neither against disfavoring conduct on the basis of religiously grounded moral belief nor, much less, against relying on religiously grounded moral belief in public argument about whether to disfavor conduct. I hope that these two conclusions will not be overread.

My arguments in this book (as I noted in the Introduction) are addressed to three groups. The *agnostics* are those who have who have no firm convictions about the proper role of religion in politics. (Again, one can be agnostic about the proper role of religion in politics without being agnostic about the existence of God, just as one can be agnostic about the existence of God without being agnostic about the proper role of religion in politics.) The *inclusionists* and the *exclusionists*, by contrast, do have firm convictions. While the inclusionists believe that religious faith may be included in the public life of the nation, the exclusionists believe that religious faith should be excluded, as much as possible, from it. The inclusionists affirm, and the exclusionists deny, that religion may play a significant role in politics. (It bears emphasis that although some religious believers are inclusionists, some others are exclusionists; and although some religious nonbelievers are exclusionists, some others are inclusionists.) My arguments in this chapter, and in the two preceding chapters, have been addressed mainly to the agnostics and the exclusionists. In the next three chapters, my arguments are addressed mainly to the agnostics and the inclusionists; they are addressed especially to those who, because they are both inclusionists and religious believers, are not at all shy about bringing their religion to bear on their politics. In the next chapter, for example, I explain why some religious believers (Christians) have good reason to be wary about relying on one kind of religiously grounded morality (biblically grounded morality) in deciding whether to oppose laws or other public policies that grant official recognition to same-sex unions.

I hope that my arguments in the next three chapters will make it clear that neither my conclusion in the preceding chapter, about the nonestablishment norm, nor my conclusion in this chapter, about the morality of liberal democracy, is meant to function as a call for religious believers, when they deliberate about or vote on proposals to outlaw or otherwise disfavor conduct, to rely uncritically, much less unhesitatingly, on religiously grounded moral belief. As I remarked in the Introduction, whereas in this and the two preceding chapters I have spoken as an inclusionist to agnostics and exclusionists, in the next three chapters I will speak to agnostics and inclusionists from the perspective of one who, though no longer an exclusionist, nonetheless shares some exclusionist concerns.

Part II

Mainly for the Agnostics and the Inclusionists, Especially Inclusionists Who Are Religious Believers

4

Christians, the Bible, and
Same-Sex Unions
An Argument for Political Self-Restraint

The reason produced for condemning the opinion that the earth moves and the sun stands still is that in many places in the Bible one may read that the sun moves and the earth stands still. Since the Bible cannot err, it follows as a necessary consequence that anyone takes an erroneous and heretical position who maintains that the sun is inherently motionless and the earth movable.

With regard to this argument, I think in the first place that it is very pious to say and prudent to affirm that the holy Bible can never speak untruth – whenever its true meaning is understood. But I believe that nobody will deny that it is often very abstruse, and may say things which are quite different from what its bare words signify. Hence if in expounding the Bible one were always to confine oneself to the unadorned grammatical meaning, one might fall into error. Not only contradictions and propositions far from true might thus be made to appear in the Bible, but even grave heresies and follies. . . .

Galileo Galilei[1]

Recall the conscientious legislator who, in deciding whether to vote to outlaw, or otherwise disfavor, particular conduct, wonders what weight, if any, she and her fellow legislators may put on what is, for them, a religiously grounded belief, namely, that the conduct is immoral. In Chapters 2 and 3, I explained that neither the nonestablishment norm nor the morality of liberal democracy stands in the way of legislators' or other policymakers' disfavoring conduct on the basis of religiously grounded moral belief. But as I emphasized at the end of Chapter 3, this does not mean that religious believers, when they deliberate about or vote on proposals to disfavor conduct, should rely uncritically on religiously grounded moral belief. In this chapter, I pursue an inquiry different from but complementary to the inquiries I pursued in Chapters 2 and 3; I explore the possibility that a Christian believer's religious tradition counsels her to be wary, in some circumstances, about disfavoring conduct on the basis of a *biblically* grounded moral belief of a certain sort: a biblically grounded belief that the conduct is immoral in the sense of contrary to the requirements of human well-being. (A person's belief that conduct is immoral is biblically "grounded" if she accepts the belief because she accepts a further belief that the Bible – the Bible understood as God-inspired and therefore authoritative – teaches that the conduct is immoral, and if she would not accept the belief if she did not also accept that further belief.) For purposes of the inquiries in Chapters 2 and 3, a fundamental aspect of the American morality of religious freedom (i.e., the nonestablishment norm) and, then, the morality of liberal democracy were paramount. But for purposes of the inquiry in this chapter, a Christian's own religious tradition is paramount. In deciding whether she should forgo or at least limit reliance on her biblically grounded moral belief, a citizen of a liberal democracy who is a Christian will want to consult the wisdom of her own religious tradition at least as much as she will want to consult either the morality of liberal democracy or, if she is a citizen of the United States, the American constitutional morality of religious freedom.

There are many examples of political controversy rooted in moral controversy. One such controversy – the moral/political controversy over same-sex unions[2] – is the principal occasion of the reflections about political self-restraint that I offer in this chapter. In the final chapter of this book, I turn to the even larger, and more difficult, moral/political controversy over abortion.

I

In the United States today, many persons, including many religious believers, hold that same-sex unions are not, as such, immoral and that the law should therefore recognize same-sex unions by extending to them the legal benefits granted to heterosexual marriage.[3] But many other persons hold that homosexual sexual conduct is, as such, always immoral – or, at least, that it is immoral in a substantial majority of cases, including a substantial majority of cases of same-sex unions – and that therefore the law should not recognize same-sex unions; for the law to do so, they argue, would be for the law both to affirm immorality and, thereby, to encourage its spread.

It bears emphasis that same-sex unions already exist; they exist in spite of the fact that the law does not recognize them.[4] The question is whether the law should recognize them. Even though, for now, the law does not recognize same-sex unions, they exist: "[C]ertain same-sex unions already are functioning in their communities as marriages. These gay and lesbian couples support and are supported by the community's practices of marriage and family as a whole. With these unions already in place, the task is not to reformulate marriage so that gays and lesbians might enter. Instead, the task is to understand how and why these same-sex unions fit so well...."[5]

I said that the question is whether the law should recognize same-sex unions. There is, however, a prior question: whether, as a constitutional matter, the law *must* recognize same-sex unions. I have argued elsewhere that a state's refusal to recognize same-sex unions violates the Fourteenth Amendment to the United States Constitution.[6] As I was drafting an earlier version of this chapter, the Supreme Court of Vermont ruled that the Vermont Constitution requires Vermont to extend to "same-sex couples . . . the benefits and protections that its laws provide to opposite-sex married couples."[7] But even if no state were constitutionally obligated to recognize same-sex unions, the question would remain whether, nonetheless, the law should recognize them – whether it should do so as a matter not of constitutional obligation but of political morality.

The moral argument at the heart of the fierce political controversy over whether the law should recognize same-sex unions – the argument about whether homosexual sexual conduct is always immoral – is at bottom an argument about the requirements of human well-being. Those who believe that homosexual sexual conduct is always (or almost always) immoral do so mainly because they believe that engaging in homosexual sexual conduct is always hostile to the authentic well-being of those who engage in it and is never, therefore, a fitting way for human beings to act. Thus, the argument about whether homosexual sexual conduct is always immoral exemplifies that, as I have explained elsewhere,[8] "moral" argument is often about this:

What is good – truly good – for those we should care about (including ourselves)? And what is bad for them? In particular: What are the requirements of one's well-being? (The "one" may be, at one extreme, a particular human being or, at the other, each and every human being.) What choices are friendly to or even constitutive of one's authentic well-being; what choices are hostile to or even destructive of it?

Many homosexual persons and others hold that same-sex unions are (or would be) truly good for many homosexual persons. But many others hold that same-sex unions are always truly bad for all persons – or, at least, that in a substantial majority of cases they are truly bad. Moreover, many persons who hold that same-sex unions are always truly bad – that they are always hostile to (authentic) human well-being – do so because they believe that the Bible teaches that homosexual sexual conduct is always hostile to human well-being. I argued in Chapters 2 and 3 that neither the morality of liberal democracy nor the nonestablishment norm counsels religious believers against disfavoring conduct on the basis of religiously grounded belief that the conduct is immoral *just in virtue of the fact that the belief is religiously grounded.* This does not mean, however, that religious believers, in deciding whether to disfavor conduct, have no reason to limit their reliance on religiously grounded moral belief. I explain in this chapter why Christians should be wary about opposing the legal recognition of same-sex unions on the basis of a biblically grounded belief that homosexual sexual conduct is always immoral. A person's belief that homosexual sexual conduct is always immoral is biblically grounded if she believes that homosexual sexual conduct is always immoral because she believes that the Bible (understood as God-inspired and therefore authoritative) teaches that homosexual sexual conduct is always immoral, and if she would not believe, or probably would not believe, that homosexual sexual conduct is always immoral if she did not believe that the Bible teaches that it is always immoral.

In my book *Love and Power*, I presented several reasons why citizens and their political representatives should be cautious about outlawing or otherwise disfavoring conduct they believe to be immoral – reasons why they should sometimes tolerate such conduct.[9] (For purposes of the reasons I presented in *Love and Power*, it doesn't matter whether the ground of the moral belief is religious or not. For the interested reader, I have excerpted the relevant passages from *Love and Power* as an appendix to this chapter.) Those reasons counsel citizens and their representatives to be cautious about disfavoring same-sex unions even if they believe (whether on a religious ground, a secular ground, or both) that homosexual sexual conduct is always immoral – that is, always hostile to human well-being. (Of course, that one should be cautious or wary about doing something does not entail that at the end of the day one should not do it.) Here my focus is more narrow: I explain why Christians should be wary about disfavoring, by opposing the legal recognition of, same-sex unions on the basis of a biblically grounded belief that homosexual sexual conduct is always immoral.

Of course, not every religious tradition is the same; not every religious tradition offers the same counsel. The particular religious tradition that informs my argument in this chapter is the one that has been formative for me: Roman Catholicism. My argument here is rooted in Catholic Christianity. My argument is meant to speak, however, not just to Catholics, but to all Christians. (As the twenty-first century begins, Christians still constitute the largest group, by far, of religious believers in the United States.)[10] I hope that my argument also speaks, even if only partially and indirectly, to religious believers who are not Christian.

II

Many persons who accept the Bible as a God-inspired text – in particular, as a text that, *inter alia,* reveals the will of God – believe that the Bible indicates that homosexual sexual conduct is always contrary to God's will – that it is always, in that fundamental sense, immoral. This belief about God's will is best understood as a belief about the requirements of human well-being. A religious believer might object that for him or her, this belief is not about (the requirements of) human well-being but only about God's will. It is implausible, however, to believe that a loving God – indeed, a God who *is* love (1 John 4:8 and 4:16) –

(1) has fashioned human nature – has defined the requirements of human well-being – in such a way that a same-sex union can be, for some, a truly and deeply fulfilling relationship for them as human beings, but at the same time

(2) has willed that no human being ever enter into such a relationship.[11]

Therefore, to believe that same-sex unions are always contrary to God's will is to believe that same-sex unions can never be truly fulfilling for anyone, that they are always hostile to authentic human well-being.

Charles Curran, the eminent Catholic moral theologian, has raised a helpful question, in correspondence, about my "emphasis on human well-being and human nature. Some people might criticize that [emphasis] as being too anthropocentric and not theocentric enough for a truly Protestant position. . . . The primary question perhaps even in the reformed tradition is what is the will of God and not what is human flourishing or human nature."[12] However, given two assumptions that few if any Christians would want to deny, the distinction between doing "what God wills or commands us to do" and doing "what fulfills our nature" is quite false. The two assumptions are, first, that human beings have a nature – indeed, a nature fashioned by God – and, second, that it is God's will that human beings act so as to fulfill or perfect their nature. As Bernard Williams has observed, "[preferred ethical categories] may be said to be given by divine command or revelation; in this form, if it is not combined with a grounding in human nature, the explanation will not lead us anywhere except into what Spinoza called 'the asylum of ignorance.'"[13] The belief that according to the Bible homosexual sexual conduct (including same-sex unions) is always contrary to God's will is, therefore, the belief that the Bible teaches – that God reveals in the Bible – that homosexual sexual conduct is always hostile to human well-being. Some religious believers hold that according to the inerrant teaching of the Bible, no kind of homosexual sexual relationship can be, for anyone, truly fulfilling.

Let me now explain why, in my judgment, Christians inclined to believe that the Bible teaches that homosexual sexual conduct is always hostile to human well-being should be wary about opposing the legal recognition of same-sex unions on the basis of that belief.

I said that many Christians believe that the Bible teaches that homosexual sexual conduct is always hostile to human well-being; they believe that the Bible teaches that no kind of homosexual sexual relationship can be, for anyone, truly fulfilling. The most relevant Old Testament passages are thought to be Genesis 19:1–29 and Leviticus 18:22 and 20:13; the most relevant New Testament passages, each from one of St. Paul's letters, are Romans 1:18–32, 1 Corinthians 6:9, and 1 Timothy 1:10. (According to Richard Hays, who believes that the Bible teaches that homosexual sexual conduct is always immoral, "[t]he most crucial text for Christian ethics concerning homosexuality remains Romans 1, because this is the only passage in the New Testament that places the condemnation of homosexual behavior in an explicitly theological context.")[14] However, many other Christians have come to believe that, properly interpreted, the Bible does *not* teach that homosexual sexual conduct is always hostile to human well-being; they have come to believe that it is a mistake to conclude that the Bible teaches that no kind of homosexual sexual relationship can

be, for anyone, truly fulfilling. There is now widespread and growing disagreement among Christians over what the Bible – in particular, the New Testament – does or does not teach about homosexual
sexual relationships. This is not a disagreement between Christians
on the one side and religious nonbelievers on the other. Nor is it a
disagreement between Christians on the one side and religious believers who are not Christian on the other. This is a disagreement
among Christians. Moreover, this disagreement among Christians is
not interdenominational but transdenominational: It is not a disagreement that divides some Christian denominations from other
Christian denominations, but one that that divides many members of
several denominations from many other members of the same denominations. (Keith Hartman provides an informative report in his book
Congregations in Conflict: The Battle Over Homosexuality [1996].) That the
disagreement is not interdenominational but transdenominational is
significant: The dissenting position that the Bible does not teach that
homosexual sexual conduct is always hostile to human well-being cannot be dismissed by the members of one denomination as just one
more lamentable example of the false (heretical) beliefs of the members of one or more other denominations. The dissenting position
that the Bible does not teach that no kind of homosexual sexual relationship can be, for anyone, truly fulfilling is a belief that grips growing
numbers of Christians largely without regard to their denominational
affiliation. This datum will give pause – indeed, should give pause – to
any reflective Christian.

The literature participating in this increasingly widespread, transdenominational disagreement is large.[15] Recent pieces defending the
traditional reading of the relevant biblical texts – the reading according to which the Bible teaches that homosexual sexual conduct is
always immoral – include:

- Charles L. Bartow, "Speaking the Text and Preaching the Gospel."[16]
- Richard B. Hays, "Awaiting the Redemption of Our Bodies: The
  Witness of Scripture Concerning Homosexuality."[17]
- Ulrich W. Mauser, "Creation, Sexuality, and Homosexuality in the
  New Testament."[18]
- Thomas E. Schmidt, "Romans 1:26–27 and Biblical Sexuality."[19]

Recent pieces dissenting from the traditional reading in favor
of a different reading – a reading according to which the Bible

does not teach that homosexual sexual conduct is always immoral – include:

- Brian K. Blount, "Reading and Understanding the New Testament on Homosexuality."[20]
- Victor Paul Furnish, "The Bible and Homosexuality: Reading the Texts in Context."[21]
- Daniel A. Helminiak, "The Bible on Homosexuality: Ethically Neutral."[22]
- Patricia Beattie Jung and Ralph F. Smith, "The Bible and Heterosexism."[23]
- Bruce J. Malina, "The New Testament and Homosexuality."[24]
- Choon-Leong Seow, "A Heterotextual Perspective."[25]
- Jeffrey S. Siker, "Homosexual Christians, the Bible, and Gentile Inclusion: Confessions of a Repenting Heterosexist."[26]

The interested reader can consult these (and kindred) pieces for herself.[27] My professional expertise does not qualify me to pass judgment here on the competing scriptural arguments – arguments about the true meaning of the relevant biblical passages. Not that I don't find some of the arguments more persuasive than others. Still, I have no professional expertise in the matter. I want simply to note that there is, and that it is *undeniable* that there is, an increasingly widespread, transdenominational disagreement among Christians over whether, according to the Bible, homosexual sexual conduct is invariably immoral – immoral without regard to any particularities of context. Indeed, some Christian ministers and communities are already "blessing" same-sex unions;[28] many more are welcoming and affirming same-sex couples as *faithful* members of their congregations.

It bears mention here that in June 1999, as I was drafting an earlier version of this chapter, "[a]n effort to repeal a law that effectively bars ordination of [noncelibate] gay men and lesbians in the Presbyterian Church (USA) was defeated by a 3-to-2 ratio ... by the church's General Assembly, the top policymaking body." What is remarkable is not that the effort was defeated but that so many "commissioners, as the assembly's delegates are called," voted to support the effort. The tally was 319 to 198.[29] One year later, in May 2000, "[t]he highest court of the Presbyterian Church (USA) ... ruled ... that its ministers may conduct religious 'holy union' ceremonies for same-sex couples, as long as the ceremonies are not regarded as marriages."[30] Then, on March 15, 2001, the Associated Press reported:

A proposal to bar Presbyterian clergy from officiating at commitment ceremonies for gay couples was defeated in a vote tally released [yesterday].... The vote is a victory for the liberal side in a conflict that has divided the 3.6 million Presbyterian Church (U.S.A.) for 24 years.... The Presbyterian measure to ban gay commitment ceremonies was passed by the church's national assembly last June and sent to 173 national legislatures, known as presbyteries, for ratification. As simply majority of 87 presbyteries was needed for passage, and the count now stands at 63 in favor and 87 opposed.... The proposal was a conservative bid to overturn a policy established by the denomination's highest court in a ruling last May.... The court said that the 1991 national assembly had defined Christian marriage as existing only between a man and a woman. But the court also said that does not bar clergy and congregations from holding same-sex ceremonies that are not readily confused with weddings.[31]

Widespread transdenominational disagreement among Christians over whether the Bible teaches about morality what some claim that it teaches is not a new phenomenon.[32] In the past, there was such disagreement over, for example, whether the Bible teaches that slavery can be morally permissible. Precisely because such disagreement is not a new thing, and because the historical experience of Christians discloses that Christians can be radically mistaken about whether in fact the Bible teaches about morality what some claim that it teaches, such disagreement – increasingly widespread disagreement among Christians, disagreement that is not interdenominational but transdenominational – should be an occasion for Christians to subject the traditional belief to careful, critical scrutiny. (Of course, doing so necessitates subjecting the emergent belief that challenges the traditional belief to such scrutiny, too.) Indeed, for Christians faced with such disagreement to fail to subject the traditional belief (that the Bible teaches so and so) to serious reexamination would be, not an act of humble fidelity, but an act of prideful infidelity. Two passages are relevant here, one from John Mahoney's magisterial book *The Making of Moral Theology: A Study of the Roman Catholic Tradition* (1987), the other from John Noonan's illuminating essay "Development in Moral Doctrine" (1993). First, Mahoney:

At any stage in history all that is available to the Church is its continual meditation on the Word of God in the light of contemporary experience and of the knowledge and insights into reality which it possesses at the time. To be faithful to that set of circumstances ... is the charge and the challenge which Christ has given to his

Church. But if there is a historical shift, through improvement in scholarship or knowledge, or through an entry of society into a significantly different age, then what that same fidelity requires of the Church is that it respond to the historical shift, such that it might be not only mistaken *but also unfaithful* in declining to do so.[33]

Now, Noonan:

One cannot predict future changes; one can only follow present light and in that light be morally certain that some obligations will never alter. The great commandments of love of God and of neighbor, the great principles of justice and charity continue to govern all development. God is unchanging, but the demands of the New Testament are different from those of the Old, and while no other revelation supplements the New, it is evident from the case of slavery alone that it has taken time to ascertain what the demands of the New really are. All will be judged by the demands of the day in which they live. It is not within human competence to say with certainty who was or will be saved; all will be judged as they have conscientiously acted. In new conditions, with new insight, an old rule need not be preserved in order to honor a past discipline. . . . In the Church there can always be fresh appeal to Christ, there is always the possibility of probing new depths of insight. . . . Must we not, then, frankly admit that change is something that plays a role in [Christian] moral teaching? . . . Yes, if the principle of change is the person of Christ.[34]

Again, such disagreement over whether the Bible teaches about morality what some claim that it teaches – increasingly widespread, transdenominational disagreement – should be an occasion for Christians to subject the traditional belief to careful, critical scrutiny. In particular, the increasingly widespread, transdenominational disagreement among Christians over whether the Bible teaches that no kind of homosexual sexual relationship can be, for anyone, truly fulfilling should be an occasion for Christians to subject to serious reexamination the traditional belief that homosexual sexual conduct is always contrary to the teaching of the Bible. How might a Christian do that? One obvious way is to examine carefully the emergent, dissident scriptural arguments that the Bible, properly interpreted, does not teach that homosexual sexual conduct is always hostile to human well-being.

That, however, is not the only way. There is another.

III

Noonan refers, in the passage just quoted, to "new conditions" and "new depths of insight." Mahoney refers to the Church's "continual meditation on the Word of God in the light of contemporary experience and of the knowledge and insights into reality which it possesses at the time." In her essay "An Ethic for Same-Sex Relations" (1983), Margaret Farley writes:

> The final source for Christian ethical insight is [contemporary human experience]. Scripture, tradition, and secular disciplines must all reflect on experiences, past and present. What differentiates the source I am calling "contemporary experience" is the unsystematic way we have access to it. In this context, I am referring primarily to the testimony of women and men whose sexual preference is for others of the same sex.[35]

There is a another, complementary way for Christians to subject the traditional belief – the belief that, according the the Bible, homosexual sexual conduct is always hostile to human well-being – to careful, critical scrutiny. It is for Christians to inquire whether any persuasive argument grounded, not on the Bible, but on contemporary human experience supports the belief that homosexual sexual conduct is always hostile to human well-being – the belief that no homosexual sexual relationship, or virtually no such relationship, can be truly fulfilling for any human being. By "persuasive," I mean persuasive to the Christian inquirer herself. If no persuasive argument grounded on contemporary human experience supports the belief that homosexual sexual conduct is always hostile to human well-being, this is reason for skepticism that such conduct is always hostile to human well-being. Given that Christians believe that what the Bible teaches about human well-being is true, this is reason too for Christians to be skeptical that the Bible teaches that homosexual sexual conduct is always hostile to human well-being.

Why should Christians (and others) put such weight on contemporary human experience? Why is such experience relevant? Authentic well-being is something that, in normal circumstances, human beings can be expected to experience. With respect to questions about the requirements of human well-being, human experience is, to say the least, probative. "Ethics will never be like physics, chemistry, or certain types of sociology, because it understands the moral reality to be about an interaction between persons and the world which can only be known from the reports of those who experience that interaction."[36] As Margaret Farley argues in her essay "The Role of Experience in Moral Discernment" (1996): "Experience is essential to both moral discernment and deliberation."[37] As John Noonan has cautioned, "[e]xperience as such, taken as 'raw experience,' the mere participation in this or that phenomenon, is . . . not the key. Raw experience carries with it no evaluation. But experience, *suffered or perceived in the light of human nature and of the gospel*, can be judged good or bad. It was the experience of unfreedom, in the gospel's light, that made the contrary shine clear."[38] Farley herself acknowledges that "[b]y itself, experience does not provide an incontestable, foundational deposit of insight in a fund of moral wisdom. . . . Interpretations of sexual experience can yield illusion and falsehood on a par with some interpretations of the Bible and of the Christian tradition."[39] Nonetheless, "there are some questions for which [contemporary experience] is an essential and even determinative source. I would argue that same-sex relations today present one of those questions."[40] Farley elaborates:

[T]here are some things important for moral discernment that simply cannot be known without experience – things like the limitations and possibilities for ourselves as moral agents, the dimensions of suffering and diminishment, the ways to hope and to love, the parameters of intimacy, the multiple consequences of injury and injustice. Moreover, all of our morally relevant knowledge (from whatever source) is modified when it partakes of experience – whether this is our knowledge of disease or of the complexities of a moral situation or of God. And there are issues of specific moral rules (and their exceptions) that cannot be resolved without access to some persons' experience – for example, issues of sexuality, of discrimination, of fidelity to covenants.[41]

In "An Ethic for Same-Sex Relations," Farley proceeds cautiously, accepting that "we have as yet no univocal voice putting to rest all of our questions regarding the status of same-sex relations." But she rightly insists that

[w]e do . . . have some clear and profound testimonies to the life-enhancing possibilities of same-sex relations and the integrating possibilities of sexual activity within these relations. We have the witness that homosexual activity can be a way of embodying responsible human love and sustaining Christian friendship. Without grounds in scripture, tradition, or any other source of human knowledge for an absolute prohibition of same-sex relations, this witness alone is enough to demand of the Christian community that it reflect anew on the norms for homosexual love.[42]

This, then, is the path I am proposing here: that Christians, faced with widespread and growing transdenominational controversy among Christians over whether the Bible really teaches about the requirements of human well-being what traditionally it has been interpreted to teach, inquire whether any persuasive argument grounded, not on the Bible, but on contemporary human experience supports the traditional belief about the Bible that is now being challenged. Let me anticipate a misunderstanding by emphasizing that this path does *not* oppose contemporary human experience to the Bible. (After all, I am speaking, in this chapter, principally to persons for whom the Bible is a God-inspired text and therefore authoritative.) Rather, this path uses contemporary experience as a helpmate in deciding what the Bible really teaches about the requirements of human well-being.

This path, this way of subjecting to serious reexamination a now-challenged but still-traditional belief about what the Bible teaches – here, the belief that according to the Bible homosexual sexual conduct is always hostile to human well-being – should be an attractive option for Christians who accept what Thomas Aquinas taught:

> Aquinas remained ... convinced that morality is essentially rational conduct, and as such it must be accessible, at least in principle, to human reason and wisdom. ... In the teaching of Aquinas, the purpose of revelation, so far as morality is concerned, appears to be essentially remedial, not absolutely necessary for man. ... [T]he Christian revelation contains in its moral teaching no substantial element over and above what is accessible to human reason without revelation. ... Revelation as such has nothing in matters of moral behaviour to add to the best of human thinking. ... [43]

The Roman Catholic religious-moral tradition follows Thomas Aquinas in embracing this position. But Aquinas's enormous influence on the Christian religious-moral tradition extends far beyond Catholic Christianity. Christians generally, and not just Catholics, would "want to argue (at least, many of them would) that the Christian revelation does not require us to interpret the nature of man in ways for which there is otherwise no warrant but rather affords a deeper understanding of man as he essentially is." [44]

For Christians who accept the Thomist understanding of the relation between "revelation" and "reason," any belief that according to the Bible such and such conduct is hostile to human well-being should be a highly suspect ground for banning or otherwise disfavoring the conduct if (a) the belief is the object of increasingly widespread, trans-denominational disagreement among Christians themselves and (b) no persuasive argument grounded on contemporary human experience supports the belief. Given the demonstrated, ubiquitious human propensity to be mistaken and even to deceive oneself about what God has revealed, including what God has revealed in the Bible, the absence of a persuasive argument grounded on human experience in support of a claim that according to the Bible such and such conduct is hostile to human well-being warrants suspicion that the claim might be false, that it might be the defective yield of that demonstrated human propensity. In particular, it warrants wariness about banning or otherwise disfavoring conduct on the basis of the claim. At least, the absence of a persuasive argument grounded on human experience in support of the claim warrants such suspicion and wariness if, as I said, the claim is the object of widespread and growing transdenominational dissensus among Christians themselves.

Some Christians might try to repress such dissensus among the members of their community of faith (dissensus about whether the Bible teaches what traditionally it has been interpreted to teach), and might try to insulate themselves from such suspicion and wariness, by means of one or more doctrines about their or their religious leaders' privileged (e.g., infallible) insight into what the Bible teaches, including what it teaches about human well-being. But any such doctrine, which will likely seem to many other Christians (and others) to be an understandable but nonetheless prideful and self-serving stratagem,[45] is conspicuously ill-suited to the politics of a religiously pluralistic democracy such as the United States. As Richard John Neuhaus has warned: "So long as Christian teaching claims to be a privileged form of discourse that is exempt from the scrutiny of critical reason, it will understandably be denied a place in discussions that are authentically public."[46] In 1988, the drafters of the Williamsburg Charter, a group that included many prominent religious believers, articulated a related contention: "Arguments for public policy should be more than private convictions shouted out loud. For persuasion to be principled, private convictions should be translated into publicly accessible claims. Such public claims should be made publicly accessible . . . because they must engage those who do not share the same private convictions. . . ."[47] Insisting on a persuasive argument grounded on human experience in support of a claim that the Bible teaches so and so about human well-being is one important way for Christians both to heed Neuhaus's warning and to abide by the counsel of the Williamsburg Charter, *especially if many Christians are themselves deeply skeptical about whether the Bible teaches what it is claimed to teach.*

Moreover, it is a relatively ecumenical way for Christians, in pursuit of the truth, to test the various statements about what the Bible teaches, and other statements about what God has revealed, that are sometimes articulated in public political debate – for example, statements that certain biblical passages " 'prove' that heterosexuality is God's exclusive intention for human sexuality and that homosexuality is an abomination before God."[48] Only a historically naive religious (or other) tradition would doubt the value of such ecumenical dialogue, which is an essential way of correcting error and broadening and deepening one's apprehension of truth – in this case, error/truth about whether the Bible teaches what traditionally it has been claimed to teach.[49] "There is, of course, much to gain by sharpening our understanding in dialogue with those who share a common heritage and common experience with us.... Critical understanding of the [religious] tradition and a critical awareness of our own relationship to it, however, is sharpened by contact with those who differ from us. Indeed, for these purposes, the less they are like us, the better."[50] Defending the moderate style of his participation in public discourse about abortion and other issues implicating what he famously called "the consistent ethic of life," the late Joseph Cardinal Bernardin, archbishop of Chicago, said:

The substance of the consistent ethic yields a style of teaching it and witnessing to it. The style should ... not [be] sectarian.... [W]e should resist the sectarian tendency to retreat into a closed circle, convinced of our truth and the impossibility of sharing it with others.... The style should be persuasive, not preachy.... We should be convinced we have *much to learn from the world* and much to teach it. A confident church will speak its mind, seek as a community to live its convictions, *but leave space for others to speak to us, to help us grow from their perspective*....[51]

IV

Again, there is now widespread and growing disagreement among Christians over whether the Bible teaches that homosexual sexual relationships are always hostile to the authentic well-being of those involved in the relationships; moreover, this disagreement is transdenominational: It divides many Christians from many other Christians without regard to denominational affiliation. According to the principle of political self-restraint I have proposed in this chapter, a faithful Christian, confronted both by this disagreement over what the Bible teaches and by the necessity of choosing whether or not to oppose the legal recognition of same-sex unions, should make the following judgment: Does contemporary human experience support the claim that according to the Bible homosexual sexual conduct is always hostile to human well-being and that therefore same-sex unions can never be truly fulfilling for anyone? Or, instead, does human experience belie that claim?

The aim, of course, is informed judgment, not ignorant judgment. Happily, in deciding whether human experience supports or, instead, belies the claim that according to the Bible same-sex unions are always hostile to human well-being, the faithful Christian – and, indeed, anyone, Christian or not, believer or not – will be aided enormously by a large literature that has emerged in recent years, a literature that inquires whether, as a matter of human experience, a same-sex union can be truly fulfilling for some persons. I refer the reader to some of that voluminous literature both in the note accompanying this sentence and in the text of the next two paragraphs.[52]

I mentioned earlier in this chapter that the particular religious tradition that has been formative for me is Roman Catholicism. The *Catechism of the Catholic Church* holds (in paragraph 2357) that "homosexual acts are intrinsically disordered" and "[u]nder no circumstances can they be approved."[53] Nonetheless, in recent years, some of the most powerful arguments to the effect that a same-sex unions can be truly and deeply fulfilling for some persons have been made by Roman Catholic thinkers.[54] One of the most important such works is Kevin T. Kelly's *New Directions in Sexual Ethics* (1998).[55] (Kelly, a Catholic priest in England with broad pastoral experience, is a moral theologian.) Other important contributions include:

- Jack A. Bonsor, "Homosexual Sexual Orientation and Anthropology: Reflections on the Category 'Objective Disorder'."[56] Bonsor teaches thelogy at Santa Clara University, a Jesuit institution.
- Margaret A. Farley, "An Ethic for Same-Sex Relations."[57] Farley, a member of the Sisters of Mercy, is the Gilbert L. Stark Professor of Christian Ethics at Yale University and a former president both of the Society of Christian Ethics and of the Catholic Theological Society of America.
- Jon D. Fuller, "The Catholic Church, Homosexuality, and Cognitive Dissonance."[58] Fuller, an associate professor of medicine at the Boston University School of Medicine, is a Jesuit priest and a member

of the adjunct faculty both at the Weston Jesuit School of Theology and at the Havard Divinity School.

- Luke Timothy Johnson, "A Disembodied 'Theology of the Body': John Paul II on Love, Sex and Pleasure."[59] Johnson, a laicized priest, is the Robert W. Woodruff Professor of New Testament at the Candler School of Theology, Emory University.
- Patricia Beattie Jung and Ralph F. Smith, *Heterosexism: An Ethical Challenge* (1993). Jung teaches theology at Loyola University of Chicago; Smith, now deceased, was an ordained Lutheran pastor who taught at Wartburg Theological Seminary (Dubuque, Iowa).
- David Matzko McCarthy, "Homosexuality and the Practices of Marriage."[60] McCarthy teaches theology at Mount Saint Mary's College (Emmitsburg, Maryland).
- Paul J. Weithman, "Natural Law, Morality, and Sexual Complementarity."[61] Weithman teaches philosophy at the University of Notre Dame.
- Richard Westley, *Morality and Its Beyond* (1984).[62] Westley teaches philosophy at Loyola University of Chicago.

Catholic writers who have recently defended the Vatican's position that homosexual sexual conduct is always hostile to human well-being include:

- John Finnis: "Law, Morality, and 'Sexual Orientation'" and "The Good of Marriage and the Morality of Sexual Relations: Some Philosophical and Historical Observations."[63] Finnis teaches law both at Oxford and at Notre Dame.
- James P. Hanigan, "Sexual Orientation and Human Rights: A Roman Catholic View."[64] Hanigan teaches theology at Duquesne University (Pittsburgh, Pennsylvania).
- Patrick Lee and Robert P. George, "What Sex Can Be: Self-Alienation, Illusion, or One-Flesh Union."[65] Lee teaches philosophy at the Franciscan University of Steubenville (Ohio); George is a member of the Department of Politics at Princeton.

It is not surprising that so many theologians, philosophers, and others in the Roman Catholic tradition are addressing the issue of same-sex unions not, or not principally, as a question about what the Bible teaches but rather as a question about what human experience discloses to be the requirements of authentic human well-being: Again, the Roman Catholic religious-moral tradition, partly because of the influence of Aquinas, is committed to the position "that the Christian revelation does not require us to interpret the nature of man in ways for which there is otherwise no warrant but rather affords a deeper understanding of man as he essentially is."[66] So, when John Finnis (for example) sets out to defend the traditional Roman Catholic teaching that homosexual sexual conduct is always antithetical to true human well-being, he does not present an argument about what the Bible teaches or even about what the Pope teaches; instead, he tries to construct an argument that is, in Finnis's own words, "reflective, critical, publicly intelligible, and rational."[67]

I said, a few paragraphs back, that in deciding whether human experience supports or belies the claim that according to the Bible same-sex unions are always hostile to human well-being, the faithful Christian (and indeed anyone) will be aided enormously by a large literature that has emerged in recent years. As the citations I have provided illustrate, much of the recent literature is moral-theological in character. It bears emphasis that the principle of political self-restraint I have proposed here does not privilege "secular" argument over moral-theological argument. (Nor, as I emphasized earlier, does the principle oppose contemporary human experience to the Bible.) In my judgment, some of the most impressive arguments about what contemporary human experience discloses about same-sex unions and human well-being – the arguments, for example, of Farley, Jung and Smith, Kelly, and McCarthy – are moral-theological; they are moral arguments rooted in a theological vision of God as Creator, of human nature as created, and of love both as the animating spirit of God's creation of human beings and as the fundamental dimension of an authentically human life, a truly and deeply human life. They are moral arguments grounded on human experience "comprehended within a theological framework built upon a doctrine of creation as the good handiwork of a creator who remains also sustainer and the ultimate redeemer of the world."[68] That an argument about human well-being – that is, an argument grounded partly on human experience – is moral-theological rather than secular is irrelevant to the principle proposed here.

It is no part of my aim in this chapter to adjudicate the political/moral controversy that frames my discussion: the controversy over same-sex unions. I do want to acknowledge, however, that in my judgment, contemporary human experience belies the claim that homosexual sexual conduct is always hostile to authentic human well-being; in particular, it belies the claim that same-sex unions can never be truly fulfilling for anyone. Not that the principle of political self-restraint that I have proposed here entails this judgment about human experience. It does not. Even if she accepts the proposed principle of political self-restraint, the faithful Christian must reach her own judgment about what human experience discloses about same-sex unions and human well-being. In any event, given the careful, thorough, and, in my view, persuasive arguments recently offered by the Catholic thinkers I have cited (in particular, by Kelly, Jung and Smith, and McCarthy)[69] it would be otiose for me to argue here that human experience discloses that same-sex unions can be truly, deeply fulfilling for some persons. (I concur in the recent judgment of the Vermont Supreme Court that for a state to extend to same-sex couples "legal protection and security for their avowed commitment to an intimate and lasting human relationship is simply, when all is said and done, a recognition of our common humanity.")[70] If contemporary human experience does indeed disclose that same-sex unions can be truly, deeply fulfilling for some persons, this constitutes a powerful reason, for Christians who believe that whatever the Bible teaches about human well-being is true, to doubt that the Bible really teaches that homosexual sexual conduct is always immoral.[71]

A growing number of Christians do not oppose the legal recognition of same-sex unions – indeed, a growing number call for its legal recognition – because they no longer believe either that human experience discloses that homosexual sexual conduct is always hostile to human well-being or, therefore, that the Bible teaches that homosexual sexual conduct is always hostile to human well-being. Many Christians, however, continue to believe both that the Bible teaches and that human experience confirms that homosexual sexual conduct (including same-sex unions) is invariably – that it is always and everywhere – hostile to human well-being. But what is a faithful Christian to do who falls between these two groups, who comes to find herself – perhaps in consequence of consulting some of the works I have cited here, both the works about what the Bible teaches and the works about what human experience discloses – uncertain about whether human experience discloses that homosexual sexual conduct is always hostile to human well-being – and therefore less sure than she was before about whether the Bible really teaches that homosexual sexual conduct is always hostile to human well-being? The principle of political self-restraint I have defended in this chapter – a principle triggered by increasingly widespread, transdenominational dissensus over what the Bible really teaches – counsels her to be wary about opposing the legal recognition of same-sex unions on the basis of a biblically grounded belief that homosexual sexual conduct is always hostile to human well-being. The principle is not an algorithm. It is perhaps better described as an attitude. How wary she should be depends on how serious her doubt has become – her doubt about whether the Bible teaches that homosexual sexual conduct is always immoral. Of course, if she has moved beyond doubt to disbelief, then she no longer accepts the principal, biblical reason that some Christians do not want the law to recognize same-sex unions. The principle/attitude of political self-restraint defended here is for Christians who have not moved beyond doubt to disbelief and who may therefore be inclined to remain opposed to the legal recognition of same-sex unions on the basis of biblically grounded belief.

As a response to doubt about what human experience discloses – and, therefore, about what the Bible really teaches – about same-sex unions and human well-being, wariness about continuing to oppose the legal recognition of same-sex unions seems especially fitting for any Christian who affirms (as many persons, perhaps most, in our society do) that, as a general matter, a competent adult is, if not always the best judge, then one of the best judges of what way of life is best for him or her. Moreover, doubt about what the Bible really teaches about same-sex unions and human well-being, in conjunction with the several reasons for political tolerance that I developed in *Love and Power* and have excerpted in the appendix to this chapter, seem to me to counsel strongly against disfavoring same-sex unions on the basis of biblically grounded belief.

v

Many Christians will be skeptical about the principle (or attitude) of political self-restraint that I have proposed in this chapter, because they are skeptical about – indeed, many Christians reject – human experience as an appropriate source of moral discernment. I now want to speak mainly to such Christians.

74

As I noted earlier, Christians still constitute, at the beginning of the twenty-first century, the largest group by far of religious believers in the United States.[72] For many Christians in the United States – including Catholics, Lutherans, Presbyterians, Episcopalians, Methodists, and others – the purported opposition between, on the one side, "faith" informed by "revelation" and, on the other, "reason" informed by "experience" is a false opposition. Many Christians understand that they do not have to choose between such "faith" and such "reason," which, for them, are neither incompatible nor even in tension. To the contrary, faith (informed by revelation) and reason (informed by experience) are, for such Christians, mutually enriching. David Hollenbach explains:

Faith and understanding go hand in hand in both the Catholic and Calvinist views of the matter. They are not adversarial but reciprocally illuminating. As [David] Tracy puts it, Catholic social thought seeks to correlate arguments drawn from the distinctively religious symbols of Christianity with arguments based on shared public experience. This effort at correlation moves back and forth on a two-way street. It rests on a conviction that the classic symbols of Christianity can uncover meaning in personal and social existence that common sense and uncontroversial science fail to see. So it invites those outside the church to place their self-understanding at risk by what Tracy calls conversation with such "classics."[73]

Hollenbach then adds, following Tracy: "At the same time, the believer's self-understanding is also placed at risk because it can be challenged to development or even fundamental change by dialogue with the other – whether this be a secular agnostic, a Christian from another tradition, or a Jew, Muslim, or Buddhist."[74]

Or, we may add, even if this be a homosexual man or woman living in a same-sex union. Recall, here, Margaret Farley's reference to "the testimony of women and men whose sexual preference is for others of the same sex." It is, she writes, "clear and profound testimon[y] to the life-enhancing possibilities of same-sex relations and the integrating possibilities of sexual activity within these relations." In what Hollenbach calls "dialogue with the other," Christian believers may come to concur in Farley's judgment that "[w]e have the witness that homosexual activity can be a way of embodying responsible human love and sustaining Christian friendship" and that "this witness alone is enough to demand of the Christian community that it reflect anew on the norms for homosexual love."[75] But whether or not a Christian believer comes to concur in that particular judgment, "dialogue with the other" is essential:

[D]isagreements actually lodged in contradictory interpretations of human experience are not without some possibilities of adjudication. Here the requirement is communication, and the potential is for enlargement of experience and expansion of its sources for interpretation. It would be naive in the extreme to suggest that all disagreements about experience are only apparent, and sufficient dialogue will in every case bring harmony. Nonetheless, what communication prevents is a premature acceptance of unbridgeable gaps. What it makes possible is the actual bringing together of diverse experiences in their concreteness and particularity.[76]

Some Christians, however, are skeptical of such communication; they are skeptical of the kind of "dialogue with the other" to which Hollenbach refers; in particular, they are skeptical of relying on human experience, including what Hollenbach calls "shared public experience": morally conservative Christians who embrace "revelation" as the virtually exclusive source of moral discernment (at least, where such revelation is understood to speak to the issue at hand).[77] There are such Christians in many denominations, but the most prominent examples of such Christians in the United States today are fundamentalist Christians, Mormons, and some evangelical Christians.[78] As Hollenbach says, "[f]aith and understanding go hand in hand in both the Catholic and Calvinist views of the matter." But for some Christians, faith and understanding do not go hand in hand but are often incompatible; in their view, human experience and human reason are often too corrupted to be trusted. For example, David Smolin, a law professor who identifies himself as an evangelical Christian, has written that

even our intellectual capacities have been distorted by the effects of sin. The pervasive effects of sin suggest that creation, human nature, and human reason are often unreliable means for knowing the law of God. . . . Thus, scripture and Christian tradition have come to have a priority among the sources of knowledge of God's will. Indeed, these sources of revelation are considered a means of measuring and testing claims made on behalf of reason, nature, or creation, in order to purify these now subsidiary means of the distortive effect of sin.[79]

However, Christians like Smolin overlook the fact that, as the history of Christianity discloses, sin can distort, and indeed often has distorted, what human beings believe about "scripture and

Christian tradition."[80] Given their belief in the "fallenness" of human nature – which is, after all, *their* nature, too – Christians should be especially alert to this dark possibility. Many Christians in the United States are, like David Smolin, social conservatives. So it is important to emphasize that this phenomenon to the contrary notwithstanding, authentically Christian premises do not yield Burkean social conservatism. "Christianity in essence is not conservative."[81] As Glenn Tinder has explained:

> [T]he consciousness of human fallibility is far keener among Christians than among conservatives, for Christians are skeptical of human arrangements that typically command deep respect in conservatives. . . . Christians cannot logically assume that the antiquity of institutions provides any assurance of their justice or efficacy. They realize, if they consult Christian principles, that long-standing customs and traditions embody not only the wisdom of generations but also the wickedness – in particular, the determination of dominant groups to preserve their powers and privileges.[82]

Christians skeptical of arguments grounded on contemporary human experience – including arguments about human well-being – would do well to reflect on Mark Noll's powerful, eloquent book, *The Scandal of the Evangelical Mind* (1994). Noll – the McManis Professor of Christian Thought at Wheaton College (Illinois), one of the foremost evangelical Christian colleges in the United States – is himself a committed evangelical Christian. Noll comments critically, in one chapter of his book, on the emergence of "creation science" in evangelical Christianity: "[I]f the consensus of modern scientists, who devote their lives to looking at the data of the physical world, is that humans have existed on the planet for a very long time, it is foolish for biblical interpreters to say that 'the Bible teaches' the recent creation of human beings." Noll explains:

> This does not mean that at some future time, the procedures of science may shift in such a way as to alter the contemporary consensus. It means that, for people today to say they are being loyal to the Bible and to demand belief in a recent creation of humanity as a sign of obedience to Scripture is in fact being unfaithful to the Bible, which, in Psalm 19 and elsewhere, calls upon followers of God to listen to the speech that God has caused the natural world to speak. It is the same for the age of the earth and for all other questions regarding the constitution of the human race. Charles Hodges's words from the middle of the nineteenth century are still pertinent: "Nature is as truly a revelation of God as the Bible, and we only interpret the Word of God by the Word of God when we interpret the Bible by science."[83]

77

Consider, too, these observations by the eminent historian George Marsden (who, like Noll, identifies himself as an evangelical Christian):

Some [historical] knowledge cuts across all theories and paradigms, and it provides all people of good sense a solid reality basis for testing some aspects of theories. So in practice there is a common ground of historical inquiry. When we look at the past, if we do it right, what we find will in large measure correspond to what other historians find.

From a Christian perspective, we may explain this phenomenon simply by observing that God in his grace seems to have created human minds with some ability to experience and know something of the real world, including the past. Furthermore, these structures are substantially common to all normal people so that, despite the notorious theoretical problems of subjectivism and point of view, we can in fact communicate remarkably well and be assured that we are talking about the same things. It may be difficult to explain, except as a matter of faith, what basis we have for reliance on these common abilities; but the fact remains that only philosophers and crackpots can long deny that often they are reliable.[84]

Why should we believe that what Noll says about the proper relation between faith and inquiry into the origins of human beings is not also true about the proper relation between faith and inquiry into the requirements of human well-being? Why should we believe that what Marsden says about historical inquiry is not also true about inquiry into the requirements of human well-being? Why should we not say, with Anthony of the Desert, a fourth-century Christian monk: "My book, O philosopher, is the nature of created things, and any time I wish to read the words of God, the book is before me."[85]

Indeed, according to Choon-Leong Seow, the Henry Snyder Gehman Professor of Old Testament Language and Literature at Princeton, "in the wisdom tradition of the Bible there is *scriptural authority* for human beings to make ethical decisions by paying attention to science and human experiences. We must not say, as we often hear in the debate about homosexuality, that 'experience has nothing to do with it' or that 'only scripture matters.' It is scriptural to take human observations and experiences seriously."[86] Professor Seow explains:

The Bible does not take human experience lightly. Neither should we. Moreover, it is not only the experience of a particular people or a faith-community that matters. To be sure, those are the concerns of most of the Bible. In the wisdom tradition, however, the concern is with the experience of the ordinary human being. Sometimes the realities of life contradict what we have always known to be true and, in the face of that contradiction, we can only admit that we do not understand all of creation.[87]

The attitude of political self-restraint I have recommended in this chapter does not presuppose that in making political choices about the morality of conduct, Christians should forget that they are Christians; it does not presuppose that they should "bracket" their Christian identity, that they should act as if they are persons who do not have the religious beliefs that they in fact do have. (I have contended against such "bracketing" elsewhere: "One's basic moral/religious convictions are (partly) self-constitutive and are therefore a principal ground – indeed, the principal ground – of political deliberation and choice. To 'bracket' such convictions is therefore to bracket – to annihilate – essential aspects of one's very self. To participate in politics and law . . . with such convictions bracketed is not to participate as the self one is but as [someone else].")[88] Rather, it is *because* they are Christians – it is because they are, *as Christians*, painfully aware of the fallenness, the brokenness, of human beings – that they should be extremely wary about banning or otherwise disfavoring conduct on the basis of a claim that according to the Bible the conduct is contrary to human well-being, if (a) the claim is the object of widespread, transdenominational disagreement among Christians themselves and (b) no persuasive argument grounded on human experience supports the claim. Christians have *their own* reasons – reasons *internal both to their own religious (theological) tradition and to their own historical experience* – to accept this modest principle of political self-restraint. It scarcely seems radical, or unfaithful, to suggest that Christians too, no less than other religious believers, must be alert to the possibility that a belief that the Bible teaches something about morality that traditionally it has been interpreted to teach is a mistaken belief – and worse. The belief that according to the Bible slavery can be morally permissible was mistaken,[89] but it was also worse than mistaken. As we can now see, that then-traditional belief about the Bible and slavery was a rationalization for a fundamentally sinful state of affairs – a state of affairs centrally constituted by an existential repudiation of the fundamental Christian commandment to "love one another just as I have loved you."[90]

The principle/attitude of political self-restraint proposed here is rooted in the realization that even some still-traditional biblical interpretations may be mistaken. In particular, the argument that according to the Bible same-sex unions are morally impermissible may be mistaken. Indeed, it may be worse than mistaken; like the argument that according to the Bible interracial marriage is morally impermissible, it may be a rationalization of sinful prejudice. Robert Bellah's claim is to that effect:

A principled rejection of gay sexuality, whether put forward by the church or any other sector of society, is morally indefensible. It has the same status today as arguments for the inferiority of women. To remain stuck in that position, as the church for the time being seems likely to do, is not only unfortunate: it makes the church collaborate in continuing forms of domination. To put it even more strongly: it makes the church collaborate in sin.[91]

In circumstances in which a large and growing number of Christians disagree deeply among themselves over whether the Bible teaches about the requirements of human well-being what traditionally it has been interpreted to teach, especially when that disagreement is transdenominational, Christians have good reason to probe contemporary human experience in their effort to discern the truth both about human well-being and, therefore, about what the Bible teaches about human well-being. ("Therefore," because for Christians, the Bible does not teach about human well-being what is contrary to the truth about human well-being. Of course, few Christians believe that the Bible's teaching about human well-being is exhaustive: The Bible does not teach *every* truth about human well-being; it does not address every question about human well-being that might arise.) They also have good reason not to ban or otherwise disfavor conduct on the ground that according to the Bible the conduct is always hostile to the well-being of those who engage in the conduct, if the reflective yield of contemporary human experience seems increasingly to put into serious question the claim that the conduct is always hostile to human well-being – and also the claim, therefore, that the Bible teaches that the conduct is always hostile to human well-being.[92] Let us end this chapter as we began it, with this observation by Galileo:

[N]obody will deny that [the Bible] is often very abstruse, and may say things which are quite different from what its bare words signify. Hence if in expounding the Bible one were always to confine oneself to the unadorned grammatical meaning, one might fall into error. Not only contradictions and propositions far from true might thus be made to appear in the Bible, but even grave heresies and follies.[93]

APPENDIX TO CHAPTER 4

[The following material is excerpted from Chapter 7 of my book *Love and Power: The Role of Religion and Morality in American Politics* (1991). I have omitted the footnotes.]

Several basic considerations counsel against pursuit of coercive political strategies. A principal such consideration is the fact that human judgment is fallible. There is always the possibility that the moral judgment in the service of which a coercive strategy has been proposed is mistaken. That possibility is especially likely with respect to paternalistic coercion. John Stuart Mill's point seems right as a *general* matter (there are always counterexamples): "[W]ith respect to his own feelings and circumstances the most ordinary man or woman has means of knowledge immeasurably surpassing those that can be possessed by anyone else. The interference of society to overrule his judgement and purposes in what only regards himself must be grounded on general presumptions which may be altogether wrong and, even if right, are as likely as not to be misapplied to individual cases, by persons no better acquainted with the circumstances of such cases than those are who look at them merely from without." The consideration of human fallibility should not be discounted. History is littered with examples of mistaken judgments that a choice or behavior different from the evaluator's own in some or many respects was not merely different but immoral. Thus, one of the most important existential prerequisites to ecumenical political dialogue – fallibilism – is also conducive to tolerance. . . .

Another important prerequisite to ecumenical political dialogue is conducive to tolerance: pluralism. To be a pluralist, in the relevant sense, is . . . to understand that a morally pluralistic context, with its attendant variety of ways of life, can often be a more fertile source of deepening moral insight than can a monistic context. Thus, a pluralist sensibility serves as a brake on the regrettable tendency to condemn and outlaw choices, behavior, and ways of life different from one's own. Fallibilism, then, in conjunction with pluralism, should make us wary about interfering, through coercion, with behavior and ways of life different from our own. Fallibilism and pluralism are conducive to tolerance. (And tolerance, like fallibilism and pluralism, is conducive to dialogue. Again, there is no or little dialogue among or with the intolerant.)

Another consideration counselling against pursuit of coercive political strategies is simple self-interest. A strong tradition or spirit of tolerance – that is, a strong wariness about political coercion – can help protect us in the event the winds change. We may be members of the politically dominant coalition today, but there is no guarantee we will be tomorrow. Governor Mario Cuomo made the point in addressing a group of fellow Catholics at Notre Dame:

> [Catholic public officials don't always] love what others do with their freedom, but . . . they realize that in guaranteeing freedom for all, they guarantee our right to be Catholics . . .
> The Catholic public official lives the political truth which most Catholics through most of American history have accepted and insisted on: the truth that to assure our freedom we must allow others the same freedom, even if it occasionally produces conduct by them which we would hold to be sinful.
> I protect my right to be a Catholic by preserving your right to believe as a Jew, a Protestant or non-believer, or as anything else you choose. We know that the price of seeking to enforce our beliefs on others is that they might some day force theirs on us. This freedom is the fundamental strength of our unique experiment in government. In the complex interplay of forces and considerations that go into the making of our laws and policies, its preservation must be a pervasive and dominant concern.

Another consideration is compassion. To coerce someone to make a choice she does not want to make is to cause her to suffer. If we are empathetic, we will be sensitive to such suffering. If we are compassionate, we will be wary about imposing that suffering on another. A related consideration is the friendship or fellowship that nourishes community. For the politically dominant coalition to coerce a member of the political community to make a choice she does not want to make is to provoke resentment in her. If we respect the other with whom we disagree, and especially if we value friendship/fellowship and the sort of community it makes possible, we will be wary about provoking such resentment, which is corrosive of community. Consider what we might call extreme coercion: coercing someone to refrain from doing something she not merely wants to do, but believes essential to her well-being, even obligatory, that she do; or coercing someone to do something she not merely does not want to do, but believes destructive of her well-being to do, even forbidden for her to do. Extreme coercion causes extreme suffering. And extreme resentment. It can tear the fabric of public civility essential to civil politics, even engender alienation from community, lack of respect for "authority" and the law, political instability, and the reactive repression that often attends political instability. (It is difficult to imagine dialogue flourishing in such a context.) Commenting on Aquinas' view of the relationship between religion and law, Mulford Sibley writes: "Human beings vary widely in their social and moral development. To make impossible demands on many of them might provoke rebellion and civil war – consummations far worse in their consequences for humanity, perhaps, than those which result from not embodying every moral offense in human law. St. Thomas is constantly emphasizing contingencies in human life, and awareness of them tends to modify what might otherwise be inflexible and absolutist principles." John Noonan has said that "[t]he central problem ... of the legal enterprise is the relation of love to power." If we are compassionate, and if we value community, we will be especially wary about relying on extreme coercion: The costs – extreme suffering and extreme resentment – are great and sometimes terrible.

Extreme coercion entails another cost as well, and another consideration, counselling against reliance on extreme coercion, concerns this cost. To coerce someone to refrain from doing something she believes herself obligated to do, or to do something she believes herself forbidden to do, is to ask her to act contrary to her conscience. A moral community that values individual conscientiousness or personal integrity – that believes that ultimately, after careful, informed deliberation, a person should choose on the basis of conscience – will be wary, therefore, about pursuing a political strategy of extreme coercion. In an essay elaborating "A Catholic Perspective on Morality and the Law," Joseph Boyle writes that the Catholic

conception of morality ... is based on the assumption that human beings have choices to make, and that it is by making the choices which they believe to be the correct ones that they become good persons. Moral norms in this conception of morality are acknowledged guidelines for choices. These norms are known within the human conscience, and human dignity lies in choosing to act in accord with these norms. [In a footnote at this point, Boyle writes: "This formulation is based on Vatical Council II, *Pastoral Constitution on The Church in the Modern World (Gaudium et Spes)*, paragraph 16."] Thus, what is morally central is making the correct choices in the light of personally acknowledged moral standards.... [The] legal imposition of moral prohibitions can have effects contrary to the moral goal of making choices that conform to one's conscience. For, it might be the case that what one person or group regards as morally prohibited is regarded by others as morally required. The legal enforcement of the moral views of some thus becomes a significant temptation for others not to act in accord with their consciences. Those who regard morality as choosing to conform to conscience can hardly regard this to be acceptable.

This concern that coercive legislation not subvert individual conscientiousness partly underlies the statement of John Courtney Murray that "the moral aspirations of the law are minimal. Law seeks to establish and maintain only that minimum of actualized morality that is necessary for the healthy functioning of the social order. It does not look to what is morally desirable, or attempt to remove every moral taint from the atmosphere of society. It enforces only what is minimally acceptable, and in this sense socially necessary."

That various considerations counsel against pursuit of coercive political strategies, and that we should therefore be wary, as a general matter, about pursuing such strategies, is not to say that no such strategy should ever be pursued. That position – radical tolerance – would be extreme and extremely silly. The principal consideration supporting, even necessitating, a coercive political strategy is the fact, if it is a fact, that the strategy is an essential means of protecting a fundamental interest or interests: interests the satisfaction of which significantly enhances one's level of well-being and the frustration of which significantly diminishes it. This consideration has special force if the coercive strategy is an essential means of protecting one or more of the fundamental interests of human beings themselves relatively incapable of protecting those interests, and if those considering the strategy are committed to protecting the weak among them ("the least of my brethren"). The protection of fundamental interests is, after all, a principal aspect of the very *raison d'etre* of government. "Thomas Aquinas, a natural lawyer if ever these was one, ... argues that the law should not seek to prohibit all vices, but only the more serious ones, and 'especially those which involve harm to others, without whose prohibition human society could not be preserved....'" ("In the heat of the civil rights debate, Martin Luther King Jr. was accused on wanting to legislate morality. He replied that the law could not make people love their neighbors, but it could stop their lynching them.") Relatedly, a coercive strategy is supported by the fact that it is an important means of safeguarding basic social institutions – the courts, for example – institutions whose effective functioning is itself crucial to the protection of fundamental interests.

Inevitably there are disagreements as to which interests are fundamental. And there are disagreements, too, as to when an entity (a slave, for example, or an unborn child) is a member, or to what extent a member, of the human community. (An instance of this disagreement looms very large in the abortion controversy.) In a religiously/morally pluralistic society like our own, however – a relatively democratic society – the views of no single religious or other moral community can be determinative, and the chance that truly idiosyncratic views might prevail is thereby diminished. . . .

[I have presented here] several considerations that militate against pursuit of coercive political strategies: fallibilism (in conjunction with pluralism), self-interest, compassion, community, and conscientiousness.

These considerations are not exhaustive, but they are, I think, the principal ones. (Others that have been mentioned include not enacting "laws which are difficult to enforce and whose enforcement tends, therefore, to be patchy and inequitable," "laws which are likely to ... produce ... evils such as blackmail," or laws "punishing people for what they very largely cannot help.") Both individually and, especially, cumulatively, the considerations set forth here ... call for a strong reluctance to rely on coercive political strategies and, so, for a tolerant political agenda. They inform a sensible, discriminating wariness about the use of coercive state power.

Catholics, the Magisterium, and Same-Sex Unions
An Argument for Independent Judgment

The two types of authority that concern us here (authority to govern and authority to teach) are, of course, distinct and can be discussed separately. In the Roman Catholic Church, however, we find that they are often intermingled, and sometimes even confused with each other. Over the centuries governing power has often been used (and misused) to bolster teaching authority. Such an approach can easily amount to little more than "we are right because we are in charge" or "we give orders, not explanations."[1]

Some Catholics concede that the church admits the principle of doctrinal development, but they accuse [John] Noonan, in Richard John Neuhaus's words, of too often equating development with "a change, or even a reversal, of doctrine." At a recent meeting of the Catholic Common Ground initiative, Noonan and theologian Avery Dulles had a polite, but sharp, exchange on the subject, with Noonan again insisting that "the record is replete with mistakes – the faithful can't just accept everything that comes from Rome as though God had authorized it."[2]

In the preceding chapter, I spoke (mainly) to Christians generally, and I spoke to them about the Bible, which is authoritative for Christians generally. In this brief chapter, which is a kind of addendum to the preceding chapter, I speak (mainly) to Roman Catholics, and I speak to them about the magisterium of the Roman Catholic Church, which is authoritative for Roman Catholics. It is sometimes observed that for Roman Catholics, it is not the Bible that is supremely authoritative but the "magisterium" of the Church: the bishops and, ultimately, the Pope.[3] (It would be misleading to reply that for Roman Catholics, as for other Christians, the Bible is supremely authoritative, because it is the Bible *as interpreted by the magisterium of the Church* that is authoritative for Roman Catholics.) Whereas in the preceding chapter, I contended against uncritical political reliance on what one imagines the Bible to say about the morality of same-sex unions, in this chapter, I contend against uncritical political reliance on what the magisterium of the

Church says about the morality of same-sex unions; in particular, I argue that Catholic citizens and legislators have good reason to make independent judgments about some moral controversies – including the controversy over the morality of same-sex unions – rather than simply yield to whatever happens to be the official position of the magisterium on the contested matter.

I have chosen to address, among all Christians, Roman Catholics in particular, both because Roman Catholicism is the religious tradition that has been formative for me and, more importantly, because Roman Catholicism is such a formidable presence in American politics. There are now over sixty-two million Catholics in the United States; in the context of American politics, "moral arguments within Catholicism about [homosexuality] will be very significant."[4]

I

In Chapters 2 and 3, I concluded that neither the nonestablishment norm nor even the morality of liberal democracy forbids legislators or other policymakers to disfavor conduct on the basis of religiously grounded moral belief. That conclusion will surely please Pope John Paul II and "the vast majority of Americans" to whom he referred on the occasion of the presentation by Lindy Boggs of her credentials as U.S. ambassador to the Vatican:[5]

> It would truly be a sad thing if the religious and moral convictions upon which the American experiment was founded could now somehow be considered a danger to free society, such that those who would bring these convictions to bear upon your nation's public life would be denied a voice in debating and resolving issues of public policy. The original separation of church and state in the United States was certainly not an effort to ban all religious conviction from the public sphere, a kind of banishment of God from civil society. Indeed, the vast majority of Americans, regardless of their religious persuasion, are convinced that religious conviction and religiously informed moral argument have a vital role in public life.[6]

So said the Pope. But there is a problem. The "vast majority of Americans" to whom the Pope referred no doubt includes the vast majority of American Catholics. As we know, however, there are in the United States many citizens, including many legislators and other policymakers, who self-identify as Catholic but who are not persuaded by the Pope's – or, if you prefer, the magisterium's – "religiously informed

87

moral argument" about one or more controversial issues. Indeed, there are many American Catholics whose own religiously grounded moral judgment about one or more such issues is contrary to the magisterium's judgment. Yet, it often seems that the Pope and the bishops – including, in the United States, the National Conference of Catholic Bishops – want Catholics, in deciding what political choice to make, not merely to give a properly respectful hearing to the magisterium's position on the moral issue at hand but to defer to the magisterium's position; it often seems that the Pope and most bishops believe that Catholic citizens/legislators/policymakers lack the competence to work out, even in respectful conversation with the teaching of the magisterium, their own positions on the moral issue at hand and do not want them to try to do so; indeed, it often seems that the Pope and the bishops believe that if a Catholic citizen/legislator/policymaker does work out her own position on the moral issue at hand, and if her position is contrary to the position of the magisterium, and if she makes a political choice on the basis of her own position rather than on the basis of the magisterium's position, she is not being a "faithful" Catholic.[7]

Although neither neither the nonestablishment norm nor the morality of liberal democracy stands in the way of legislators or other policymakers outlawing or otherwise disfavoring conduct on the basis of a religiously grounded belief that the conduct is immoral, this does not mean that religious believers, when they deliberate about or vote on proposals to disfavor conduct, should rely uncritically on religiously grounded moral belief. In this chapter, I will particularize the point by arguing that *with respect to moral issues that have become widely controversial among those Catholics and other Christians engaged by the issues*, it is important for a Catholic citizen/legislator/policymaker to work out her own position on the moral issue at hand, albeit in conversation with the teaching of the magisterium, and then to make a political choice on the basis of her own position, even if her position is contrary to the position of the magisterium. Moreover, for a Catholic to do so does not entail that she is not being a "faithful" Catholic. There is no contradiction between being a faithful Catholic – a faithfull Catholic, a Catholic who is full of faith – and being a Catholic who exercises her faith in a critical, discriminating way. One can be both a faith-full Catholic and a mind-full Catholic. Recall John Noonan's reply to Avery Dulles: "[T]he record is replete with mistakes – the faithful can't just accept everything that comes from Rome as though God had authorized it."[8]

I do not add casually the proviso "albeit in conversation with the teaching of the magisterium." The proviso is important: It makes no sense for a citizen/legislator/policymaker *to self-identify as Catholic* and then, in struggling with a difficult moral issue (capital punishment, e.g., or physician-assisted suicide, or abortion),[9] to fail to enter into conversation with the teaching of the magisterium – and with the reflections of the Pope and, more locally, the National Conference of Catholic Bishops. Bernard Hoose has written recently that most Catholic theologians "accept that . . . teachings emanating from members of the hierarchy, especially the pope, have a special status that calls for bias in the direction of assent."[10] The following passages from a statement issued in 2000 by the Assembly of (Catholic) Bishops of Quebec, *Annoncer l'Évangile dans la culture actuelle au Québec*, help to explain why it is important to enter into conversation with the teaching of the magisterium on the moral issue at hand:

> For our contemporaries, truth may come from tradition, but it is also the fruit of their own work of exploration. It is received, but it is also discovered. It may remain beyond us, but it comes to us by way of the subject's own activity on a personal journey. In this view, tradition and teaching may have a role to play in a person's pursuits, in the quest of a subject. Tradition and teaching are not imposed as a kind of final or definitive word, but function as memory, reference points and markers or as a word which questions and confronts one's own discoveries, a word which evokes a response from the subject. Statements from tradition are critiqued before being taken up by the subject. Tradition no longer represents a catalogue of timeless, ready-made answers from which one has only to pick and choose. . . .
>
> . . . Tradition is not first and foremost a source for answers. It puts us in dialogue with the quests and pursuits of individuals from the past, who, in given situations, produced a given faith-filled meaning. Conceived of in this way, tradition no longer elicits a negative response from many of our contemporaries who see in it something other than an authority which short-circuits our own attempts at discovery by providing, in advance, answers to all our questions, both now and in the future. Better yet, understood in this way, tradition allows the subject to shift her centre of concern outside the self and enter into a fruitful dialogue with other points of view which find expression in tradition.[11]

As the Quebec bishops obviously understand, however, in their insightful portrayal of the role of tradition in an individual's moral discernment, to say that a Roman Catholic should enter into conversation with "tradition" – in particular, with the traditional teaching of the magisterium – is not to say that she should, at the end of the day, assent to, or even defer to, that teaching – for example, the teaching that is the principal subtext for my discussion in this chapter, namely, that "homosexual acts are intrinsically disordered" and "[u]nder no circumstances can they be approved."[12]

II

Most of what I said in the preceding chapter, about the role of human experience in moral discernment, is directly relevant to, and supportive of, my argument in this chapter. (Again, "[e]xperience as such, taken as 'raw experience,' the mere participation in this or that phenomenon, is ... not the key. Raw experience carries with it no evaluation. But experience, *suffered or perceived in the light of human nature and of the gospel,* can be judged good or bad. It was the experience of unfreedom, in the gospel's light, that made the contrary shine clear.")[13] Recall, from the preceding chapter, the late Joseph Cardinal Bernardin's statement that the Roman Catholic Church "should be convinced we have *much to learn from the world* and much to teach it. A confident church will speak its mind, seek as a community to live its convictions, *but leave space for others to speak to us, to help us grow from their perspective. . . .*"[14]

Predictably, however, some Catholics, both clergy and laity, will reply that with respect to the question of the morality of same-sex unions, we Catholics have no need for further moral discernment based on human experience, because we now know, ultimately on the authority of the magisterium, that same-sex unions are always and everywhere hostile to the true human well-being of those who are parties to such unions. These Catholics will insist that with respect to the morality of same-sex unions, Catholics have nothing "to learn from the world"; they know all they need to know, namely, that according to the clear and authoritative teaching of the magisterium, same-sex unions are always and everywhere immoral. They will argue that the proper inquiry for a citizen/legislator/policymaker *qua* Catholic is not whether same-sex unions are immoral, but only how to persuade enough others that same-sex unions are immoral to keep the law from affirming the contrary view.[15] For a Catholic citizen/legislator/policymaker to conclude, against the teaching of the magisterium, that same-sex unions are not immoral (i.e., that such unions are not immoral in

90

virtue of the fact that they are same-sex) and then to make a policy choice on the basis of that view is for her to fail in her calling to be a "faithful" Catholic.

This way of thinking about a Catholic's political role is deeply misconceived. The place to begin, in making this clear, is an important statement issued in 2000 by the International Theological Commission: "Memory and Reconciliation: The Church and the Faults of the Past."[16] The statement distinguishes between "the indefectible fidelity of the church" – the Church understood theologically and analogically as Holy Mother – and "the weaknesses of her members, clergy or laity, yesterday and today."[17] The Church, which in the words of the ITC statement is "the bride of Christ 'with neither blemish nor wrinkle ... holy and immaculate'," must be neither confused nor conflated with the Church's "children, pardoned sinners, called to permanent *metanoia*, to renewal in the Holy Spirit."[18] The statement acknowledges that the Church's "sons and daughters," when acting "in the name of the church," can do things – and from time to time have done things – "in contradiction to the Gospel."[19] Commenting on the ITC statement in the Jesuit weekly *America*, Francis A. Sullivan, SJ, a professor of ecclesiology at the Pontifical Gregorian University in Rome from 1956 to 1992 and now a professor of theology at Boston College, writes:

[T]he hierarchical structure of the church is such that there have always been those who were authorized to act and speak "in the name of the church," and in her name have proclaimed the church's doctrine, enacted its laws and determined its official policy. The ITC. text recognizes the possibility that what was done "in the name of the church" could have been done "in contradiction to the Gospel." ... [O]bviously, it is only members of the hierarchy who have been authorized to act and speak "in the name of the church," and only they could be meant as those who, in doing so, have acted in contradiction to the Gospel.... [Those] things in the history of the church that call for repentance and a request for forgiveness are the official policies and practices that were established or sanctioned by those who were authorized to act and speak in the name of the church, but that were objectively "in contradiction to the Gospel." ... What is needed is the frank recognition that some official policies and practices of the church have been objectively in contradiction to the Gospel and have caused harm to many people.[20]

We may say, in the light of the ITC statement, that for a Catholic to dissent from one or more of the doctrines, policies, and practices established by the hierarchy in the name of the Church, which can be, and some of which have been, in contradiction to – and in that sense unfaithful to – the Gospel, is not for her to compromise her calling to be faithful to the Church as Holy Mother, possessed of "indefectible fidelity," the church as "the bride of Christ 'with neither blemish nor wrinkle . . . holy and immaculate'." Not that this understanding of "the Church" is unproblematic.[21] It is, however, the understanding of "the Church" advanced by the present Pope and by the ITC, and therefore I want to work with it here.

How are Catholics to judge whether an official Church doctrine (or policy or practice) that some Catholics fear might be untrue to the Gospel is true to the Gospel – or, instead, betrays the Gospel? Clearly, the fact that the doctrine is official – the fact that the doctrine bears the imprimatur of the magisterium – cannot be conclusive, because, *pace* the ITC statement, official Church doctrines can be, as some have been, "in contradiction to the Gospel." An example: the once-official Church doctrine "that war gives a right to enslave and that ownership of a slave gives title to the slave's offspring."[22] ("Six different popes justified and authorised the use of slavery.")[23] Another: the once-official Church doctrine "that error has no rights and that fidelity to the Christian faith may be physically enforced."[24] ("Pope Leo X . . . declared that the burning of heretics is in accord with the Holy Spirit.")[25] Another: "the explicit centuries-long papal teaching that Jews and heretics go to hell unless they convert to the Catholic faith."[26]

Again: How are Catholics to judge whether an official Church doctrine (policy, practice) is in conformity with the Gospel? Some claim that the official Church doctrine that homosexual sexual conduct is always immoral, because always hostile to human well-being, is a betrayal of the Gospel. Recall, from the preceding chapter, Robert Bellah's conclusion:

A principled rejection of gay sexuality, whether put forward by the church or any other sector of society, is morally indefensible. It has the same status today as arguments for the inferiority of women. To remain stuck in that position, as the church for the time being seems likely to do, is not only unfortunate: it makes the church collaborate in continuing forms of domination. To put it even more strongly: it makes the church collaborate in sin.[27]

How are Catholic citizens/legislators/policymakers to judge whether official Church doctrine about homosexual sexual conduct is in conformity to the Gospel – or is, instead, a betrayal of it?

I quoted, in the preceding chapter, Margaret Farley's reference to "the testimony of women and men whose sexual preference is for others of the same sex." It is, she writes, "clear and profound testimon[y] to the life-enhancing possibilities of same-sex relations and the integrating possibilities of sexual activity within these relations." In what David Hollenbach has called "dialogue with the other,"[28] Christian believers may come to concur in Farley's judgment that "[w]e have the witness that homosexual activity can be a way of embodying responsible human love and sustaining Christian friendship" and that "this witness alone is enough to demand of the Christian community that it reflect anew on the norms for homosexual love."[29] But whether or not a Christian believer comes to concur in that particular judgment, "dialogue with the other" is essential:

[D]isagreements actually lodged in contradictory interpretations of human experience are not without some possibilities of adjudication. Here the requirement is communication, and the potential is for enlargement of experience and expansion of its sources for interpretation. It would be naive in the extreme to suggest that all disagreements about experience are only apparent, and sufficient dialogue will in every case bring harmony. Nonetheless, what communication prevents is a premature acceptance of unbridgeable gaps. What it makes possible is the actual bringing together of diverse experiences in their concreteness and particularity.[30]

With respect to the issue of the morality of same-sex unions, however, what would be the point of such "communication" if Catholics, on condition of being "faithful," were required to give "religious assent" to the position of the magisterium?[31] What would be the point of "dialogue with the other" if Catholics, in order to be "faithful," had to deem the issue closed? In any event, such an understanding of the requirements of "faithfulness" is mistaken. Again, and as the statement of the International Theological Commission on "the church and the faults of the past" makes clear, Catholics are called to be faithful to the Church. We may also say that Catholics, like all Christians, are called to be faithful to the Gospel; they are called to be faithful both to the person and to the teaching of Jesus Christ. This call obviously demands that Catholics be discriminating in the exercise of their faith. (Recall, from the preceding chapter, John Mahoney's point: "[I]f there is a historical shift, through improvement in scholarship or knowledge, or through an entry of society into a significantly different age, then what that same fidelity requires of the Church is

93

that it respond to the historical shift, such that it might be not only mistaken *but also unfaithful* in declining to do so.")[32] As I said, this call must not be confused or conflated with a call to indiscriminate obedience to the Church's "sons and daughters," even when they are promulgating doctrines, policies, or practices "in the name of the church."

Bellah's point, I take it, is that fidelity to the Gospel – to the person and teaching of Jesus Christ – is objectively inconsistent with fidelity to the position of the magisterium on the morality of same-sex unions. Now, Bellah may be wrong, but Catholics are not required, as a condition of being "faithful" to the Church, to conclude that Bellah must be wrong *just because he has come to reject the position of the magisterium.* "Faithful" Catholics may and indeed should decide for themselves, in conversation with the teaching of the magisterium, whether Bellah is wrong – and they should make a political choice on the basis of their own judgment about the matter, even if their own judgment is a "dissenting" judgment. The Roman Catholic Church should not – though the Vatican sometimes seems to[33] – aspire to "the ideological unanimity of a totalitarian political movement." I concur in the judgment implicit in the questions that Margaret O'Brien Steinfels posed about ten years ago:

If one doubts whether real communion implies dissent, imagine a church where dissent had been rendered unthinkable, impermissible, or inexpressible. Would such a church be likely to resemble the interpersonal, vital, ever-deepening, always outstretching encounter of hearts and minds that is communion? Or would it be more likely to resemble the bureaucracy of a government, the conformity of a corporation, the discipline of an army, of even the ideological unanimity of a totalitarian political movement?[34]

I concur, too, in Steinfels' further point – she says she "take[s] it for granted" – "that somewhere a line must be drawn between the dissent that is an inevitable and healthy aspect of communion and the dissent that is no longer compatible with communion." (Like Steinfels, "I do not question the efforts of bishops and theologians (it is important to include both) to resolve where, exactly, that line should be drawn in principle.")[35] Indeed, the position I am recommending here – namely, that a Catholic citizen/legislator/policymaker should work out her own position on the moral issue at hand, albeit in conversation with the teaching of the magisterium, and then make a political choice on the basis of her own position even if her position is contrary to the position of the magisterium – contains this important proviso: *with respect to moral issues that have become widely controversial among those Catholics and other Christians engaged by the issues.* The morality of slavery, for example, is not widely controversial among Christians – not any longer. Nor is the question of the true and full humanity of nonwhites, or of women, widely controversial among Christians. The morality of same-sex unions, however, is now widely controversial among Christians; it is, moreover, controversial not interdenominationally but transdenominationally. Such a datum, as I emphasized in the preceding chapter, should give pause to any reflective Christian – and, therefore, to any reflective Catholic.[36]

III

Some citizens of the United States are not religious believers. Of these, some, perhaps because they are hostile to religious belief, would like to fence religion out of politics – or to fence it out as much as possible.[37] Consider, for example, the American philosopher Richard Rorty, who has written approvingly of "privatizing religion – keeping it out of . . . 'the public square,' making it seem bad taste to bring religion into discussions of public policy."[38] Of the large majority of citizens of the United States who are religious believers, some – including some American Catholics – are in the grip of older, more authoritarian modes of religious believing (I am tempted to say, more monarchical modes of religious believing) that fit uneasily, if at all, the culture of liberal democracy, which, *at its best*, encourages ecumenical and self-critical deliberation of the sort suggested by, among others, David Hollenbach and Margaret Farley.

Today most American Catholics seem to me to stand somewhere between these two groups – between those, like Rorty, who would fence religion out of politics, and those who would bring an authoritarian ("dogmatic") religion into politics. Recall the question to which, I said, this chapter is a (partial) response – the question I gleaned from the U.S. bishops' most recent statement on "political responsibility": "What does it mean to be a Catholic and a citizen of the United States in the year 2000 and beyond?" Those Catholic citizens (including legislators and other policymakers) who stand between the two groups must forge for themselves a vision of their proper role in politics that is true *both* to their citizenship in a liberal democracy (the United

95

States) *and* to their membership in a community of faith (the Roman Catholic Church). In forging that vision, Catholic citizens should understand and insist, against Richard Rorty and kindred spirits, that, as I argue in Chapters 2 and 3 of this book, neither the morality of liberal democracy nor the establishment clause counsels them (or other religious believers) against banning or otherwise disfavoring conduct on the basis of a religiously grounded belief that the conduct is immoral (even if the belief lacks plausible, independent secular grounding). But at the same time, they should understand and insist – against some in their own Church – that, as I have argued in this chapter, a Catholic citizen/legislator/policymaker does not compromise her fidelity to the Church when, in conversation with the teaching of the magisterium, she works out her own position on the moral issue at hand, *a moral issue that has become widely controversial among those Catholics and other Christians engaged by the issue,* and then makes a political choice on the basis of her own position – even if, in the end, her position is contrary to the position of the magisterium. Again, one can be – like John Noonan, Margaret Farley, David Hollenbach, and countless others – both a faithful Catholic and a Catholic who exercises her faith in a critical, discriminating way.

After drafting an earlier version of this chapter, I had occasion to read the statement by the bishops of Quebec that I quoted earlier in this chapter. I was both struck and consoled by the extent to which my reflections in this chapter seem to be nourished by the same spirit that animates the Quebec bishops' argument. Consider, for example, these passages:

These modern sensibilities affect the way in which we think about the institutions of Christianity, whose vocation clearly sets them apart from bureaucratic structures and from the mechanisms of standardization which are the province of large public administrations. The nature of Christian institutions ought to favor relationships based on equality and brotherhood/sisterhood and to value attitudes that welcome and liberate...

The democratic spirit builds a new relationship to the truth. The Church is to proclaim the Gospel in a relevant way. It is not sufficient to insist that the church is not a democracy, even if that statement is correct. Integration into the Church in a democratic society leads to a new relation to authority and a different manner of proclaiming the Gospel. What is required is a certain degree of participation and a careful listening to all the voices that want to be heard. Nothing can be imposed simply by authority: there is no single word. [Rien ne s'impose d'autorité et il n'y a pas de parole unique.][39]

In 1989, the historian David O'Brien suggested, in his book *Public Catholicism*, that "after two centuries of organized existence in the United States, the American church has not evolved a coherent understanding of its public role and responsibilities."[40] In 1975, in what should be understood partly as an effort to repair this state of affairs, the U.S. bishops began their practice of issuing "a reflection on 'political responsibility' in advance of each presidential election."[41] In October 1999, in the conclusion to their most recent such reflection, the bishops asked: "What does it mean to be a believer and a citizen in the year 2000 and beyond?"[42] Let me suggest this as a more precise formulation of the question the bishops meant to ask: "What does it mean to be a Catholic and a citizen of the United States in the year 2000 and beyond?" This chapter is a response – a partial response – to that question. One of my aims in this chapter has been to do what Kenneth Himes, past president of the Catholic Theological Society of America, has urged Catholics to do: "reflect on the experience of being faithful disciples and free citizens in a democratic nation."[43] In my judgment, the passages I quoted in the preceding paragraph, from the Quebec bishops' statement, should be a principal guide for Catholic citizens as they participate in the politics of their liberal democracy and contend there with difficult, contested issues of morality and justice.

Religion, Politics, and Abortion

We can approach a solution of the problem of relating religious commitments to political decisions by excluding two answers. . . . The one wrong answer is to find no relevance at all between our faith and our political actions. This answer is wrong because it denies the seriousness of our political decisions and obscures our Christian responsibilities for the good order and justice of our civil community.

The other answer stands at the opposite extreme. It is to equate religious and political commitments and to regard every political decision as simply derived from our faith. This is a wrong answer because political issues deal with complex problems of justice, every solution for which contains morally ambiguous elements. . . . The tendency to equate our political with our Christian convictions causes politics to generate idolatry.

Reinhold Niebuhr[1]

The contemporary American debate about religion in politics is animated and shaped, in part, by two large controversies that are at once both moral and political in character: the controversies over same-sex unions and abortion. Addressing the issue of religion in politics without addressing those two controversies would be like staging *Hamlet* without the prince. In Chapter 4, I discussed same-sex unions as a political issue for Christians; and in Chapter 5, I used the controversy over the morality of same-sex unions to frame my argument about the responsibility of Catholic citizens and legislators. In this chapter, still speaking mainly to religious believers who hold (as I do) that political reliance on religiously grounded morality is neither illegitimate in a liberal democracy nor unconstitutional in the United States, I turn to the moral/political controversy that, in the last generation, has been the most difficult and divisive of all: abortion. Indeed, "many consider [abortion] to be the most divisive American issue since slavery. . . ."[2] To an even greater extent than the controversy over same-sex unions, the abortion controversy looms large in the background, it looms large as a subtext, of the debate about the proper role of religion in the politics of the United States. More than any other American political controversy in the second half of the twentieth century, the abortion controversy has been a principal, if sometimes unspoken, occasion of the debate about religion in politics.[3] My overarching aim here is to address the abortion controversy in a way that is true to each of the two propositions advanced by Reinhold Niebuhr in the epigraph to this chapter. First: A citizen's religious faith has a legitimate, important role to play in her politics. Second: "[P]olitical issues deal with complex problems of justice, every solution for which contains morally ambiguous elements."

I

There are many controversial questions, or sets of questions, about abortion. In the context of this chapter – and of this book – three questions are fundamental.

- The "moral" question: Which abortions are immoral? All or most abortions – even, for example, in cases of rape? Or is abortion often a morally acceptable option?
- The "policy" question: Of the abortions that a legislature (legislative majority) believes to be immoral, which abortions should the legislature criminalize (or otherwise disfavor)?[4]
- The "constitutional" question: Of the abortions that a legislature wants to criminalize, which abortions is it constitutionally free to criminalize?

To believe that most (if not all) abortions are immoral is not necessarily to believe that a legislature should criminalize most abortions. To believe that it would be better for the legislature to criminalize most abortions – to believe, for example, that our society would be more just if the legislature criminalized most abortions – is not necessarily to believe that the legislature is constitutionally free to criminalize most abortions. To believe that the legislature is constitutionally free to criminalize most abortions is not necessarily to believe that it should do so, or even to believe that most abortions are immoral. Arguments about abortion are often confused enough without adding to the confusion by failing to distinguish among these three very different questions – the moral question, the policy question, and the constitutional question.

99

Because I have addressed it at length elsewhere, I want to say just a few words here about the constitutional question. On January 22, 1973, in *Roe v. Wade*, the Supreme Court of the United States famously decreed that under the Fourteenth Amendment, no state may outlaw abortion during the period of pregnancy prior to the time at which the fetus becomes "viable," that is, "[capable] of meaningful life outside the mother's womb."[5] (In January 1998, on the eve of the twenty-fifth anniversary of *Roe v. Wade*, the *New York Times* reported that because of advances "in neonatology, most experts place the point of fetal viability at 23 or 24 weeks.")[6] Although, according to the Court's decree, a state may outlaw abortion during the post-viability period of pregnancy, it must provide an exception for any abortion "necessary to preserve the life or health of the mother."[7] No constitutional decision by the Supreme Court since the end of World War II has been more controversial – certainly none has been more persistently controversial – than the Court's ruling in *Roe*. Even after almost a third of a century, the legitimacy of the Court's decision is widely and furiously contested.[8]

In my book *We the People: The Fourteenth Amendment and the Supreme Court*, I argued that the Court's ruling in *Roe* was mistaken;[9] in my judgment, state legislatures *are* constitutionally free to criminalize most pre-viability abortions. There is no need to rehearse my argument here. (I hope the interested reader will borrow a copy of *We the People* and consider my argument in its entirety.)[10] Here I want to address not the constitutional question, but the other two questions: the moral question and, especially, the policy question. That state legislatures and other policymakers are constitutionally free to do something does not entail that, all things considered, they *should* do it. Even if, *arguendo*, state legislatures are free to criminalize most pre-viability abortions, the question remains: Should they do so? Assuming that there is no constitutional impediment to their criminalizing the pre-viability abortions that they want to criminalize, which, if any, pre-viability abortions should state legislatures criminalize (or otherwise disfavor)?

A word of clarification: Few persons dispute what the Supreme Court's ruling in *Roe* acknowledges, namely, that state legislatures are constitutionally free to criminalize most *post-viability* abortions. And most state legislatures do in fact ban most post-viability abortions.[11] Putting aside (as we have just done) the question of constitutionality, the serious policy question is which, if any, *pre-viability* abortions state legislatures should criminalize. Hereafter, when I say simply "abortions," I am usually referring to pre-viability abortions.

II

Let's turn first to the moral question, which, as a practical matter, is prior to the policy question. That one believes that all or most (pre-viability) abortions in a particular category are immoral – for example, in cases of rape – does not necessarily mean that one believes that the law ought to criminalize abortions in that category. One may have reasons for concluding that the law ought not to criminalize abortions in a particular category even though one believes that (all or most) abortions in that category are immoral. Nonetheless, if one believes that abortions in a particular category are immoral, that is one reason to want the law to criminalize those abortions. Moreover, unless one believes that abortions in a particular category are immoral, one has little if any reason to want the law to criminalize those abortions.

It is worth noting that the moral question in this chapter – the question of the morality of abortion – is a different kind of moral question from the one that engaged us in Chapters 4 and 5: the question of the morality of same-sex unions. As I explained early in Chapter 4:

The moral argument at the heart of the fierce political controversy over whether the law should recognize same-sex unions – the argument about whether homosexual sexual conduct is always immoral – is at bottom an argument about the requirements of human well-being. Those who believe that homosexual sexual conduct is always (or almost always) immoral do so mainly because they believe that engaging in homosexual sexual conduct is always hostile to the authentic well-being of those who engage in it and is never, therefore, a fitting way for human beings to act. Thus, the argument about whether homosexual sexual conduct is always immoral exemplifies that ... "moral" argument is often about this:

What is good – truly good – for those we should care about (including ourselves)? And what is bad for them? In particular: What are the requirements of one's well-being? (The "one" may be, at one extreme, a particular human being or, at the other, each and every human being.) What choices are friendly to or even constitutive of one's authentic well-being; what choices are hostile to or even destructive of it?

By contrast, the argument about the morality of abortion is not an argument about the requirements of human well-being. It is instead an argument about which human beings are subjects of justice – about which are inviolable. As I have noted elsewhere,[12] "moral" argument is often, and most fundamentally, about this:

> Which human beings ought we to care about – which ones, that is, besides those we already happen to care about, those we already happen to be emotionally or sentimentally attached to: ourselves, our families, our tribes, and so on? Which human beings ought to be the beneficiaries of our respect; the welfare, the well-being, of which human beings ought to be the object of our concern? Which human beings are inviolable; which are subjects of justice? All human beings, or just some?

Those who argue that most or even all abortions are immoral – that is, all abortions not necessary to save the mother's life[13] – typically argue that unborn human beings, no less than born human beings, are inviolable; they typically argue that human fetuses, even during the period of pregnancy prior to viability, are inviolable; indeed, they argue that human embryos and even human zygotes are inviolable.[14] (To say that one is "inviolable" is to say that one is "not to be violated; not liable or allowed to suffer violence; to be kept sacredly free from profanation, infraction, or assault.")[15] Robert George has written: "Opponents of abortion . . . view all human beings, including the unborn . . ., as members of the community of subjects to whom duties in justice are owed. . . . The real issue of principle between supporters of abortion . . . and opponents . . . has to do with the question of who are subjects of justice." In George's view, "The challenge to the orthodox liberal view of abortion . . . is to identify nonarbitrary grounds for holding that the unborn . . . do not qualify as subjects of justice."[16] George then adds: "Frankly, I doubt that this challenge can be met."[17]

By contrast, those who argue that abortion is often a morally acceptable option typically argue that human fetuses, at least during the pre-viability period of pregnancy (and, a fortiori, human zygotes and human embryos), do not have the same moral status as other human beings: they are not subjects of justice, they are not inviolable.

Why do some believe that human fetuses (and human zygotes and human embryos) are inviolable – and others, that they are not? Is this moral disagreement amenable to what I shall call, for want of a better term, adjudication? On what basis?

Let's look first at the argument that (most or even all) abortions are immoral because human fetuses are inviolable – because, in George's terms, "the unborn . . . qualify as subjects of justice." That is, let's look at a particular argument to that effect: the argument made by, among others, several contemporary Roman Catholic ethicists – perhaps most fully by Patrick Lee,[18] but also by many others, including Germain Grisez,[19] John Finnis,[20] and Robert George.[21] For convenience, I call this the "pro-life" argument – though I do not mean to suggest that there are no other arguments on the pro-life side of the abortion controversy. (I was tempted to call it the "Catholic" argument, but this would have been misleading, because the argument does not comprise any specifically Catholic religious premises.)[22] I want to consider the pro-life argument, because it is the most widely shared argument among those who are morally opposed to abortion; it is, in that sense, the least sectarian antiabortion argument. The pro-life argument is accepted by many religious believers who are not Catholic and even by many persons who are not religious believers.[23]

The pro-life argument begins with a judgment that many Americans, including many who believe that abortion is often a morally acceptable option, do not want to deny: It is immoral to attack a born human being for the purpose of killing him or her. (This is not to say that it is immoral to attack a born human being for some other purposes – for example, to defend oneself or another from an unjust aggressor – even if the attack is foreseeably lethal.)[24] This judgment gives rise to the question: *Why* is it immoral to attack a born human being for the purpose of killing him or her? The pro-life argument gives this answer: Because each and every born human being is inviolable. But this answer gives rise to a further question: *Why – in virtue of what –* is each and every born human being inviolable? The pro-life argument responds: Each and every born human being is inviolable because a sufficient condition of an entity's being inviolable is that the entity be a human being (i.e., a *living* human being). Affirming that a human fetus is a human being,[25] the argument concludes that a human fetus is inviolable. (According to this argument, that a human fetus – or a human zygote or a human embryo – is an *unborn* human being is morally irrelevant, because a sufficient condition of an entity's being inviolable is not that the entity be a *born* human being, but simply that it be a human being.) The further conclusion follows that no one may attack a human fetus for the purpose of killing – of destroying – the human fetus. (This is a sketch of the pro-life argument; for an elaboration of the argument, see Patrick Lee's book, *Abortion and Unborn Human Life* [1996].) Again, this argument is the most widely shared argument among those, whether Catholic or not – indeed, whether religious believers or not – who hold that all or most abortions are immoral.[26]

Now, let's look at the argument that abortion is often a morally acceptable option. The most credible versions of this argument do not deny that a human fetus is a human being. (As one of the most prominent "pro-choice" theorists, the Harvard law professor Laurence Tribe, has written: "[T]he fetus is alive. It belongs to the human species. It elicits sympathy and even love, in part because it is so dependent and helpless.")[27] Although some may want to deny that prior to fourteen days, the embryo is a human being,[28] this denial doesn't explain why one concludes that abortion is often a morally acceptable option during the twenty-one to twenty-two weeks after fourteen days but before viability. In any event, the most credible versions of the argument that pre-viability abortion is often a morally acceptable option do not deny that a human fetus (at least, a human fetus after fourteen days) is a human being; instead, they deny that a sufficient condition of an entity's being inviolable is that the entity be a human being. The most credible versions of the argument insist that some additional criterion (or criteria) must be satisfied before a human being, born or unborn, is inviolable. Because this additional criterion is not satisfied in the case of a human fetus – at least, a human fetus during the pre-viability period of pregnancy – a human fetus, at least during the pre-viability period, does not have the same moral status as some other human beings; it is not *yet* a subject of justice, it is not *yet* inviolable.

The "not yet inviolable" argument is often cast as an argument about when a human fetus, understood as a human being, becomes a human "person," understood as a human being who has achieved the status of inviolability.[29] Three years before the Supreme Court's decision in *Roe v. Wade*, Daniel Callahan presented such an argument in his book *Abortion, Law, Choice and Morality*: "[Abortion] is not the destruction of a human person – for at no stage of its development does a conceptus fulfill the definition of a person, which implies *a developed capacity for reasoning, willing, desiring, and relating to others* – but is the destruction of an important and valuable form of human life."[30] Many such arguments – many variations on the kind of argument Callahan presented – have been presented in the years since *Roe v. Wade* was decided.[31]

There is widespread skepticism *both* about the pro-life argument *and* about the "not yet inviolable" argument. (At least, there is serious skepticism about most versions of the "not yet inviolable" argument.) The most serious skepticism about the pro-life argument focuses on the claim that a sufficient condition of an entity's being inviolable is that the entity be a human being, and that it is therefore irrelevant to the question of whether a human being is inviolable that the human being is a zygote, an embryo, or a fetus at an early stage of development. Patrick Lee has written that "[t]he pro-life argument is that although there are several differences between killing a two-year-old child and killing a human embryo or fetus, there is no *morally significant* difference between them.... Whatever makes [intentionally] killing a two-year-old child wrong is equally present in the [intentional] killing of a human embryo or fetus."[32] But many people find it difficult, even impossibly difficult, to accept this argument; for many people, it is deeply counterintuitive that a human zygote, or a human embryo, or a human fetus at an early stage of development, has precisely the same moral status – namely, inviolability – as a human being at a much later stage of human development (e.g., a ten-year-old child). Consider these passages from an essay that Peter Steinfels, then editor of the Catholic weekly *Commonweal*, published in *Commonweal* in 1981:

[T]he right-to-life movement is naively overconfident in its belief that the existence of a unique "genetic package" from conception onwards settles the abortion issue. Yes, it does prove that what is involved is a human individual and not "part of the mother's body." It does not prove that, say, a twenty-eight-day-old embryo, approximately the size of this parenthesis (–), is *then and there* a creature with the same claims to preservation and protection as a newborn or an adult.... Although it is not *logically* impossible, for example, to consider the great number of fertilized eggs that fail to implant themselves in the uterus as lost "human beings," a great many people find this idea totally incredible. Similarly, very early miscarriage usually does not trigger the sense of loss and grief that [later] miscarriage does. Can we take these instinctive responses as morally helpful? ... It is simply *not* the case that a refusal to recognize Albert Einstein or Anne Frank as human beings deserving of full legal rights is equivalent to the refusal to see the same status in a disc the size of a period or an embryo one-sixth of an inch long and with barely rudimentary features.[33]

Whereas the most serious skepticism about the pro-life argument focuses on the claim that being a human being is a sufficient condition of an entity's being inviolable, skepticism about the "not yet inviolable" argument focuses on the claim that no human being – not even a *born* human being, according to some versions of the argument – is inviolable (or is a "person" and therefore inviolable) unless and until he or she possesses the proposed property (e.g., in Callahan's version of the argument, "a developed capacity for reasoning, willing, desiring, and relating to others"). Many people find it difficult, even impossibly difficult, to accept this claim if the proposed property is one that even human infants and some other born human beings, in addition to human fetuses, lack. (In most versions of the "not yet inviolable" argument, the proposed property fits that profile.) For many people, it is deeply counterintuitive that an infant or, for example, a severely mentally disabled adult lacks the moral status – inviolability – the possession of which they believe to be the fundamental reason that it is gravely morally wrong to attack a human being for the purpose of killing him or her.

> [I]n their emphasis ... on social, interpersonal, relational, and rational criteria for "humanness," prochoice arguments almost always deny the fetus any moral standing in such a way that, except for sheer arbitrariness (and instinctive decency, one might add), moral status should also be denied the newborn. Those familiar with the philosophical literature [regarding abortion] know that, logic being logic, defenses of infanticide are no longer uncommon.[34]

I said that there is widespread skepticism both about the pro-life argument and about the "not yet inviolable" argument.[35] Indeed, many people are, at one and the same time, skeptical both about the pro-life argument and about the "not yet inviolable" argument. *They are unable to embrace either argument.* There are many who do not believe that, much less act as if, human beings are inviolable – even normal adult human beings. But among many who do believe that *some* human beings, at least, are inviolable, there is fundamental uncertainty both about what it is that makes a human being inviolable and, therefore, about when a human being becomes inviolable. This uncertainty afflicts even many religious believers. Listen, for example, to Garry Wills, who is a Catholic: "I cannot be certain when personhood begins, any more than Augustine was certain when the soul was infused."[36] Wills adds: "[A]gainst all those who tell us, with absolute assurance, when [personhood] begins, we should entertain some knowledge of our limits. On the whole subject of the origins of life, [Augustine] said, 'When a thing obscure in itself defeats our capacity, and nothing in Scripture comes to our aid, it is not safe for humans to presume that they can pronounce on it.'"37

This uncertainty is pervasive even among many contemporary secular moral philosophers who rely on the idea of human inviolability. An example: In an otherwise laudatory review of a book by the moral philosopher Frances Kamm, Jeff McMahan, referring to "Kamm's central contention ... that people must be regarded as inviolable, as ends-in-themselves," observes that "[Kamm's] arguments often raise difficult questions that the book fails to address. A conspicuous instance of this is Kamm's failure to identify the basis of our moral inviolability."38 It is revealing that Kamm, one of the principal neo-Kantian moral philosophers now writing, "conspicuously" fails in her otherwise rigorously argued book to tell her audience why – in virtue of what – people are inviolable. The issue is anything but marginal: As McMahan states, "[u]nderstanding the basis of our alleged inviolability is crucial both for determining whether it is plausible to regard ourselves as inviolable, and for fixing the boundaries of the class of inviolable beings."39

A failure to "understand[] the basis of our alleged inviolability" is not always consequential. Even without this understanding, we can say that if white human beings (for example) are inviolable, then non-white human beings are inviolable, too, because *whatever* the basis of human inviolability, we are confident that it has nothing whatsoever to do with the color of one's skin, any more than it has to do with the color of one's eyes or hair. May we say, too, that whatever the basis of human inviolability, we are confident that it has nothing whatsoever to do with the stage of one's biological development – nothing to do, that is, with whether one is a human zygote, embryo, or fetus rather than a normal adult human being? Whereas the conviction that the basis of human inviolability has nothing to do with skin color is very widespread among us citizens of liberal democracies, the claim that the basis of human inviolability has nothing to do with whether one is a human zygote rather than a normal adult human being is widely disputed among us. (Even in the United States and some other predominantly Christian countries, Christians denominations are divided as to whether the basis of human inviolability makes relevant the stage of biological development.)40 "Understanding the basis of our alleged inviolability" is crucial for determining whether human zygotes, embryos, and fetuses are inside or outside "the class of inviolable beings."

I have suggested elsewhere that contemporary secular moral philosophy, insofar as it is secular, lacks the resources to explain why – in virtue of what – human beings (whether all or some) are "not to be violated; not liable or allowed to suffer violence; to be kept sacredly free from profanation, infraction, or assault."[41] A religiously grounded moral philosophy, insofar as it is religiously grounded, does not lack those resources. (That this is so does not entail that every religious explanation, or indeed any religious explanation, is credible.) But, of course, a particular religious explanation of the basis of human inviolability is destined to be sectarian in a religiously pluralistic society like the United States.

In any event, it is undeniable that among the citizens of contemporary liberal democracies such as the United States, there is widespread uncertainty about what it is that makes a human being – a normal young woman, say – inviolable. (And even among those blessed with certainty, "there are [competing] views about what characteristic is the source of human 'dignity'.")[42] Is she inviolable because she, like every human being, unborn as well as born, is a beloved "child" of God and a sister to oneself, created in the image of God? Or because she, like every normal human being a certain number of years beyond infancy, is a "rational" creature? Or is it enough if one has what even normal unborn human beings have: the potential to become rational? Or, *pace* Callahan, is it because she, like every normal human being a certain number of years beyond infancy, has "a developed capacity for reasoning, willing, desiring, and relating to others"? Or is it enough if one has the potential to develop such a capacity?[43] And so on. The issue is genuinely daunting. ("[T]he moral status of the fetus in its early development is a genuinely difficult problem. It is so of its nature, as a unique and boundary-line situation, and not because of the blindness or self-interest of those examining the problem.")[44] This is why so many people – including many religious believers – are simply unable to be confident partisans in the debate about the precise moral status of human zygotes, embryos, and fetuses. Not that there are no confident partisans in the debate. Of course there are. But a majority of Americans is unable to embrace *either* the pro-life claim that being a human being is a sufficient condition of an entity's being inviolable *or* the competing claim that a human being is not inviolable (or not a "person" and so not inviolable) unless and until he or she possesses a particular property.

Is the moral conflict between partisans of the pro-life claim (such as Patrick Lee) and partisans of one or another version of the "not yet inviolable" claim (such as Daniel Callahan) amenable to adjudication?[45] I suspect that if one is to try to adjudicate the conflict, one must make a judgment about one or more contested theological issues. As I noted earlier, it is far from clear on what basis one who is not a religious believer, one who is an agnostic or even an atheist, can claim that every human being, *or indeed that any particular human being(s),* is inviolable.[46] I am inclined to concur in R. H. Tawney's view: "The essence of all morality is this: to believe that every human being is of infinite importance, and therefore that no consideration of expediency can justify the oppression of one by another. But to believe this it is necessary to believe in God."[47] (We may say, too, that to believe, not that every human being is inviolable, but just that some particular human beings are inviolable, "it is necessary to believe in God.") It bears emphasis that one need not be a religious believer to concur in this view. Jeffrie Murphy, for example, insists that it is, for him, "very difficult – perhaps impossible – to embrace religious convictions," but he nonetheless claims that "the liberal theory of rights requires a doctrine of human dignity, preciousness and sacredness that cannot be utterly detached from a belief in God or at least from a world view that would be properly called religious in some metaphysically profound sense." Murphy continues: "[T]he idea that fundamental moral values may require [religious] convictions is not one to be welcomed with joy [by nonreligious enthusiasts of the liberal theory of rights]. This idea generates tensions and appears to force choices that some of us would prefer not to make. *But it still might be true for all of that.*"[48]

That there may be no way to adjudicate the conflict between the pro-life argument and one or another version of the "not yet inviolable" argument that does not involve a judgment about one or more contested theological issues is a conclusion destined to displease certain partisans of the pro-life argument, such as Patrick Lee, John Finnis, and Robert George: They want to believe (and do believe) that the pro-life argument does not rely on theology; they want to believe that the pro-life argument is atheological – that it is, in Finnis's words, "reflective, critical, publicly intelligible, and rational."[49] They want to believe this, because they want to believe that the pro-life argument is beyond religious sectarianism. But it seems to me that the pro-life argument, as a pro-life thinker recently suggested in *First Things*, is fundamentally religious in character: "[M]ost pro-life activists would concede that the fetus, especially in the early stages of its development, is not *self-evidently* (I repeat: not *self-evidently*) a human person; that there very well may be an element of religious belief that informs their conviction that human life begins at the moment of conception."[50]

In any event, my aim here is not to try to adjudicate the (intractable?) moral conflict between partisans of the pro-life argument and partisans of one or another version of the "not yet inviolable" argument. (Whatever the basis on which that conflict might be amenable to adjudication, I am like a majority of Americans – indeed, like a majority of American Catholics[51] – in this respect: I am unable to be a confident partisan in this debate even though I believe abortion to be gravely morally problematic.) Rather, my aim, in the remainder of this chapter, is twofold. In the next section, I want to sketch how the widespread uncertainty about the moral status of unborn human life has played itself out both in the attitudes of (a majority of) the American people toward abortion and, relatedly, in their preferences concerning the legal regulation of abortion. Then, in the final two sections, I want to think about how religious believers (and others) who are morally opposed to abortion should respond, politically and otherwise, to the state of affairs constituted by those majoritarian attitudes and preferences.

III

Recall Patrick Lee's statement of the pro-life position: "[A]lthough there are several differences between killing a two-year-old child and killing a human embryo or fetus, there is no *morally significant* difference between them.... Whatever makes [intentionally] killing a two-year-old child wrong is equally present in the [intentional] killing of a human embryo or fetus." That a majority of Americans is unable to accept this claim does not mean that a majority is unable to accept a different but related claim: that because it intentionally destroys a human life, abortion is a morally problematic act – gravely so.[52] (Even pro-choice advocates can accept this claim – and *should* accept it, argues Naomi Wolf in a powerful, sobering essay, "Our Bodies, Our Souls: Rethinking Pro-Choice Rhetoric.")[53] That a majority of Americans does in fact accept this claim – especially with respect to a pre-viability abortion performed during the second three months of pregnancy – is revealed in the results of a New York Times/CBS News poll conducted and published in January 1998, "[t]wenty-five years and nearly 30 million abortions after the Supreme Court's landmark Roe v. Wade decision."[54] The article accompanying the polling results reported that "public opinion has shifted notably away from general acceptance of legal abortion and toward an evolving center of gravity: a more nuanced, conditional acceptance that some call a 'permit, but discourage' model."[55] According to the polling data:

- A substantial majority of Americans – 61 percent – said that the law should permit a woman to have an abortion during the first three months of pregnancy; but only 15 percent said that the law should permit a woman to have an abortion in the second three months.
- However, a majority also said that abortion should not be "generally available" but available only "under stricter limits" – that is, limits stricter than the permissive regime now in place in consequence of the Supreme Court ruling in *Roe v. Wade*. Among women, 44 percent said "available, but under stricter limits"; only 32 percent said "generally available." Among men, the results were substantially identical: 45 percent said "available, but under stricter limits"; only 31 percent said "generally available." Among Protestants, 48 percent said "available, but under stricter limits"; only 28 percent said "generally available." Among Catholics, the results were (surprisingly?) similar: 43 percent said "available, but under stricter limits"; 31 percent said "generally available."
- What did those who supported availability "but under stricter limits" have in mind? "[W]hen people were asked [in 1989] whether a pregnant women should be able to get a legal abortion if her pregnancy would force her to interrupt her career, 37 percent said yes and 57 percent said no; in 1998, only 25 percent said yes and 70 percent said no. Similarly, in 1989, 48 percent thought an interrupted education was enough to justify a teen-age girl's abortion; that dropped to 42 percent [in 1998]. Support remained overwhelming, however, for women who sought abortions because they had been raped, their health was endangered, or there was a strong chance of a defect in the baby."[56]

II. Mainly for the Agnostics and the Inclusionists

This polling data strongly suggests that a substantial majority of the American people does not accept the pro-life argument. (Indeed, the data suggests that even a substantial majority of American Catholics does not accept the argument.)[57] In particular, a substantial majority does not believe that abortion in the first three months of pregnancy is the moral equivalent of abortion after the first three months, much less the moral equivalent of the intentional destruction of born human life. But the data also reveals that only a small minority of Americans would deny that abortion – even early abortion – is a gravely morally problematic act. Indeed, when you add together the number of respondents who said that the law should forbid abortion even in the first three months of pregnancy and the number who said that abortion should be "available, but under stricter limits," it seems clear that a substantial majority of the American people supports a significantly stricter regime of legal regulation of abortion than the Court's decision in *Roe v. Wade* permits state legislatures to adopt. The polling results "and other findings appear to indicate that the country's [twenty-five years' worth of] experience with legal abortion – more than 1 million are performed each year – is not leading to growing sympathy or acceptance."[58]

IV

The "policy" question, again, is this: Which, if any, abortions should the law criminalize (or otherwise disfavor)? The polling data just presented suggests the American people's answer – a part of their answer – to the policy question: Too many Americans are unable to accept what Patrick Lee has called the "pro-life" position ("[w]hatever makes [intentionally] killing a two-year-old child wrong is equally present in the [intentional] killing of a human embryo or fetus") to make it politically attractive to them, or politically possible for their representatives, to outlaw all the abortions that, according to the position, are immoral. Many Americans, however, do accept the pro-life position (as Lee has described it), and do so on one or another religious basis: e.g., "Every human being, unborn no less than born, is a beloved 'child' of God and a sister/brother to oneself, created in the image of God...." (Although religious believers are not the only ones who accept the pro-life position, they are the principal ones. According to the New York Times/CBS News poll, Americans who say that religion is "extremely important" in their daily lives are the ones who are most supportive of strict legal limits on abortion: 43 percent of this group say that abortion should be "not permitted"; 38 percent say that abortion should be "available, but under stricter limits.")[59] How ought such Americans to respond politically to the fact that, as I said, too many other Americans cannot accept the pro-life position to make it politically possible to outlaw all the abortions that, according to the position, are immoral?

Let's begin by recalling the lessons of Chapters 2 and 3: Nothing in the morality of liberal democracy – nothing in liberal democracy's constitutive commitments to the true and full humanity of every person and to certain basic human freedoms – forbids legislators or other policymakers to make a political choice to ban or otherwise disfavor conduct on the basis of religiously grounded moral belief *just in virtue of the fact that the belief is religiously grounded.* Nor does the nonestablishment norm forbid them to do so. (This is so, I explained, even if the moral belief lacks plausible, independent secular grounding.) Therefore, it is not inappropriate, insofar as the morality of liberal democracy and the nonestablishment norm are concerned, for pro-life religious believers to call for a state legislature to outlaw most abortions, or for a state legislature actually to outlaw most abortions, on the basis of a religiously grounded belief that unborn human life is inviolable.

Indeed, if a pro-life religious believer (call her Hannah) holds that an unborn human being is no less a "person" – and therefore no less inviolable – than a born human being, then what I said at the close of Chapter 3 applies to Hannah:

[N]othing in the morality of liberal democracy forbids legislators or other policymakers to disfavor conduct on the basis of a religiously grounded moral belief just in virtue of the fact that the belief is religiously grounded. But an even stronger claim commands our assent: One particular religiously grounded belief – one fundamental religiously grounded moral claim – is not only a legitimate ground of political choice in a liberal democracy but a most fitting ground. . . .

As I noted earlier in this chapter, one of the two constitutive commitments of liberal democracy – one of the two commitments that make a democracy "liberal" – is the commitment to the true and full humanity of *every* person, without regard to race, sex, religion, and so on. (The second constitutive commitment, grounded in part on the first, is to certain basic human freedoms.) This commitment is responsive to the "which human beings ought we to care about" inquiry: It is axiomatic, for liberal democracy, that every person (without regard to race,

etc.) is a subject of justice – that every person is inviolable. Of course, the proposition that every person is inviolable is embraced by many who do not count
themselves religious believers, but, as I have explained elsewhere, it is obscure *on
what basis* one who is not a religious believer, one who is an agnostic or even an
atheist, can claim (indeed, can believe) that every person is inviolable: *Why* is it
the case – *in virtue of what* is it the case – that every person is "not to be violated;
not liable or allowed to suffer violence; to be kept sacredly free from profanation,
infraction, or assault"? . . . In any event, that every person is inviolable is, for many
religious believers, a religiously embedded tenet. And, in a liberal democracy, it
is altogether fitting – it is altogether "liberal" – for religious believers to make
political choices, including *coercive* choices – choices to ban or require conduct –
on the ground of what is, for them, a religious claim: that each and every person
is sacred, that all persons are subjects of justice.

Of course, the position that an unborn human being is no less a
"person" than a born human being is controversial, but that's beside
the point. What matters here is that *Hannah* believes that an unborn
human being is no less a person. If Hannah wants the law to ban most
abortions because (1) she embraces the constitutive liberal commitment to the sacredness – the inviolability – of every person and (2) she
believes that an unborn human being *is* a person, then Hannah's pro-
life stance is liberal, not illiberal. Hannah might insist, as one liberal
activist who opposes abortion has insisted: "I see a liberal as one who
embraces life, whether it's women, the poor, gays and lesbians, the
people on death row or the unborn. It is antithetical for liberals to
exlude a class of persons from our embrace."[60]

To say that Hannah's stance is liberal is not to say that it is the only
liberal stance on the issue: We liberals can and do disagree among
ourselves – sometimes passionately and deeply – about many things.
Moreover, to say that Hannah's pro-life stance is liberal is not to say
that every pro-life stance is liberal. Not every pro-life stance is liberal.
But then, not every pro-choice stance is liberal, either. That is, some
who are pro-choice are pro-choice in part because they reject the idea
that any human being, born or unborn, is inviolable. Such a stance is
not liberal in the relevant sense.

In any event, it follows from the arguments I made in Chapters 2
and 3 that neither the morality of liberal democracy nor even the
American morality of religious freedom (i.e., the nonestablishment
norm) stands in the way of a pro-life religious believer's basing her call
for a state legislature to outlaw most abortions, or of a state legislature's
basing its decision to outlaw most abortions, on a religiously grounded

belief that unborn human life is inviolable. Nonetheless, a religious believer's own religious tradition might counsel her against calling, on the basis of a religiously grounded belief that unborn human life is inviolable, for a state legislature to outlaw most abortions. As I said in the opening paragraph of Chapter 4:

Recall the conscientious legislator who, in deciding whether to vote to outlaw, or otherwise disfavor, particular conduct, wonders what weight, if any, she and her fellow legislators may put on what is, for them, a religiously grounded belief, namely, that the conduct is immoral. In Chapters 2 and 3, I explained that neither the nonestablishment norm nor the morality of liberal democracy stands in the way of legislators' or other policymakers' disfavoring conduct on the basis of religiously grounded moral belief. But as I emphasized at the end of Chapter 3, this does not mean that religious believers, when they deliberate about or vote on proposals to disfavor conduct, should rely uncritically on religiously grounded moral belief. In this chapter, I pursue an inquiry different from but complementary to the inquiries I pursued in Chapters 2 and 3; I explore the possibility that a Christian believer's religious tradition counsels her to be wary, in some circumstances, about disfavoring conduct on the basis of a *biblically* grounded moral belief of a certain sort: a biblically grounded belief that the conduct is immoral in the sense of contrary to the requirements of human well-being.... For purposes of the inquiries in Chapters 2 and 3, a fundamental aspect of the American morality of religious freedom (i.e., the nonestablishment norm) and, then, the morality of liberal democracy were paramount. But for purposes of the inquiry in this chapter, a Christian's own religious tradition is paramount. In deciding whether she should forgo or at least limit reliance on her biblically grounded moral belief, a citizen of a liberal democracy who is a Christian will want to consult the wisdom of her own religious tradition at least as much as she will want to consult either the morality of liberal democracy or, if she is a citizen of the United States, the American constitutional morality of religious freedom.

I suggested, in Chapter 4, that with respect to the question of the law recognizing same-sex unions, Christians do in fact have *their own* reasons – reasons *internal both to their own religious (theological) tradition and to their own historical experience* – to accept the modest principle of political self-restraint I presented in the chapter. Does that principle of self-restraint apply not only to the controversy over same-sex unions but also to the controversy over abortion? Is the latter controversy, as well as the former, within the jurisdiction of the principle?

The answer is no – for two reasons. First, the principle of political self-restraint presented in Chapter 4 is meant to apply to *biblically grounded* argument about the morality of the conduct at issue (e.g., homosexual sexual conduct); the principle calls for self-restraint, under certain conditions, in basing a political choice to disfavor the conduct on such argument. But the principal argument that most abortions are immoral – the pro-life argument I have described here – is not biblically grounded. Although the Bible speaks of homosexual sexual conduct, "[t]he Bible in its Hebrew and Christian forms does not mention 'abortion' or provide explicit guidance about whether the practice is permitted or prohibited."[61]

Second, the principle of political self-restraint presented in Chapter 4 is meant to apply to (biblically grounded) argument about the requirements of human well-being; the principle calls for reliance, under certain conditions, on contemporary experience – subjective experience, experience from the inside (as it were) – of human well-being (or of the lack of it). The principle is thus relevant to the controversy over same-sex unions in a way that it is not relevant to the controversy over abortion. The moral controversy over same-sex unions is a controversy over the requirements of human well-being – and, as I explained in Chapter 4, contemporary human experience is probative with respect to questions about the requirements of human well-being. (Authentic human well-being is something that, in normal circumstances, human beings can be expected to experience.) By contrast, the moral controversy over abortion is a controversy not about the requirements of human well-being, but about which human beings are subjects of justice, which are inviolable. Thus, although one's experience of one's own well-being (or lack of it) is probative with respect to the question of the morality of homosexual sexual conduct, it is not probative with respect to the very different kind of question at issue in the abortion controversy: the question of the status – the inviolability *vel non* – of unborn human life. One's experience of one's own well-being is not probative with respect to the question of the status of unborn human life, any more than it is probative with respect to the question, for example, of the age of the earth.

Neither the morality of liberal democracy, nor the American morality of religious freedom, nor even the principle of political self-restraint presented in Chapter 4 stands in the way of a religious believer's basing her call for a state legislature to outlaw most abortions on her religiously grounded belief that unborn human life is inviolable. Still, the fact remains that too many Americans are unable to accept the pro-life argument to make it politically possible to outlaw all the abortions that, according to the argument, are immoral.

How ought pro-life religious believers to respond politically to this state of affairs? Of course, some of them may want to bear witness to their religious convictions about the inviolability of unborn human life by continuing to insist that the law should ban most abortions. But is there another – an alternative – political response that pro-life religious believers should consider?

The several public policies suggested by Cathleen Kaveny, of the Notre Dame Law School, merit serious consideration. Observing that "the pro-life conviction of the immorality of abortion too often translates into a call for stringent criminal penalties," Kaveny contends that "this call ignores the proper differences between moral and legal sanctions.... To say that the law cannot be *indifferent* to the well-being of the unborn ... does not mean that stringent criminal penalties for abortion are the best way for [the law] to express its concern."[62] Kaveny then poses this question: "What sort of legislative response to abortion would manifest proper sensitivity to its [i.e., abortion's] moral dimension?"[63] Drawing on the thinking of Thomas Aquinas about the proper relation between morality and law, Kaveny, a Catholic, sketches an agenda of several related public policies. Based on the polling data presented earlier, Kaveny's proposals, which richly deserve quotation in full, seem to be ones – some of them, at least – that a majority of the American people could plausibly be expected to support:

[T]he law as a whole should clearly express a bias on behalf of unborn life. Yet, at the incipient stages of instituting a pro-life legislative policy, criminal sanctions should be reserved to solidify the moral consensus that already exists. Moreover, they should be directed primarily at physicians rather than women, who are likely to be obtaining even the most morally dubious abortions under conditions of duress. For example, all third trimester abortions except those strictly necessary to preserve the mother's life could be prohibited in the criminal code. Moreover, the law could mandate that the technique used to perform the abortion be the one most likely to produce a living fetus. Since there is sturdy consensus in our society that live-born infants are vested with full legal status, adequate procedures should be instituted to protect the best interests of those infants whose "birth" is a late-term abortion.

Mid-term abortions in response to tests revealing serious genetic abnormalities in the fetus are a wrenchingly difficult situation in which to forge an adequate legal response. On the one hand, the quality-of-life judgments implicit in many of these abortion decisions are [morally problematic]. Moreover, these abortions are performed relatively late in pregnancy, at a fairly advanced stage in fetal development. On the other hand, in our culture, this situation is a paradigmatic example of how doing the right thing can sometimes require an extraordinary amount of virtue. The resources to aid parents with handicapped children are scant, and the burden could easily seem intolerable to many persons. The first response of pro-lifers, therefore, should be to increase substantially aid to families with mentally or physically damaged offspring. Yet the fact that the limits of the criminal law are the limits of ordinary virtue weighs against the institution of penal sanctions. In the grim meantime, the law should certainly make clear that its refusal to implement criminal penalties in such cases is a matter of excuse, not justification.

What of early abortions? Again, I reluctantly conclude that the inherent limits of the criminal law make penal sanctions inappropriate in this case. The extreme lack of consensus regarding this class of abortions means that laws which do institute such sanctions are likely to be unstable. The ready availability of illegal abortions means that laws against them are likely to be ineffective. Instead, in this case above all, the burden must rest upon the pedagogical function of the law in supporting and gradually extending a pro-life consensus. As a first "lesson," informed consent requirements conjoined with a short mandatory waiting and reflection period could be instituted. The state's concern for both unborn life and vulnerable pregnant women could be manifested in stress on information not about anatomical details and abortion procedures but about practical alternatives to abortion. In short, counselors could be trained to put together a "pro-life package," attempting to show a woman how she could feasibly carry her child to term while getting on with her own life.

For such a package to be more than a pathetic and half-hearted stab at a pervasive social problem, intense effort and imagination will be needed. First, a concerted attempt must be made effectively to hold fathers equally responsible with mothers for the well-being of their offspring. For Aquinas, this would not be a discretionary matter but a question of justice, going to the heart of a pro-life legal policy's legitimacy. In the face of any gross unfairness, the mere fact that a given policy was designed to further a virtuous societal response to the unborn would not be sufficient to insure its moral acceptability. Of situations "when burdens are imposed unequally on the community, although with a view to the common good," Aquinas declares, "the like are acts of violence rather than laws; because as Augustine says, 'a law that is not just, seems to be no law at all.'"

Secondly, we need to restructure our adoption laws so that deciding not to mother a baby after it is born does not seem to be such a draconian option. Worthy of serious consideration are recent experiences in less secretive adoption proceedings, where the birth mother has some influence upon the choice of adoptive parents and maintains some contact with the adoptive family as the child she bore grows to adulthood.

Thirdly, we need to insist that both public and private institutions dealing with young women provide easily available help so that those who find themselves pregnant can carry their fetuses to term while continuing with their own lives. For example, how many Catholic colleges have on their staffs an advocate specifically designated for women with problem pregnancies, someone who will facilitate the arrangement of alternative housing and medical care, run interference with professors and deans, organize a support network, and provide financial counseling?

Fourth, and most generally, we need to foster the plausibility of pro-life sentiment with respect to abortion by nurturing the relevant virtues with regard to other issues as well. In the words of the Roman Catholic Bishops' pastoral letter on warfare, "When we accept violence in any form as commonplace, our sensitivities become dulled. . . . Violence has many faces: oppression of the poor, deprivation of basic human rights, economic exploitation, sexual exploitation and pornography, neglect or abuse of the aged and the helpless, and innumerable other acts of inhumanity." A lenient attitude toward abortion, then, should finally be viewed as a prismatic and poignant example of a callousness toward life in general, a callousness that must be eradicated in all its forms.[64]

Again, it is politically impossible to outlaw all the abortions that, according to the pro-life argument, are immoral, because too many Americans are unable to accept that argument. I asked above how pro-life religious believers – religious believers who accept the pro-life argument – ought to respond, politically, to that state of affairs. Cathleen Kaveny is herself a pro-life religious believer; her thoughtful list of public policy proposals is, in my judgment, a sensitive and powerful political response, worthy of the most serious deliberation.

V

This state of affairs – a majority of citizens unable to accept the pro-life argument and the political impossibility, therefore, of outlawing all the abortions that, according to the argument, are immoral – is not unique to the United States but has become increasingly pervasive throughout the liberal democracies of the world in the last twenty-five to thirty years. The following "Western" countries, for example, all permit categories of pre-viability abortion (though not all permit exactly the same categories) that, according to the pro-life argument, are immoral: Australia,[65] Austria, Belgium, Canada, Denmark, Finland, France, Germany, Great Britain, Greece, Italy, Luxembourg, Malta, The Netherlands, New Zealand, Portugal, Spain, Sweden, and Switzerland.[66] It certainly seems to be the case, then, not merely in the United States but in liberal democracies generally, that a majority of citizens does not accept the pro-life argument presented by Patrick Lee and others. (The Republic of Ireland is a prominent exception,[67] but even there attitudes toward abortion and preferences concerning its legal regulation are in transition.[68]) The citizens of the

United States self-identify as religious believers to a much larger extent than do the citizens of most other liberal democracies; indeed, *most* Americans self-identify as religious believers.[69] One might wonder whether this makes a difference. It doesn't. As the polling data reported earlier discloses, most religious believers in the United States do not accept the pro-life position described by Lee.

Remarkably, the polling data reveals that even a majority of Catholics in the United States does not accept the argument, even though the argument represents the official position of the Roman Catholic Church.[70] Dissent from the position is not uncommon even among professional Catholic ethicists. A recent example: Writing in the Jesuit weekly *America* about "how one understands the moral status of early human life," Kevin Wildes, a Jesuit priest who is a professor of bioethics at Georgetown University and associate director of Georgetown's Joseph and Rose Kennedy Institute of Ethics, states that

Catholicism is not monolithic. . . . Many Catholics accept the genetic criteria for personhood. . . . This school of thought argues that the embryo should be treated as a person from the moment of conception. . . . Another view is also represented in Catholicism: the developmental school. . . . This school argues that while the early human embryo is worthy of respect, it ought not to be given personal moral status until there has been sufficient development of the embryo.[71]

Wildes reports that the developmental view "is shared by many Protestant traditions as well as by the Jewish and Islamic religious traditions. . . . "[72] Wildes then goes on to express his judgment that

[t]he developmental view . . . represents a richness in Catholic moral thought. . . . In my view, at the blastocyst stage, . . . the embryo does not yet possess sufficient biological unity to be a person. At the same time, one ought to be very cautious about adopting a genetic model, as the [Catholic] bishops and others have done. This model opens the door to a genetic reductionism that is very popular in American culture.[73]

My point here is not that (one or another instance of) "the developmental view" is right and the "genetic model" is wrong. My point is that the fundamental claim on which the pro-life position described by Lee relies – that the stage of development of unborn human life is morally irrelevant, that from the moment of conception unborn human life is no less inviolable than born human life – is controversial among religious believers in the United States (who are overwhelmingly Christian), a majority of whom do not accept the claim. The claim is not accepted even by a majority of Catholics in the United States. Of course, that the pro-life claim is controversial – even that it lacks majoritarian support – does not entail that the claim is mistaken. Patrick Lee, John Finnis, Robert George, and many others do not believe that the claim – that from the moment of conception unborn human life is no less inviolable than born human life – is mistaken. Still, a majority of Americans – indeed, a majority of the citizens of most liberal democracies – is unable to accept the claim.

How ought those religious believers who *do* accept the claim to understand the character of this disagreement? How ought they to judge those who cannot accept the position? Is it a disagreement between the morally informed on the one side and the morally ignorant on the other? Worse, is it a disagreement between the morally righteous – the children of light – on the one side and the morally corrupt – the children of darkness – on the other? Between those who embrace a "culture of life" and those who embrace a "culture of death"?[74] Between those who accept "the Gospel of Life" and those who reject it?[75] Listen, in that regard, to Jean Porter, a professor of theology at the University of Notre Dame:

What can we [Catholics] say to convince men and women of good will who do not share our theological convictions or our allegiance to church teaching that early-stage embryos have exactly the same moral status as we and they do? It will not serve us to fall back at this point on blanket denunciations such as "the culture of death." Naturally, these tend to be conversation stoppers. What is worse, they keep us from considering the possibility that others may not be convinced by what we are saying because what we are saying is – not convincing.[76]

It bears repetition: In the United States, most citizens self-identify as religious believers, and a majority of them is unable to accept the claim that from the moment of conception unborn human life is no less inviolable than born human life. Even a majority of American Catholics is unable to accept the claim. Let me suggest an understanding of the disagreement less dark than that indicated by the polar terms used in the preceding paragraph. The disagreement about the moral status of unborn human life at an early stage of development is, at bottom, a *religious* controversy:[77] There is no way to adjudicate the disagreement between those who, like Patrick Lee, give the pro-life answer to the question of whether unborn human life is inviolable from the moment of conception and those who, like Kevin Wildes, reject the pro-life answer in favor of a "not yet inviolable" answer that does not involve a judgment about one or more contested theological issues. (Jean Porter has noted that "[t]he argument between defenders of immediate and delayed hominization involves fundamental philosophical and theological issues that do not depend on scientific facts in any obvious and non-question-begging way.")[78] John Paul II's encyclical *Evangelium Vitae* (The Gospel of Life) is illustrative of the point: "*Evangelium Vitae* is addressed to 'all men and women of good will.' Yet one of the central arguments of the letter is rooted in the Christian experience of God and is articulated in very particular, theological categories.... The argument from human dignity in *Evangelium Vitae* ... is built on a particular theological anthropology...."[79]

Because the disagreement about the moral status of unborn human life is a religious controversy, it is far from clear why we should understand the disagreement in the dark, polar terms suggested two paragraphs back (e.g., culture of life vs. culture of death). More precisely, it is far from clear why we should understand this particular religious controversy in darker terms than we understand many other contemporary religious controversies. At least as much as many other religious controversies that divide us, this particular religious controversy – "the moral status of the fetus, and especially the conceptus" – is, as the philosopher Robert Audi, who is a Christian, has said, "a clear case of a question on which conscientious reasonable people can disagree."[80] Kevin Wildes, discussing the controversy over the moral status of unborn human life at an early stage of development, makes much the same point: "[I]t is not clear that by an appeal to reason we can reach agreement on who is to be counted 'human' and who has human dignity and human rights."[81] Therefore, we Americans, who pride ourselves on respecting our religious differences – at least, our differences about those matters as to which "conscientious reasonable people can disagree" – should be especially wary about understanding and characterizing *this* religious controversy in the dark, polar terms just suggested, terms that have served, however unwittingly, to nourish a violent response on the part of a few on the pro-life side of the abortion controversy.

Moreover, that the disagreement about the moral status of unborn human life at an early stage of development is, at bottom, a religious controversy is an additional, substantial reason for wondering, with Cathleen Kaveny, whether, even if one or another state legislature might be able to succeed in enacting them into law, "stringent criminal penalties for [early] abortion are the best way for [the law] to express its concern [for the well-being of the unborn]."[82] Because I agree with Joan Callahan that "[t]he abortion issue is one about which reasonable people can disagree," I am drawn to her counsel:

> Trying to decide public policy ... must involve sensitive deliberation which takes carefully into account the deeply felt and morally reasonable concerns of a variety of perspectives. And the effort must lead to thoughtful decisions that persons in a pluralistic society can respect, no matter what policies they would prefer to see. Defenders and opponents of a policy of elective abortion must realize that we share a large common moral ground. We must begin to work from that common ground to come to an agreement on policies that can respectfully govern us all.[83]

As I said earlier in this chapter, Cathleen Kaveny's thoughtful list of public policy proposals are worthy of the most serious deliberation. Based on available polling data, many of them are proposals that a majority of the American people could plausibly be expected to support. Moreover, even though many advocates of abortion rights would strenuously oppose all or most of them, Kaveny's proposals are nonetheless, in my judgment, "policies that can respectfully govern us all."

I said at the beginning of this chapter that my overarching aim was to address the abortion controversy in a way that is true to the two propositions advanced by Reinhold Niebuhr in the epigraph to this chapter. The first proposition, which I defended in Chapters 2 and 3, is that a citizen's religious faith has a legitimate, important role to play in her politics. The second proposition is perhaps more powerfully illustrated by the moral/political controversy over abortion than by any other moral/political controversy in our time: "[P]olitical issues deal with complex problems of justice, every solution for which contains morally ambiguous elements."

Conclusion
"This Nation, Under God"

I began this book by recalling the speech that vice-presidential candidate Joseph Lieberman delivered to the congregation of the Fellowship Chapel on August 27, 2000 – the speech in which, as the *New York Times* reported the next morning, Lieberman "bluntly made the case for allowing faith into politics."[1] Although "the Constitution wisely separates church from state," said Lieberman, "the Constitution guarantees freedom *of* religion, not freedom *from* religion."[2] Senator Lieberman's speech was an uncompromising rejection of the exclusionist position that religious faith has little if any legitimate role to play in American politics. Lieberman was on target, in my judgment. The exclusionist position does not survive careful scrutiny. As I explained in Part One of this book, neither the American constitutional ideal of nonestablishment nor the morality of liberal democracy calls for fencing religious faith out of American politics. This does not mean, however, that when religious believers participate in politics, whether as policymakers or just as citizens, they should rely uncritically on religiously grounded moral belief; religious believers sometimes have good reasons, including reasons internal to their own religious traditions, to moderate or even to forgo political reliance on religiously grounded moral belief. I developed this point in Part Two.

I said that the exclusionist position doesn't survive careful scrutiny; there is even a sense in which the position is – dare I say it? – un-American. Consider the Declaration of Independence, which marks the first formative moment in the emergence of the United States of America. The Declaration famously relies – explicitly so – on belief in God: "We hold these truths to be self-evident, that all men are *created* equal, that they are endowed by their *Creator* with certain inalienable rights . . ." (emphasis added). How strange that the citizens of a nation whose very birth was rooted in belief in a Creator God should now be told that it is, at best, "bad taste to bring religion into discussions of

124

public policy."[3] As John Paul II lamented, "[i]t would truly be a sad thing if the religious and moral convictions upon which the American experiment was founded could now somehow be considered a danger to free society, such that those who would bring these convictions to bear upon your nation's public life would be denied a voice in debating and resolving issues of public policy."[4]

If the Declaration marks a formative moment in the birth of the United States, two texts of Abraham Lincoln mark formative moments in the nation's rebirth:[5] the Gettysburg Address, with its resolve that "this nation, under God, shall have a new birth of freedom," and the Second Inaugural Address, which is surely one of the most theologically intense political speeches in American history. "The Almighty," said Lincoln in his Second Inaugural, "has his own purposes. 'Woe unto the world because of offences! for it must needs be that offences come; but woe to that man by whom the offence cometh!'" Lincoln continued:

If we shall suppose that American Slavery is one of those offenses which, in the providence of God, must needs come, but which, having continued through his appointed time, He now wills to remove, and that He gives to both North and South, this terrible war, as the woe due to those by whom the offence came, shall we discern there any departure from those divine attributes which the believers in a Living God always ascribe to Him? Fondly do we hope – fervently do we pray – that this mighty scourge of war may speedily pass away. Yet, if God wills that it continue, until all the wealth piled by the bond-man's two hundred and fifty years of unrequited toil shall be sunk, and until every drop of blood drawn with the lash, shall be paid by another drawn by the sword, as was said three thousand years ago, so still it must be said "the judgments of the Lord, are true and righteous altogether." With malice toward none; with charity for all; with firmness in the right, as God gives us to see the right, let us strive on to finish the work we are in. . . .

How strange that the citizens of a nation whose rebirth was rooted in belief in a God whose "judgments . . . are true and righteous altogether" should now be told that it is uncivil or impolite, if not constitutionally or morally illegitimate, to bring their religion to bear as they participate in politics. What Reinhold Niebuhr said out of his Christian tradition was surely right – and could just as accurately be said by those speaking out of other religious traditions: It is no "solution of the problem of relating religious commitments to political decisions . . . to find no relevance at all between our faith and our political actions. This answer is wrong because it denies the seriousness of our political decisions and obscures our Christian responsibilities for the good order and justice of our civil community."[6] Niebuhr could have reminded his readers, at this point, of the abolitionists.

Although we citizens of the United States of America don't recite the Declaration, the Gettysburg Address, or Lincoln's Second Inaugural, we *do* recite, frequently, the Pledge of Allegiance.[7] In 1954, the words "under God" were added to the Pledge,[8] so that the Pledge now echoes Lincoln at Gettysburg ("this nation, under God, shall have a new birth of freedom"). According to the Pledge, the United States of America is a nation "under God": a nation that, as Lincoln insisted in his Second Inaugural, stands under the judgment of a righteous God. (Politicians and others are fond of asking God to "bless" America. Lincoln understood that the God who can, in judgment, bless America can also, in judgment, damn her: "He gives to both North and South, this terrible war, as the woe due to those by whom the offence came. . . . [A]s was said three thousand years ago, so still it must be said 'the judgments of the Lord, are true and righteous altogether.'") How very strange that the citizens of such a nation, a nation that proclaims itself to stand under the judgment of a righteous God, should now be told that they should privatize their religion, that they should keep it to themselves – in particular, that they should keep their religion out of the public square. This prescription, which has the smell of the lamp about it, makes precious little sense in the real world of the United States. The United States, after all, is not only a nation with "under God" in its Pledge; it is also a nation with "In God We Trust" as its motto, inscribed on its coins and paper currency;[9] a nation whose legislatures, state and federal, open their sessions with a prayer;[10] a nation whose Supreme Court opens its sessions with the invocation "God save the United States and this Honorable Court";[11] a nation whose President, at the direction of Congress, issues annual Thanksgiving Day proclamations.

How might an exclusionist respond? Perhaps by insisting that "under God" in the Pledge, "In God We Trust" as the national motto, prayers at the beginning of legislative and judicial sessions, Thanksgiving Day proclamations, and the like are all deeply inconsistent with the American constitutional commitment to nonestablishment. The problem with this response, as I have argued elsewhere, is that it relies on an implausible reading – an overreading – of the nonestablishment norm.[12] I will not rehearse my argument here. Suffice it to say that no construal of the nonestablishment norm according to which "under God" in the Pledge or any other practice just mentioned is unconstitutional will be taken seriously by more than a relatively few citizens of the United States;[13] nor will such a construal be taken seriously by the Supreme Court of the United States.[14]

I suspect that some exclusionists are growing weary of pressing arguments that persuade only those who are already converted. Their hope, I suspect, is that the phenomenon of religion in politics will become increasingly marginal because religious faith will itself become an increasingly marginal phenomenon among citizens of the United States. This is wishful thinking. Recent survey data indicates that even now, at the beginning of the twenty-first century, the American people remain overwhelmingly religious; there is no evidence that religious faith is gradually disappearing from the American scene. Results of a *U.S. News* poll published in May 2002, as I was drafting these concluding comments, confirm that "the wealthiest, most powerful, and best educated nation on Earth is still one of the most religious. . . . [T]he United States may well be, as many experts claim, the most religious of the Western democracies."[15] The following figures are striking:

[Ninety] percent of Americans tell pollsters they believe in God or a higher power. Sixty percent say they pray every day. Even half the people who profess no religion say they pray, too. The number of these so-called seculars – atheists, agnostics, and others unchurched – is going up: one survey says it is now 14 percent. But the overwhelming majority of Americans say they are religious and 80 percent identify themselves as Christians, worshipping in 300,000 congregations in more than 4,000 denominations.[16]

From a storefront tabernacle in South Central Los Angeles to a Gothic cathedral in upper Manhattan, there are more churches, synagogues, temples, and mosques per capita in the United States than in any other nation on Earth: one for about every 865 people.[17]

A clarification is in order: "The minority of American adults who claim no religious preference doubled from 7 percent in 1991, its level for almost 20 years, to an unprecedented 14 percent in 1998."[18] However, as the sociologists Michael Hout and Claude Fischer go on to explain:

[T]he evidence ... indicates how the new religious dissenters have distanced themselves from the churches, not from God. The data offer no support for conjecture that a long-expected secularization has finally asserted itself. The majority of adults who prefer no religion continue to believe in God and an afterlife. Few are atheists or agnostics. Most pray. Many reject the "religious" label, but they think of themselves as "spiritual." They seldom if ever attend religious services or read the Bible. In short, the critical feature of most such people is not their beliefs or personal piety but their estrangement from organized religion.[19]

It is exceedingly unlikely – in any event, there is no evidence to suggest – that religious faith will become a marginal phenomenon among citizens of the United States at any time in the foreseeable future, much less that religious faith in the United States will "wither away."[20]

Although religious faith is not gradually disappearing from the American scene, the religious landscape of the United States is undergoing a significant transformation. In addition to the growing number of religious believers who claim no religious preference, religious faith in the United States is an increasingly diverse phenomenon. Indeed, the United States may well have become, in the last decade, the most religiously diverse nation on earth.[21] "Since the Immigration Act of 1995 eliminated quotas linked to national origin, Muslims, Buddhists, Hindus, Sikhs, Jains, Zoroastrians, and others have arrived in increasing numbers, dramatically altering the religious landscape of many communities. . . . Nationwide, there are now more Buddhists than Presbyterians and nearly as many Muslims as Jews."[22] Given the changing religious landscape of America, those who bring their religion into the public square face ever more difficult challenges.

That neither the American constitutional ideal of nonestablishment nor the morality of liberal democracy calls for marginalizing the role of religious faith in, much less excluding it from, American politics does not mean that religious participation in politics is unproblematic. To bring one's religion to bear as one participates in politics – to rely on religiously grounded moral belief in the course of deliberating about or making political choices – is not necessarily to do so in an appropriate way. I first addressed the subject of religion in politics in my book *Love and Power*; I sketched there the ideal of "ecumenical politics," which, as I explained, comprised both ecumenical political dialogue and ecumenical political tolerance.[23] As I have noted more than once in this book, I have abandoned the exclusionism I defended in *Love and Power*. Nonetheless, ecumenical politics still seems to me the right ideal for those in the United States – indeed, in any liberal democracy – who would bring their religion to bear on their politics. The mirror image of ecumenical politics is sectarian politics. Sectarian politics is precisely the wrong ideal.

Consider a mode of religious participation in politics that is bereft of ecumenical generosity – a mode that disdains open-minded engagement with religious views different from one's own and that is little inclined to tolerate ways of life, choices, and acts different from those sanctioned by one's own religious views and conscience. Such a mode of religious participation is not likely to fare well in the increasingly diverse religious environment of the United States. Assume, however, that a sectarian mode of religious participation can sometimes succeed in achieving its political objective(s). Religious believers should nonetheless consider whether what the late Joseph Cardinal Bernardin, archbishop of Chicago, said about his religious community isn't equally applicable to their own: "[The Roman Catholic Church] should be convinced we have *much to learn from the world* and much to teach it. A confident church will speak its mind, seek as a community to live its convictions, *but leave space for others to speak to us, to help us grow from their perspective. . . .*"[24] Moreover, a sectarian mode of religious participation in politics is more likely, when successful in achieving its political objective, to tear the bonds of political community than to strengthen them.

This distinction between ecumenical politics and sectarian politics raises important and difficult issues. I touched on some of them in Part Two of this book, in discussing the moral/political controversies over same-sex unions and abortion. I am merely gesturing toward the issues here; a fuller, more careful consideration must await another day.[25] For now, we are left with this question: In the years ahead, as this "nation under God" becomes even more religiously diverse, what role will religious faith play, on balance, in our politics? We hope, of course, that it will play a constructive role – even, perhaps, an ennobling role: "Politics that does not contain theology within itself, however little considered, may often be shrewd but remains in the end no more than a business."[26] Hope, however, is not expectation. Many of us will be content if religion plays a role that is not destructive, because we know from history what religion in politics at its worst has been: a highly combustible mixture that can, when ignited, maim or destroy those in its proximity.

If the trajectory of American history – or, at least, the present circumstances of the United States – yielded a serious possibility that in the years ahead religious faith will play a destructive role in American politics, it would make sense for us to reject Senator Lieberman's "case for allowing faith into politics" and to consider ways to marginalize the role of faith in politics. But the possibility that religion will play a destructive role is more remote than serious. The same survey data that shows that the United States is an increasingly religiously diverse society – perhaps the most religiously diverse society in the world – also shows that today most citizens of the United States are much more tolerant of their religious differences than were previous generations of Americans, and that they consider the religious diversity of the United States not as a problem to be endured or overcome but as a source of the nation's strenth.[27] These are not the attitudes that fueled the religious wars of the sixteenth century; as John Courtney Murray admonished, we shouldn't "project into the future of the Republic the nightmares . . . of the past."[28] As I said in Chapter 3, a rapprochement between religion and politics forged in the crucible of a time or place very different from our own is not necessarily – not even probably – the best arrangement for our time and place. If in the years ahead the predominant mode of religious participation in politics is more ecumenical than sectarian, as befits a society as religiously diverse as the United States, the chance is slim to nonexistent that the mixture – religion and politics – will ignite.[29]

Notes

INTRODUCTION

1. Richard Pérez-Peña, "Lieberman Seeks Greater Role for Religion in Public Life," *New York Times*, Aug. 28, 2000, at A1. The Gore-Lieberman campaign never published or otherwise made available a draft of Senator Lieberman's speech. But a later, similar speech by Senator Lieberman has now been published: Senator Joe Lieberman, "Vision for America: A Place for Faith," *The Responsive Community*, Winter 2000/01, at 41.
2. Lindy Boggs was married to the the late Hale Boggs, a U.S. representative from Louisiana, and is the mother of the journalist Cokie Roberts.
3. "John Paul II on the American Experiment," *First Things*, April 1998, at 36–37 (quoting John Paul's speech, which was delivered in Rome on Dec. 17, 1997).
4. ADL Press Release, "ADL to Senator Lieberman: Keep Emphasis on Religion Out of Campaign," Aug. 29, 2000. See Gustav Niebuhr, "The Religion Issue: Lieberman Is Asked to Stop Invoking Faith in Campaign," *New York Times*, Aug. 29, 2000, at A24.
5. In one of the more interesting op-ed pieces, Eleanor Brown, identified as a lawyer and a fellow at the New American Foundation, suggested "why Mr. Lieberman is so important":

> By severing the connection between religious devotion and political conservatism, he has injected a new force into the wider political debate. Although much has been made of his moral rhetoric, he receives high ratings from liberal groups and on many issues holds views diametrically opposed to those of the religious right. Mr. Lieberman demonstrates that people of religious faith can, and do, disagree on important political issues that imply deeply held moral beliefs. More important, he represents a willingness – rarely seen among liberals at the national level – to ground his political positions in specific religious commitments. (Eleanor Brown, "Lieberman's Revival of the Religious Left," *New York Times*, Aug. 30, 2000.)

For a vigorously critical reaction to Senator Lieberman's position – and to other efforts to amplify religion's voice in politics – see Ellen Willis, "Freedom from Religion: What's at Stake in Faith-Based Politics," *The Nation*, Feb. 19, 2001, at 11. For a critical response to Willis's piece, see Margaret O'Brien Steinfels,

"Public Religion: Not Around Here, Says Ellen Willis," *Commonweal*, March 9, 2001, at 7.

6. On October 18, however, after about six weeks of "speak[ing] far less about religion," Senator Lieberman returned to the theme of religious faith in American politics. See Richard Pérez-Peña, "Lieberman Cites Religion as Foundation of Environmentalism," *New York Times*, Oct. 19, 2000, at A1. Then, on October 22, two weeks to the day before the presidential election, Lieberman gave a speech at the University of Notre Dame emphasizing the importance of religious faith in the life of the nation. See Associated Press, "Lieberman Urges Religious Faith," October 24, 2000. Lieberman's speech at Notre Dame was published in February 2001: Lieberman, "Vision for America."

7. Though not the same exclusionist position in each book: I defended a thoroughgoing exclusionist position in *Love and Power: The Role of Religion and Morality in American Politics* (New York: Oxford University Press, 1991). I defended a more moderate exclusionist position, but an exclusionist position nonetheless, in *Religion in Politics: Constitutional and Moral Perspectives* (New York: Oxford University Press, 1997).

8. For a fuller definition of the "magisterium", see Chapter 5, note 3, this volume.

9. Patricia Beattie Jung, "Introduction," in Patricia Beattie Jung with Joseph Andrew Coray, eds., *Sexual Diversity and Catholicism: Toward the Development of Moral Theology* (Collegeville, Minn.: Liturgical Press, 2001), at x, xxix n. 31.

10. Carey Goldberg with Janet Elder, "Public Still Backs Abortion, But Wants Limits, Poll Says," *New York Times*, Jan. 16, 1998, at A1.

11. See generally Elizabeth Mensch and Alan Freeman, *The Politics of Virtue: Is Abortion Debatable?* (Durham, N.C.: Duke University Press, 1993).

12. Larry Rasmussen, ed., *Reinhold Niebuhr, Theologian of Public Life* (San Francisco: Harper and Row, 1989), at 127.

13. See "Faith in America," *U.S. News*, May 6, 2002, at 40–49.

CHAPTER 1

1. 122 S. Ct. 2460 (2002).

2. This is not to say that I agree with every aspect of the Court's reasoning. In particular, I don't think that the direct/indirect aid distinction is a sensible one. See note 35.

3. Cf. Elisabeth Bumiller, "Bush Calls Ruling about Vouchers a 'Historic' Move," *New York Times*, July 2, 2002: "Although Mr. Bush had tried to include vouchers in a major education bill he signed early this year, he quickly gave up when he saw that there was not enough support from Congressional leaders for the program."

4. See Marshall Breger et al., *In Good Faith: A Dialogue on Government Funding of Faith-Based Social Services* (Philadelphia: Feinstein Center for American Jewish History, Temple University, 2001), at 3 n. 2. "The terms 'faith-based organization' or 'religious organization' are used here as umbrella terms encompassing any organization that is motivated by faith,

affiliated with a faith tradition, or that incorporates religion in its activities in any way. The term applies, therefore, to a range of organizational forms including houses of worship as well as separately incorporated nonprofits."

5. A report issued by the White House Domestic Policy Council on Aug. 16, 2001, "Unlevel Playing Field," argues that there are significant inappropriate "barriers to participation by faith-based and community organizations in federal social service programs." See Elizabeth Becker, "Report Finds Bias Against Religious Groups," *New York Times*, Aug. 17, 2001.

For a clarification of the issues involved in the "charitable choice" debate, see *In Good Faith*, at 3–4:

"Charitable choice" is a term of art that refers to a specific legislative proposal first enacted by Congress in the 1996 federal welfare reform law. [See Welfare Reform Act, P.L. 104–193, Sec. 104, 110 Stat. 2161–63 (1996).] Although the concept is often used loosely to refer to government funding of faith-based social service programs in general, in fact it refers more particularly to the new statutory conditions under which states may enter into funding relationships with religious organizations that provide social services using federal or state funds that originated with enactment of the TANF [Temporary Assistance for Needy Families] Program in 1996. Other legislative initiatives also popularly referred to a "charitable choice" have since been introduced in Congress and the states, and some have been enacted. These apply variations of the TANF language to other program areas, such as drug rehabilitation or housing.

The new idea represented by "charitable choice" is not the involvement of faith communities in the social service area, as many religious organizations have a history of involvement in such services. Nor is government funding of religious social service providers in itself an innovation, as many organizations with a religious affiliation [e.g., Catholic Charities USA] have long received government funds to carry out their work. Before "charitable choice," governments at all levels awarded grants and contracts to religiously affiliated organizations. There are no uniform statutory provisions regarding the participation of religious providers, and there was and remains controversy over whether an organization could be a pervasively religious entity (such as a house of worship) and receive government money to provide social services.

"Charitable choice" alters previous practice through new federal statutory language that specifically addresses the participation of religious providers. "Charitable choice" permits all faith-based organizations to compete for government social service funding, regardless of their religious nature. Thus "charitable choice" significantly broadens the scope and extent of government financial collaboration with faith-based organizations. This change is welcome to some but highly problematic to others. The legal, philosophical, and ethical dimensions of the change have generated substantial controversy.

According to those who favor "charitable choice":

The past approach was, roughly, for government to permit funds only to religiously affiliated organizations providing secular services in a secular setting. "Pervasively religious" organizations, which displayed an integral religious character, were excluded. "Charitable choice" instead permits religious and secular organizations alike to participate as government-funded social service providers. "Charitable choice" enables government to fulfill its constitutional obligation not to establish religion and its constitutional duty to protect the religious liberties of beneficiaries without imposing illegitimate secularizing requirements on religious social service providers. (11)

According to those who oppose "charitable choice":

"Charitable choice" is designed to allow houses of worship and other organizations that integrate religion into their social services to receive funds generated through taxation. When the government funds these institutions, it inevitably results in government funding and advancing religion itself, which is unconstitutional. (13)

For a clarification of Bush's "charitable choice" proposal, see Ira C. Lupu and Robert Tuttle, "The Distinctive Place of Religious Entities in Our Constitutional Order," 47 Villanova L. Rev. 37, 45–47 (2001):

Prior to the 1996 federal welfare reforms, lawyers generally believed and counselled that religious providers could participate in public programs only if they were first "scrubbed" of their religious characteristics. Religious providers set up distinct legal entities to receive and adminsiter public welfare funds – entities that engaged in no religious worship, proselytizing or instruction. In operating government-supported programs, religious providers eliminated explicit religious imagery and references....

... [T]he welfare reforms enacted by Congress in 1996 launched, at the federal level, the regime known as Charitable Choice. Reduced to its simplest terms, Charitable Choice authorizes religious entities, as well as other community groups, to participate as contractors in the administration of the new federal welfare program.... The right of religious organizations to participate in government programs, however, is hardly novel. For religious entities, the legislation's major innovation is its affirmation that they may retain their religious character, rather than operate under a legal duty to mask or dilute it. They are not required to provide these services separate and apart from their religious premises. Instead, church personnel may provide services directly from church itself....

President George W. Bush, in his first few weeks in office, took steps to broaden the notion of Charitable Choice. Drawing on the expansive Texas experience with Charitable Choice, Bush's executive orders [Executive Order, "Establishment of White House Office of Faith-Based and Community Initiatives," Jan. 29, 2001; Executive Order, "Agency Responsibilities with Respect to Faith-Based and Community Initiatives,"

Jan. 29, 2001] contemplate a wide range of service to people in need by faith-based and community organizations financed, in whole or in part, by the government. One key element in Bush's initiative is its emphasis on results, without discrimination as to the method of obtaining them. Described more directly, the Bush philosophy appears to contemplate government-financed social services, such as drug counseling and prisoner rehabilitation, which use explicitly religious methods. In the past, proponents of Charitable Choice have pointed to the successes of the Inner Change Freedom Initiative in reducing criminal recidivism, and Teen Challenge, an evangelical Christian program, in treating teenage drug abuse. Such programs represent a large step beyond the 1996 welfare reform package, which tolerated religious trappings but did not itself finance explicitly religious means of achieving secularly desirable ends. Moreover, and quite consistently with the overarching philosophy of harnessing the spiritual energy of faith-based groups, the Bush vision contemplates that religious organizations will be free to hire only co-religionists to implement their programs. [The authors state, in a footnote, that "[t]he 1996 Act explicitly permits this hiring preference . . . [and t]he proposed Community Solutions Act of 2001 includes an identical provision."]

Professors Lupu and Tuttle then inquire:

Would the Bush philosophy, if fully implemented, undermine long-standing prohibitions on the relationship between the state and religious institutions? May the government finance faith-based methodologies of social and personal transformation? May the government subsidize programs that openly engage in religious discrimination in hiring? Planned Parenthood most assuredly has a philosophy of responsible sexuality, which the government may help to support with programs for adolescent counseling, and Planned Parenthood no doubt limits its hiring to those who share its secular views. Are religious entities constitutionally distinguishable from entities like Planned Parenthood, such that state support for their substantive ideologies or their hiring preferences should be barred? (47)

6. So, for example, after the Supreme Court's five to four decision in the Cleveland school voucher case, Senator Edward Kennedy said that "[p]rivate school vouchers may pass constitutional muster, but they fail the test when it comes to improving our nation's schools. It's flat wrong to take scarce taxpayer dollars away from public schools and divert them to private schools." Bumiller, "Bush Calls Ruling about Vouchers a 'Historic' Move."

7. See John Hart Ely, "Another Such Victory: Constitutional Theory and Practice in a World Where Courts Are No Different from Legislatures," 77 Virginia L. Rev. 833 (1991).

8. A voluminous and growing literature addresses the question of whether, even if constitutional, school vouchers are, all things considered, a good idea. On school vouchers and other kinds of "school choice" programs, especially charter schools, see, e.g., Paul E. Peterson and Bryan C. Hassel, eds., *Learning*

from School Choice (Washington, D.C.: Brookings Institution Press, 1998). See also James E. Ryan and Michael Heise, "The Political Economy of School Choice," 111 Yale L. J. 22043 (2002).

9. On the idea of constitutional "bedrock," see Michael J. Perry, *We the People: The Fourteenth Amendment and the Supreme Court* (New York: Oxford University Press, 1999), at 20–23.

10. See Michael J. Perry, *Religion in Politics: Constitutional and Moral Perspectives* (New York: Oxford University Press, 1997), at 10–12. On the controversial question of whether the Fourteenth Amendment was meant to make the First Amendment's "free exercise" and "nonestablishment" norms applicable to the states, see Kurt T. Lash, "The Second Adoption of the Free Exercise Clause: Religious Exemptions under the Fourteenth Amendment," 88 Northwestern U. L. Rev. 1106 (1994); Kurt T. Lash, "The Second Adoption of the Establishment Clause: The Rise of the Nonestablishment Principle," 27 Arizona St. L. J. 1085 (1995). Lash argues that the Fourteenth Amendment was meant to make applicable to the states both a broad free exercise norm and a nonestablishment norm. For an argument that the Fourteenth Amendment was not meant to make the First Amendment's nonestablishment norm applicable to the states, see Jonathan P. Brose, "In Birmingham They Love the Governor: Why the Fourteenth Amendment Does Not Incorporate the Establishment Clause," 24 Ohio Northern U. L. Rev. 1 (1998). For an argument that the Fourteenth Amendment was not meant to make any First Amendment norm applicable to the states, see Jay S. Bybee, "Taking Liberties with the First Amendment: Congress, Section 5, and the Religious Freedom Restoration Act," 48 Vanderbilt L. Rev. 1539 (1995).

11. See Michael W. McConnell, "Accommodation of Religion: An Update and Response to the Critics," 60 George Washington L. Rev. 685, 690 (1992): "The government may not 'establish' religion and it may not 'prohibit' religion." McConnell explains, in a footnote attached to the word "establish", that "[t]he text [of the First Amendment] states the 'Congress' may make no law 'respecting an establishment' of religion, which meant that Congress could neither establish a national church nor interfere with the establishment of state churches as they then existed in the various states. After the last disestablishment in 1833 and the incorporation of the First Amendment against the states through the Fourteenth Amendment, this 'federalism' aspect of the Amendment has lost its significance, and the Clause can be read as forbidding the government to establish religion." (690, n. 19)

12. See Michael J. Perry, "Freedom of Religion in the United States: Fin de Siècle Sketches," 75 Indiana L. J. 295, 297–302 (2000).

13. See *Everson v. Board of Education*, 330 U.S. 1 (1947).

14. Justice Thomas has noted that "our Establishment Clause jurisprudence is in hopeless disarray...." *Rosenberger v. Rector and Visitors of University of Virginia*, 515 U.S. 819, 861 (1995) (Thomas, J., concurring). Many scholars concur in this judgment. See, e.g., Jesse H. Choper, *Securing Religious Liberty: Principles for Judicial Interpretation of the Religion Clauses* (Chicago: University of Chicago

Press, 1995), at 174–76. Akhil Amar has referred to "the many outlandish (and contradictory) things that have been said about [the nonestablishment norm] in the *United States Reports*." Akhil Reed Amar, "Foreword: The Document and the Doctrine," 114 Harvard L. Rev. 26, 119 (2000).

15. See *Rosenberger v. Rector and Visitors of University of Virginia*, 515 U.S. 819 (1995) (five to four decision); *Agostini v. Felton*, 521 U.S. 203 (1997) (five to four decision); *Mitchell v. Helms*, 530 U.S. 793 (2000) (six to three decision; no majority opinion); *Zelman v. Simmons-Harris*, 122 S. Ct. 2460 (2002) (five to four decision).

16. For a sketch of different kinds of religious establishment, from extreme to moderate, see W. Cole Durham, Jr., "Perspectives on Religious Liberty: A Comparative Framework," in Johan D. van der Vyver and John Witte, Jr., eds., *Religious Human Rights in Global Perspective: Legal Perspectives* (The Hugue: Martinus Nijhoff Publishers, 1996), at 1, 19ff.

17. Cf. Amar, "Foreword," at 119: "Let us recall the world the Founders aimed to repudiate, a world where a powerful church hierarchy was anointed as the official government religion, where clerics ex officio held offices in the government, and where members of other religions were often barred from holding government posts."

18. What is the present reality? See Cheryl Saunders, "Comment: Religion and the State," 21 Cardozo L. Rev. 1295, 1295 (2000):

> The special status of the Church of England manifests through legal links with the British crown. Under legislation, the reigning queen or king is "supreme governor" of the church and swears a coronation oath to maintain it. As such, the monarch may not be a Catholic, or marry a Catholic, and must declare on accession to the throne that he or she is a Protestant.
>
> This is surprising enough in a western liberal democracy at the end of the twentieth century. But there is more. The monarch also appoints the archbishops and other reigning church dignitaries. Twenty-six of these "Lords Spiritual" sit in the upper house of the legislature, the House of Lords. The British Parliament can legislate for the church and can prescribe modes of worship, doctrine and discipline. And the church has delegated legislative authority in relation to church affairs. Measures initiated by the church may be accepted or rejected, but not amended, by the Parliament and override earlier inconsistent law.

Professor Saunders then states:

> As usual with the British system of government, however, what you see is not exactly what you get. In advising the crown on appointments to church positions, the prime minister draws names from a list provided by church authorities. As a practical matter, Parliament is unlikely to veto legislative measures initiated by the church, or to act unilaterally in relation to other church affairs. Vernon Bogdanor draws attention to a House of Commons debate on the ordination of women priests in 1993, in which several Members expressed the view that the House should not be discussing the view at all. (1295–6)

Clearly, and happily, that England has an established church does not
mean everything it once meant. But that England *still* has an established
church *is* problematic. See Clifford Longley, "An Act That Holds Us Back,"
The Tablet [London], March 17, 2001, at 362; Clifford Longley, "Establishment – It's Got to Go," *The Tablet* [London], May 11, 2002, at 2. Cf. Brian
Barry, *Justice as Impartiality* (New York: Oxford University Press, 1995), at
165 n. *c*.

> We must, of course, keep a sense of proportion. The advantages of estab-
> lishment enjoyed by the Church of England or by the Lutheran Church
> in Sweden are scarcely on a scale to lead anyone to feel seriously dis-
> criminated against. In contrast, denying the vote to Roman Catholics or
> requiring subscription to the Church of England as a condition of entry
> to Oxford or Cambridge did constitute a serious source of grievance.
> Strict adherence to justice as impartiality would, no doubt, be incom-
> patible with the existence of an established church at all. But departures
> from it are venial so long as nobody is put at a significant disadvantage,
> either by having barriers put in the way of worshipping according to the
> tenets of his faith or by having his rights and opportunities in other mat-
> ters (politics, education, occupation, for example) materially limited on
> the basis of his religious beliefs.

19. However, neither the nonestablishment norm nor the free exercise norm
    should be understood to call into question the following proposition: Gov-
    ernment may make a policy choice on the basis of a position that one or
    more churches happen to reject, even though the policy choice has the ef-
    fect of disfavoring those churches relative to other churches that do not reject
    the position. (For a discussion of this in connection with the free exercise
    norm, see Perry, "Freedom of Religion in the United States," at 297–302.)
    An example of such a position: Racist ideologies are false and evil. Another:
    The theory of evolution should be presented to high school students. (This
    does not entail that competing perspectives on evolution shouldn't be pre-
    sented, too.) Thus, a state may exclude from its voucher program any school,
    whether or not religiously affiliated, that teaches that some persons are "natu-
    rally" inferior to others by virtue of race. (The Ohio Pilot Project scholarship
    program at issue in the Cleveland school voucher case excludes schools that
    discriminate on the basis of race, religion, or ethnic background, or that ad-
    vocate or foster unlawful behavior, or that teach hatred of a person or group
    on account of race, ethnicity, national origin, or religion. Ohio Rev. Code
    Ann. 3313.976[A][6].) To say that government may not take any action that
    favors one or more churches in relation to one or more other churches, or in
    relation to no church at all, on the basis of the view that the favored church
    is, as a church – as a community of faith – better along one or another di-
    mension of value (truer, for example, or more efficacious spiritually, or more
    authentically American) is *not* to say that government may not take a stand
    on an issue that is opposed to a stand that one or more churches happen
    to take. Obviously, such a rule would be not merely extreme, but extremely
    silly.

20. *Marsh v. Chambers*, 463 U.S. 783, 821 (1983) (Brennan, J., joined by Marshall, J., dissenting).

21. For an example of a position that privileges the Christian church generally, see "Other Faiths Are Deficient, Pope Says," *The Tablet* [London], Feb. 5, 2000, at 157: "The revelation of Christ is 'definitive and complete', Pope John Paul affirmed to the Congregation for the Doctrine of the Faith, on 28 January. He repeated the phrase twice in an address which went on to say that non-Christians live in 'a deficient situation, compared to those who have the fullness of salvific means in the Church'." The harsh doctrine that there is no salvation outside the church has been revised, however. "[Pope John Paul II] recognised, following the Second Vatican Council, that non-Christians can reach eternal life if they seek God with a sincere heart. But in that 'sincere search' they are in fact 'ordered' towards Christ and his Church."

22. Cf. Douglas Laycock, "Freedom of Speech That Is Both Religious and Political," 29 U. California, Davis L. Rev. 793, 812–13 (1996) (arguing that "[a]t the core of the Establishment Clause should be the principle that government cannot engage in a religious observance or compel or persuade citizens to do so").

    What the nonestablishment norm forbids is one question. Another, and different, inquiry arises when we have answered the question of what the nonestablishment norm forbids: Is it a good thing that the nonestablishment norm is part of our constitutional law, or is it a bad thing? I have argued elsewhere that it is a good thing. See Perry, "Freedom of Religion in the United States," at 326–32. Most Americans believe that it is a good thing. But there is, among Americans, not just one answer to the question why it is a good thing, and not every answer will appeal to every person. For example, although some secular answers may appeal to some religious believers, religiously grounded answers will not appeal to nonbelievers.

23. On charter schools programs and differences among them, see Paul E. Peterson, "School Choice: A Report Card," in Peterson and Hassel, eds., *Learning from School Choice*, at 3, 7. For an argument in support of charter schools, see Bryan C. Hassel, "The Case for Charter Schools," in Peterson and Hassel, eds., *Learning from School Choice*, at 33.

24. Under the program, if a qualifying family opts to send a child to a public school outside the family's own school district, that school will receive not only the voucher money for which the family qualifies, but also the per-pupil financial contribution that the state makes to every public school in the state for every child enrolled there. Cf. Ohio Rev. Code Ann. 3313.976(C), 3317.03(I)(1).

25. The Ohio Pilot Project scholarship program at issue in the Cleveland school voucher case gives preference to students from low-income families, defining them as families whose income is less than 200 percent of the poverty level. Ohio Rev. Code Ann. 3313.978(A) and (C)(1).

26. The Ohio Pilot Project Scholarship Program at issue in the Cleveland school voucher case excludes schools that discriminate on the basis of race, religion,

or ethnic background, or that advocate or foster unlawful behavior, or that teach hatred of a person or group on account of race, ethnicity, national origin, or religion. Ohio Rev. Code Ann. 3313.976(A)(6).

27. Cf. note 3.

28. In the sense in which I mean it here, to base a political choice on a belief – to make the choice "on the basis of" the belief – is to make a political choice that one would not make in the absence of the belief. To base a political choice partly, not solely, on a belief is still to make a political choice that one would not make in the absence of the belief.

29. In *Rosenberger*, the Supreme Court noted and then quickly dismissed such a possibility: "The governmental program here is neutral toward religion. There is no suggestion that the University created it to advance religion or adopted some ingenious device with the purpose of aiding a religious cause." *Rosenberger v. Rector and Visitors of University of Virginia*, 515 U.S. 819, 840 (1995).

30. The inquiry here – the inquiry into the possibility of a covert establishment of religion – is analogous to the inquiry into the possibility of covert racial discrimination. See *Village of Arlington Heights v. Metropolitan Housing Development Corp.*, 429 U.S. 252, 270 n. 21 (1977); Michael J. Perry, "Modern Equal Protection: A Conceptualization and Appraisal," 79 Columbia L. Rev. 1023, 1036–40 (1979).

According to the voucher program I sketched earlier in this chapter, the amount of a voucher may not exceed, in any school year, the local school district's average per-pupil expenditure during the preceding school year. This feature responds to the concern that funding vouchers at too high a level would be constitutionally problematic. Would funding them at too low a level be constitutionally problematic? For an affirmative answer, see *Simmons-Harris v. Zelman*, 234 F.3d 945, 959 (6th Cir. 2000), rev'd, 122 S. Ct. 2460 (2002): "Practically speaking, the tuition restrictions mandated by the statute [$2,250] limit the ability of nonsectarian schools to participate in the program, as religious schools often have lower overhead costs, supplemental income from private donations, and consequently lower tuition needs." The court then added this citation: "*See* Martha Minow, *Reforming School Reform*, 68 Fordham L. Rev. 257, 262 (1999) (finding that voucher funding levels typically 'approximate[] the tuition level set by parochial schools [which] reflects subsidies from other sources')." The court erred, in my judgment. Funding vouchers at $2,250 is not constitutionally fatal unless it can be shown that the funding level was chosen on the basis of the belief that the favored church(es) is, as such, better than one or more other churches or than no church at all. In any event, and as the Supreme Court pointed out in its own opinion in the Cleveland school voucher case:

> The program here in fact creates financial *dis*incentives for religious schools, with private schools receiving only half the government assistance given to community schools and one-third the assistance given to magnet schools. Adjacent public schools ... are also eligible to receive

two to three times the state funding of a private religious school. Families too have a financial disincentive to choose a private religious school over other schools. Parents that choose to participate in the [voucher] program and then to enroll their children in a private school (religious or nonreligious) must copay a portion of the school's tuition. Families that choose a community school, a magnet school, or traditional public school pay nothing. Although such features are not necessary to its constitutionality, the clearly dispel the claim that the program "creates . . . financial incentives[s] for parents to choose a sectarian school." (*Zelman v. Simmons-Harris,* 122 S. Ct. 2460 [2002] [slip op'n at 12].)

In commenting on this chapter, Fred Gedicks asked:

> Why not an establishment clause prophylactic as well? You endorse the *Arlington Heights* inquiry into legislative motivation, but given the general difficulty of establishing with any certainty whether a government actor established a facially neutral aid program in order to aid a church or religion generally because of a values-based belief in its superiority, why not reinforce the establishment clause norm with a rule providing that when the beneficiaries of a financial aid program are substantially/primarily/overwhelmingly – the precise line matters little – sectarian or religious, then the aid program should be understood as having as its principal purpose endorsement of the moral superiority of the aided religions in violation of the establishment clause. . . . This rule need not be understood as "religious discrimination" – which, I agree, should be prohibited, if we can only agree on what it is – but merely as a wise prophylactic even when the aid is distributed directly to students or their parents according to secularly defined benefit categories. This seems particularly appropriate if, as you suggest, we wish to avoid "judicial inquiry into the subterranean attitudes of legislators." (Letter from Frederick Gedicks to Michael Perry, Dec. 13, 2000.)

The problem with this approach, I think, is that one can easily imagine a voucher program (indeed, many voucher programs) about which two things are true: (1) The beneficiaries of the program – that is, the secondary beneficiaries; the primary beneficiaries are the students/families who receive the vouchers – are, substantially, religiously affiliated schools. (2) It is exceedingly unlikely that either those who lobbied for or those who enacted the voucher program had as their "principal purpose endorsement of the moral superiority of the aided religions." (I disagree that it is difficult to establish "with any certainty whether a government actor established a facially neutral aid program in order to aid a church or religion generally because of a values-based belief in its superiority.") In my judgment, therefore, the suggested prophylactic approach is draconian. Now, this is not to deny the possibility that a particular voucher program has as its "principal purpose endorsement of the moral superiority of the aided religions" – the possibility, that is, that the program is based on the belief that one or more other churches are, as such, better than one or more other churches or than no church at all. (Indeed, my second criterion is designed to defend against just that possibility.) If so, the voucher program violates the nonestablishment norm.

31. See *Mitchell v. Helms*, 530 U.S. 793, 801 (2000) (plurality op'n, written by Thomas, J., joined by Rehnquist, C.J., Scalia and Kennedy, JJ.).

32. As the three different opinions in *Mitchell v. Helms* disclose, the position of Justices Stevens, Souter, and Ginsburg is the most demanding; it is more demanding than the position of Justices O'Connor and Breyer, because the criteria that Justices Stevens, Souter, and Ginsburg apply include all the criteria that Justices O'Connor and Breyer apply and then some. See ibid. at 836 (O'Connor, J., concurring in judgment, joined by Breyer, J.); and ibid. at 867 (Souter, J., dissenting, joined by Stevens and Ginsburg, JJ.). Justice Thomas, in his plurality opinion, observed: "The dissent serves up a smorgasbord of eleven factors that, depending on the facts of each case 'in all its particularity,' could be relevant to the constitutionality of a school-aid program. And those eleven are a bare minimum. We are reassured that there are likely more. Presumably they will be revealed in future cases, as needed. . . . " Ibid. at 825 (Thomas, J., joined by Rehnquist, C.J., Scalia and Kennedy, JJ.). For the dissenting justices' several criteria, see ibid. at 877 (Souter, J., dissenting, joined by Stevens and Ginsburg, JJ.):

> At least three main lines of enquiry addressed particularly to school aid have emerged to complement evenhandedness neutrality. First, we have noted that two types of aid recipients heighten Establishment Clause concern: pervasively religious schools and primary and secondary religious schools. Second, we have identified two important characteristics of the method of distributing aid: directness or indirectness of distribution and distribution by genuinely independent choice. Third, we have found relevance in at least five characteristics of the aid itself: its religious content; its cash form; its divertibility or actual diversion to religious support; its supplantation of traditional items of religious school expense; and its substantiality.

Five years earlier, Justice Souter, in a dissenting opinion joined by Justices Stevens, Ginsburg, and Breyer, had spoken of "the primacy of the no-direct-funding rule over the evenhandedness principle. . . . " *Rosenberger v. Rector and Visitors of University of Virginia*, 515 U.S. 819, 885 (1995).

33. See *Mitchell v. Helms*, 530 U.S. 793, 843–44 (2000) (O'Connor, J., concurring in judgment, joined by Breyer, J.).

34. For a thoughtful discussion of the matter, see Laura S. Underkuffler, "Vouchers and Beyond: The Individual Causative Agent in Establishment Clause Jurisprudence," 75 Indiana L. J. 167 (2000).

35. I am not persuaded by Justice O'Connor's defense, in *Mitchell*, of the direct/indirect distinction. See *Mitchell v. Helms* at 2559–60 (O'Connor, J., concurring in judgment, joined by Breyer, J.). The plurality's position, rejecting the direct/indirect distinction as formalistic, seems to me quite sound. See ibid. at 815–20 (Thomas, J., joined by Rehnquist, C.J., Scalia and Kennedy, JJ.). As the plurality opinion put the point at the beginning of its

critique of the distinction:

> If aid to schools, even "direct" aid, is neutrally available and, before reaching or benefitting any religious school, first passes through the hands (literally or figuratively) of numerous private citizens who are free to direct the aid elsewhere, the government has not provided any "support of religion." . . . Although the presence of private choice is easier to see when aid literally passes through the hands of individuals . . ., there is no reason why the Establishment Clause requires such a form. (Ibid. at 2544–45.)

36. *Simmons-Harris v. Zelman*, 234 F.3d 945,948 (6th Cir. 2000), rev'd, 122 S. Ct. 2460 (2002).

37. See Carl H. Esbeck, "A Constitutional Case for Government Cooperation with Faith-Based Social Service Providers," 46 Emory L. J. 1 (1997); Douglas Laycock, "The Underlying Unity of Separation and Neutrality," 46 Emory L. J. 43 (1997). The four most relevant recent cases are *Rosenberger v. Rector and Visitors of University of Virginia*, 515 U.S. 819 (1995); *Agostini v. Felton*, 521 U.S. 203 (1997); *Mitchell v. Helms*, 530 U.S. 793 (2000); and *Zelman v. Simmons-Harris*, 122 S. Ct. 2460 (2002). In *Rosenberger*, the Court stated:

> A central lesson of our decisions is that a significant factor in upholding governmental programs in the face of Establishment Clause attack is their neutrality toward religion. We have decided a series of cases addressing the receipt of government benefits where religion or religious views are implicated to some degree. . . . We have held that the guarantee of neutrality is respected, not offended, when the government, following neutral criteria and evenhanded policies, extends benefits to recipients whose ideologies and viewpoints, including religious ones, are broad and diverse. (*Rosenberger v. Rector and Visitors of University of Virginia*, 515 U.S. 819, 839 [1995].)

See also *Agostini v. Felton*, 521 U.S. 203, 231 (1997) (arguing that it is constitutionally significant that the challenged aid "is allocated on the basis of neutral, secular criteria that neither favor nor disfavor religion and is made available to both religious and secular beneficiaries on a nondiscriminatory basis").

38. See John T. McGreevy, "Thinking on One's Own: Catholicism in the American Intellectual Imagination, 1928–1960," *Journal of American History*, June 1997, at 97, 122–26.

39. Especially Justices Souter, Stevens, and Ginsburg. See *Mitchell v. Helms*, 530 U.S. 793, 867 (2000) (Souter, J., dissenting, joined by Stevens and Ginsburg, JJ.). See also *Agostini v. Felton*, 521 U.S. 203, 240 (1997) (Souter, J., dissenting, joined by Stevens, Ginsburg, and Breyer, JJ.).

40. For recent examples, see Steven K. Green, "Private School Vouchers and the Confusion over 'Direct' Aid," 10 George Mason U. Civil Rights L. J. 47 (2000); Marci A. Hamilton, "Power, the Establishment Clause, and Vouchers," 31 Connecticut L. Rev. 807 (1999); Marc D. Stern, "School Vouchers – The Church-State Debate That Really Isn't," 31 Connecticut L. Rev. 977 (1999). See also

"Establishment Clause – School Vouchers – Wisconsin Supreme Court Upholds Milwaukee Parental Choice Program," 112 Harvard L. Rev. 737 (1999) (criticizing the Wisconsin Supreme Court's decision in *Jackson v. Benson*, 578 N.W.2d 602 (Wisc. 1998), cert. denied sub nom. *Gilbert v. Moore*, 525 U.S. 997 [1998]); "Government Aid to Religious Schools," 114 Harvard L. Rev. 239 (2000) (criticizing the U.S. Supreme Court's decision in *Mitchell v. Helms*, 530 U.S. 793 [2000]).

41. For example, the editorial board of the *New York Times*. See the editorial's "Breaching the Church-State Wall," *New York Times*, June 12, 1998, at A22 (criticizing the Wisconsin Supreme Court's decision in *Jackson v. Benson*, 578 N.W.2d 602 [Wisc. 1998], which held, in part, that the Milwaukee voucher program, which includes religiously affiliated schools, does not violate the federal nonestablishment norm); "Vouchers for Parochial Schools," *New York Times*, Nov. 11, 1998, at A30 (criticizing the U.S. Supreme Court's denial of certiorari in *Jackson v. Benson*, sub nom. *Gilbert v. Moore*, 525 U.S. 997 [1998]); and "The Wrong Ruling on Vouchers," *New York Times*, June 28, 2002 (criticizing the U.S. Supreme Court's decision in the Cleveland school voucher case).

42. Akhil Amar has observed that according to Justice Souter and the two other justices (Stevens and Ginsburg) who joined his dissenting opinion in *Mitchell v. Helms*, 530 U.S. 793 (2000), government aid may not go directly to religiously affiliated primary and secondary schools "even if this aid does not single out [such schools] for any preferential treatment." Amar, "Foreword," at 119.

43. See McGreevy, "Thinking on One's Own," at 122–26; Thomas C. Berg, "Anti-Catholicism and Modern Church-State Relations," 33 Loyola U. Chicago L. Rev. 121 (2001); Laycock, "The Underlying Unity of Separation and Neutrality," at 50ff. See also *Mitchell v. Helms*, 530 U.S. 793, 828–29 (2000) (plurality op'n).

44. Laycock, "The Underlying Unity of Separation and Neutrality," at 58. The tract Justice Douglas cited: Loraine Boettner, *Roman Catholicism* (Philadelphia: Presbyterian and Reformed Publishing, 1962). (Laycock has emphasized that he is not a Catholic or even a religious believer. See Douglas Laycock, "Religious Liberty as Liberty," 7 J. Contemporary Legal Issues 313, 352ff. [1996].) For a fuller account, see Brief of the Becket Fund for Religious Liberty as *Amicus Curiae* in Support of Petitioners, *Mitchell v. Helms*, 530 U.S. 793 (2000).

45. Cf. Eugene Volokh, "Equal Treatment Is Not Establishment," 13 Notre Dame J. L., Ethics & Public Policy 341, 341 (1999):

> Casting the matter in terms of discrimination frames the issue in a stark light, but such a characterization is accurate: Discrimination is indeed what it's all about. Fair-minded people may argue that the Constitution does require such discrimination; not all discrimination is bad. But there should be no denying that a constitutional rule excluding religious schools from generally available benefits rests on the theory that discrimination is constitutionally mandated.

46. See 530 U.S. 793, 867 (2000) (Souter, J., dissenting, joined by Stevens and Ginsburg, JJ.).
47. Amar, "Foreword," at 119.
48. Ibid.
49. Justice O'Connor has noted that "[t]he Religion Clauses prohibit the government from favoring religion, but they provide no warrant for discriminating *against* religion." *Board of Ed. of Kiryas Joel Village School Dist. v. Grumet*, 512 U.S. 687, 717 (O'Connor, J., concurring in part and concurring in judgment).
50. Esbeck, "A Constitutional Case for Government Cooperation," at 18.
51. Michael W. McConnell, "Political and Religious Disestablishment," 1986 Brigham Young U. L. Rev. 405, 413. Cf. *McDaniel v. Paty*, 435 U.S. 618, 640–41 (1978) (Brennan, J., concurring in judgment):

    That public debate of religious ideas, like any other, may arouse emotion, may incite, may foment religious divisiveness and strife does not rob it of constitutional protection.... The mere fact that a purpose of the Establishment Clause is to reduce or eliminate religious divisiveness or strife, does not place religious discussion, association, or political participation in a status less preferred than rights of discussion, association and political participation generally.... The State's goal of preventing sectarian bickering and strife may not be accomplished by regulating religious speech and political association.... Government may not as a goal promote "safe thinking" with respect to religion.... The Establishment Clause, properly understood, ... may not be used as a sword to justify repression of religion or its adherents from any aspect of public life.

52. Cf. Esbeck, "A Constitutional Case for Government Cooperation," 18. "If the answer is that we are protecting a religiously informed conscientious right not to have one's taxes go toward the support of religion, the Supreme Court has already rejected such a claim [citing Tilton v. Richardson, 403 U.S. 672, 689 (1971)]."
53. Stephen G. Gilles, "Why Parents Should Choose," in Peterson and Hassel, eds., *Learning from School Choice*, at 395, 404.
54. Ibid.
55. See Kathleen M. Sullivan, "Religion and Liberal Democracy," 59 U. Chicago L. Rev. 195, 208–14 (1992); Brief of Baptist Joint Committee on Public Affairs, National Council of Churches of Christ in the USA, American Jewish Congress, Union of American Hebrew Congregations, Hadassah, the Women's Zionist Organization of America, Inc., People for the American Way, and National Coalition for Public Education and Religious Liberty as *Amicus Curiae* in Support of Respondents, *Rosenberger v. Rectors and Visitors of University of Virginia*, 515 U.S. 819 (1995).

    In the words of Kathleen Sullivan, "the establishment clause necessarily requires that government 'disfavor' religion in relation to secular programs," because "government [may not] make us pay taxes to be used for religious indoctrination in faiths we may not share." Or, as the ACLU argued, the Wisconsin Supreme Court's upholding an evenhanded school choice program should be condemned because under it "Wisconsin taxpayers will be coerced into supporting religions, including sects and cults, with which they may not agree." (Volokh, "Equal Treatment Is Not Establishment," at 342.)

56. *Rosenberger v. Rectors and Visitors of University of Virginia*, 515 U.S. 819, 856–57, 863 (Thomas, J., concurring). (The majority opinion made the same point. See ibid. at 840 [op'n of Court].) See also Volokh, "Equal Treatment Is Not Establishment," at 351; Steffen N. Johnson, "A Civil Libertarian Case for the Constitutionality of School Choice," 10 George Mason U. Civil Rights L. J. 1, 5–10 (1999/2000). Akhil Amar recently rehearsed Justice Thomas' explanation: "In past church-state opinions, the *Mitchell* dissenters have tried to wrap themselves in the mantle of James Madison. But the kind of governmental aid to religion that Madison and his allies opposed was aid to religion *as such*, through laws that explicitly singled out some religious sects or institutions or practices ('Protestants' or 'Christians' or 'churches' or 'prayer,' for example)." Amar, "Foreword," at 120.

57. For a discussion of this, see Joseph P. Viteritti, "School Choice and State Constitutional Law," in Peterson and Hassel, eds., *Learning from School Choice*, at 409. In *Jackson v. Benson*, the Wisconsin Supreme Court tamed such a state constitutional provision. See *Jackson v. Benson*, 578 N.W.2d 602 (Wisc. 1998), cert. denied sub nom. *Gilbert v. Moore*, 525 U.S. 997 (1998).

58. This, I think, is the deep meaning of certain "state action" cases. See, e.g., *Shelley v. Kramer*, 334 U.S. 1 (1948); *Burton v. Wilmington Parking Authority*, 365 U.S. 715 (1961).

59. On the idea of human rights, see Michael J. Perry, *The Idea of Human Rights: Four Inquiries* (New York: Oxford University Press, 1998).

60. Thus, I disagree with Laura Underkuffler that "[i]f we publicly fund parochial schools, Quaker schools, Jewish schools, and other mainstream institutions – actions which most citizens would, in all likelihood, find quite benign – then we must also fund the private religious schools that preach religious hatred, racial bigotry, the oppression of women, and other views." Laura S. Underkuffler, "The Price of Vouchers for Religious Freedom," 78 U. Detroit Mercy L. Rev. 463, 475–76 (2001).

61. See Michael W. McConnell, "Governments, Families, and Power: A Defense of Educational Choice," 31 Connecticut L. Rev. 847, 855, 858 (1999):

> The government may fund only government schools, or it may extend its funding neutrally, but it may not discriminate between students on the basis of the religious viewpoint or character of the schools.... If a legislature passed a bill forbidding students to use their college grants at any institution where Marxism is espoused, it would be struck down in an instant. There is no more justification for forbidding students to use their educational grants at institutions where Christianity or Judaism is espoused.

See also Volokh, "Equal Treatment Is Not Establishment," at 365–67; Johnson, "A Civil Libertarian Case for the Constitutionality of School Choice," at

31–36; Allan E. Parker, Jr., and R. Clayton Trotter, "Hostility or Neutrality? Faith-Based Schools and Tax-Funded Tuition: A GI Bill for Kids," 10 George Mason U. Civil Rights L. J. 83, 101–05 (1999/2000). Cf. *Rosenberger v. Rector and Visitors of the University of Virginia*, 515 U.S. 819, 845 (1995): "The neutrality commanded of the State by the separate Clauses of the First Amendment was compromised by the University's action [denying financial support to an evangelical student organization]."

62. For several possible constitutional arguments, see Volokh, "Equal Treatment Is Not Establishment," at 365–73; Parker and Trotter, "Hostility or Neutrality?".

63. See *Employment Division, Department of Human Resources of Oregon v. Smith*, 494 U.S. 872 (1990); *Church of the Lukumi Babalu Aye, Inc. v. City of Hialeah*, 508 U.S. 520 (1993).

64. For my understanding of (the Court's understanding of) the free exercise norm, see Perry, "Freedom of Religion in the United States," at 297–302. I summarized as follows:

> What does it mean to say that government may not discriminate against religion – or, equivalently, that the free exercise norm is an antidiscrimination norm? The answer is twofold. Government may not oppose one or another kind of conduct either
>
> - because, or in part because, the conduct is, for some, (a) a religious practice (b) animated by a religious belief or beliefs thought to be false or otherwise objectionable, or
> - because, or in part because, of hostility/indifference to the religious group (or groups) for whom the conduct is a religious practice – because of a failure to include the group within the circle of religious groups that government normally treats with active respect and concern. (302)

In 1947, when it first applied the nonestablishment norm to the states, the Supreme Court wrote:

> [The First] Amendment requires the state to be neutral in its relationship with groups of religious believers and non-believers; it does not require the state to be their adversary. State power is no more to be used to handicap religions than it is to favor them. . . . [The state] cannot exclude individual Catholics, Lutherans, Mohammedans, Baptists, Jews, Methodists, Non-believers, Presbyterians, or the members of any other faith, *because of their faith, or lack of it,* from receiving the benefits of public welfare legislation. (*Everson v. Board of Education*, 330 U.S. 1, 16, 18 [1947] [passages rearranged].)

Given that the free exercise norm is a religion-specific antidiscrimination norm, it is unnecessary to rely, in this context, on the equal protection clause, which is a more general antidiscrimination norm. See Perry, "Modern Equal Protection."

65. See, e.g., Viteritti, "School Choice and State Constitutional Law," at 419–21. See also Johnson, "A Civil Libertarian Case for the Constitutionality of School Choice," at 10–11.

66. In a recent decision by the Supreme Court of Maine, the court's ruling that Maine did not act unconstitutionally in discriminating against religiously affiliated schools was based on an inaccurate understanding of what the non-establishment norm forbids. See *Bagley v. Raymond School Dept.*, 728 A.2d 127 (Maine 1999), cert. denied, 528 U.S. 947 (1999). (Accord, *Strout v. Albanese*, 178 F.3d 57 (1st Cir. 1999), cert. denied, 528 U.S. 931 [1999].) In the same year, the Supreme Court of Vermont made the same mistake. See *Chittenden Town School Dist. v. Vermont Dept. of Educ.*, 738 A.2d 539 (Vermont 1999), cert. denied, 528 U.S. 1066 (1999). Cf. *KDM ex rel. WJM v. Reedsport School District*, 196 F.3d 1046 (9th Cir. 1999), cert. denied, 531 U.S. 1010 (2000) (although the challenged regulation "treats [students in religiously affiliated schools] differently by denying them state services on school grounds," no free exercise violation existed because plaintiff did not prove any substantial "burden" on his religious conduct). For a critical comment on *KDM ex rel. WJM v. Reedsport School District*, see "Constitutional Law – Free Exercise Clause – Ninth Circuit Upholds Oregon Regulation Limiting Special Education Services to Religiously Neutral Settings," 114 Harvard L. Rev. 954 (2001). "[T]he Ninth Circuit's decision insulates a wide range of official state action targeting religion from meaningful judicial review, thereby weakening the guarantee of religious liberty at the heart of the Free Exercise Clause."
67. See note 65.
68. See *Church of the Lukumi Babalu Aye, Inc. v. City of Hialeah*, 508 U.S. 520 (1993).
69. See note 61.
70. See Steven D. Smith, "Free Exercise Doctrine and the Discourse of Disrespect," 65 U. Colorado L. Rev. 519 (1994).
71. For a contrary view, see Underkuffler, "The Price of Vouchers for Religious Freedom"; Laura S. Underkuffler, "Public Funding for Religious Schools: Difficulties and Dangers in a Pluralistic Society," 27 Oxford Rev. Education 577 (2001).
72. Joseph P. Viteritti, "A Truly Living Constitution: Why Educational Opportunity Trumps Strict Separation on the Voucher Question," 57 New York U. Annual Survey of American L. 89, 112 (2000). See ibid. at n. 127 (referring to Australia, Belgium, Canada, Denmark, England, France, Germany, Holland, Iceland, Israel, Scotland, Spain, Sweden, and New Zealand). "For years Catholics have pointed out to American lawmakers that Britain, France, Canada, Australia and other countries support church-related schools." Robert Drinan, SJ, "Mr. Bush Backs the Gospel on the Streets," *The Tablet* [London], Feb. 10, 2001, at 176, 177.

CHAPTER 2

1. 29 Cong. Globe 656 (1854); quoted in John T. Noonan, Jr., and Edward McGlynn Gaffney, Jr., *Religious Freedom: History, Cases, and Other Materials on the Interaction of Religion and Government* (New York: Foundation Press, 2001), at 263.

2. If political choices disfavoring conduct on the basis of religiously grounded moral belief do not violate the nonestablishment norm, it is difficult to see how political choices that do not disfavor conduct, if based on religiously grounded conduct, violate the nonestablishment norm.

3. A state legislature would be constitutionally free to re-criminalize most abortions, however, only if the United States Supreme Court overruled *Roe v. Wade*, 410 U.S. 113 (1973).

4. For a list of such reasons, see Robert P. George, *Making Men Moral: Civil Liberties and Public Morality* (New York: Oxford University Press, 1993), at 42–43. The United States Constitution has been interpreted to forbid government to ban abortion, which is conduct many believe to be immoral. See *Roe v. Wade*, 410 U.S. 113 (1973). (I comment on the Supreme Court's decision in *Roe* in my book, *We the People: The Fourteenth Amendment and the Supreme Court* [New York: Oxford University Press, 1999].) Cf. Richard A. Posner, "Reply to Critics of *The Problematics of Moral and Legal Theory*," 111 Harvard L. Rev. 1796, 1814 (1998): "That a case involves a moral issue does not mean that the court must resolve that issue in order to decide the case."

5. As the Supreme Court noted in one of the physician-assisted suicide cases it decided in June 1997, "[the New York State Task Force on Life and the Law] expressed its concern that, because depression is difficult to diagnose, physicians and medical professionals often fail to respond adequately to seriously ill patients' needs. Thus, legal physician-assisted suicide could make it more difficult for the State to protect depressed and mentally ill persons, or those who are suffering from untreated pain, from suicidal impulses." *Washington v. Glucksberg*, 521 U.S. 702, 731 (1997). The Court then added:

> [T]he State has an interest in protecting vulnerable groups – including the poor, the elderly, and disabled persons – from abuse, neglect, and mistakes. . . . We have recognized . . . the real risk of subtle coercion and undue influence in end-of-life situations. Similarly, the New York Task Force warned that "legalizing physician-assisted suicide would pose profound risks to many individuals who are ill and vulnerable. . . . The risk of harm is greatest for the many individuals in our society whose autonomy and well-being are already compromised by poverty, lack of access to good medical care, advanced age, or membership in a stigmatized social group." . . . If physician-assisted suicide were permitted, many might resort to it to spare their families the substantial financial burden of end-of-life health-care costs.
>
> The State's interest here goes beyond protecting the vulnerable from coercion; it extends to protecting disabled and terminally ill persons from prejudice, negative and inaccurate stereotypes, and "societal indifference." The State's assisted-suicide ban reflects and reinforces its policy that the lives of terminally ill, disabled, and elderly people must be no less valued than the lives of the young and healthy, and that a seriously disabled person's suicidal impulses should be interpreted and treated the same way as anyone else's. (731–32)

6. See, e.g., George, *Making Men Moral*. It bears emphasis here that, as Kent Greenawalt has observed, "much legal enforcement of morality is uncontroversial and rarely discussed. Disagreement arises only when the law enforces aspects of morality that do not involve protecting others from fairly direct harms. More precisely, people raises questions about legal requirements (1) to perform acts that benefit others, (2) to refrain from acts that cause indirect harm to others, (3) to refrain from acts that cause harm to themselves, (4) to refrain from acts that offend others, and (5) to refrain from acts that others believe are immoral." Kent Greenawalt, "Legal Enforcement of Morality," 85 J. Criminal L. & Criminology 710, 710 (1995).

7. In a recent, important piece, Scott Idleman argues that existing nonestablishment doctrine – doctrine articulated by the Supreme Court and by other federal courts as well – leaves ample room for government to disfavor conduct on the basis of religiously grounded belief. Idleman also argues, on the basis of "overarching principles of democratic legitimacy," in support of this state of affairs. See Scott C. Idleman, "Religious Premises, Legislative Judgments, and the Establishment Clause," Cornell Journal of Law & Public Policy, forthcoming.

8. However, neither the nonestablishment norm nor the free exercise norm should be understood to call into question the following proposition: Government may make a policy choice on the basis of a position that one or more churches happen to reject, even though the policy choice has the effect of disfavoring those churches relative to other churches that do not reject the position. See Chapter 1, note 19.

9. For an example of a position that privileges the Christian Church generally, see Chapter 1, note 21.

10. It bears mention that no generation of "We the People" ever established, as part of our constitutional law, any such rule. The first part of the constitutional text – the Preamble – declares: "We the People of the United States, in Order to form a more perfect Union, establish Justice, insure domestic Tranquility, provide for the common defence, promote the general Welfare, and secure the Blessings of Liberty to ourselves and our Posterity, do ordain and establish this Constitution for the United States of America." In American constitutional culture, few if any persons – even, remarkably, few if any constitutional theorists – disagree that the Constitution comprises at least some directives issued by – that is, some norms "ordained and established" by – "We the People." More to the point, few disagree that the Constitution comprises some such norms partly because the norms were "ordained and established" by "We the People." It is now a convention – an axiom – of American constitutional culture that "We the People of the United States" not only "do ordain and establish this Constitution for the United States of America" but *may* ordain and establish it. This is not to say that *only* "We the People" may establish norms as constitutional. Nor is it to deny that a norm never established as constitutional by "We the People" can become constitutional bedrock for us. For a discussion of all this, see Perry, *We the People*, at 15–23.

11. *Edwards v. Aguillard*, 482 U.S. 578, 615 (1987) (Scalia, J., dissenting). "Today's religious activism may give us the Balanced Treatment Act [which according to the majority in *Aguillard* violated the nonestablishment norm], but yesterday's resulted in the abolition of slavery, and tomorrow's may bring relief for famine victims." Ibid.

12. See, e.g., Kathleen M. Sullivan, "Religion and Liberal Democracy," 59 U. Chicago L. Rev. 195, 197 (1992): "[T]he negative bar against establishment of religion implies the affirmative 'establishment' of a civil order for the resolution of public moral disputes. . . . [P]ublic moral disputes may be resolved only on grounds articulable in secular terms."

    Recall that, as I noted at the beginning of this chapter, the religious grounding *vel non* of a moral belief is person-relative: A moral belief that is religiously grounded for one person may not be for another. A belief that conduct is immoral is religiously "grounded" for a person if she would not believe the conduct to be immoral if she did not credit one or more religious premises that support the belief – for example, the premise that the Bible (understood as God-inspired and therefore authoritative) teaches that the conduct is immoral.

13. See James Bradley Thayer, "The Origin and Scope of the American Doctrine of Constitutional Law," 7 Harvard L. Rev. 129 (1893). See, generally, "One Hundred Years of Judicial Review: The Thayer Centennial Symposium," 88 Northwestern U. L. Rev. 1–468 (1993).

14. See, e.g., *U.S. Railroad Retirement Bd. v. Fritz*, 449 U.S. 166 (1980); *FCC v. Beach Communications, Inc.*, 508 U.S. 307 (1993).

15. See *Loving v. Virginia*, 388 U.S. 1 (1967).

16. See Perry, *We the People*, at 131–49.

17. See Patricia Beattie Jung and Ralph F. Smith, *Heterosexism: An Ethical Challenge* (Albany: State University of New York Press, 1993).

18. See Perry, *We the People*, at 88–97 (racist belief), 131–49 (heterosexist belief). Government may not disfavor conduct based on a racist (or homophobic) belief – for example, the belief that interracial marriage is immoral – not because the belief is false, or believed to be false, but simply because for government to do so would be for it to act unconstitutionally; it would be for government to make a judgment that it is not constitutionally free to make. Of course, that the Constitution forbids government to make a particular judgment – that interracial marriage is immoral, for example, or that the Pope is the Antichrist and Roman Catholicism a false religion – may well be due, at least in part, to the fact many believe the judgment to be false. But it may also be due solely to the fact that many believe that whether or not the judgment is false, it is no part of the proper business of government to make the judgment.

19. See Michael J. Perry, "Protecting Human Rights in a Democracy: What Role for the Courts?" (Wake Forest Law Review, forthcoming). See also Jeremy Waldron, *Law and Disagreement* (New York: Oxford University Press, 1999), Chapters 10–13.

20. As Andrew Koppelman, for example, thinks I have. See Andrew Koppelman, "Secular Purpose," 88 Virginia L. Rev. 87, 117 n. 100 (2002).

21. When we are engaged in what we understand to be "moral" argument, most of us seem to be arguing about one or more of these three basic questions. In my Gianella Lecture, in the course of commenting on the controversy among legal academics and contemporary moral philosophers as to what the subject matter of morality is, I sketched the three questions. See Michael J. Perry, "What Is 'Morality' Anyway?" 45 Villanova L. Rev. 69, 98–105 (2000) (the 1999 Donald M. Giannella Memorial Lecture).

22. Koppelman, "Secular Purpose," at 114. Koppelman writes: "The most obvious way in which the government expresses an opinion is through the passage of legislation. . . . Through legislation, the government can, and often does, express a point of view." Ibid. at 112.

23. See Michael J. Perry, *The Idea of Human Rights* (New York: Oxford University Press, 1998), Chapter 1.

24. See Perry, "Freedom of Religion in the United States," at 329–32. See also Douglas Laycock, "The Benefits of the Establishment Clause," 42 DePaul L. Rev. 373, 380 (1992): "There is no need for the government to make decisions about Christian rituals versus Jewish rituals versus no religious rituals at all. For government to make that choice is simply a gratuitous statement about the kind of people we really are. By making such statements, the government says the real American religion is watered-down Christianity, and everybody else is a little bit un-American."

25. Compared to the citizenries of the world's other advanced industrial democracies, the citizenry of the United States is one of the most religious – perhaps even the most religious. According to recent polling data, "[a]n overwhelming 95% of Americans profess belief in God." Richard N. Ostling, "In So Many Gods We Trust," *Time*, Jan. 30, 1995, at 72. Moreover, "70% of American adults [are] members of a church or synagogue." "Religion and *Roe*: The Politics of Exclusion," 108 Harvard L. Rev. 495, 498 n. 21 (1994). Cf. Andrew Greeley, "The Persistence of Religion," *Cross Currents*, Spring 1995, at 24.

26. See note 20.

27. See note 12.

28. The argument I make in this chapter competes with an argument I made six years ago. See Michael J. Perry, *Religion in Politics: Constitutional and Moral Perspectives* (New York: Oxford University Press, 1997), at 30–38. For critical commentary on my earlier argument, see Laycock, "Freedom of Speech That Is Both Religious and Political."

29. E-mail message from Andrew Koppelman ⟨akoppelman@law.northwestern.edu⟩ to Michael Perry ⟨mperry@law.wfu.edu⟩, June 27, 2000.

30. E-mail message from Andrew Koppelman ⟨akoppelman@law.northwestern.edu⟩ to Michael Perry ⟨mperry@law.wfu.edu⟩, July 31, 2000.

31. One might be tempted to respond along these lines: The nonestablishment norm, understood as Koppelman understands it, is concerned with "legislative outcomes rather than [with] legislative inputs." See Koppelman, "Secular

Purpose," at 119. Therefore, no one who shares Koppelman's understanding of the norm need dispute the claim that legislators are constitutionally free to proceed on the basis of the ground(s) in which they have the most confidence, in which they place the most trust, even if the ground is religious. The problem with this response is that according to Koppelman's understanding of the nonestablishment norm, if at the end of the day the legislature decides to disfavor the conduct on the basis of the belief that the conduct is immoral, and if there is no plausible, independent secular ground for that belief, the legislature's decision violates the nonestablishment norm. So, under the nonestablishment norm as Koppelman understands it, a legislature is *not* constitutionally free to proceed on the basis of a moral belief that has only religious grounding – a moral belief that lacks plausible, independent secular grounding.

32. Christopher J. Eberle, "Why Restraint Is Religiously Unacceptable," 35 Religious Studies 247, 261–62 (1999).

33. Cf. Michael J. Perry, *Love and Power: The Role of Religion and Morality in American Politics* (New York: Oxford University Press, 1991), at 10. (criticizing Bruce Ackerman's conception of "neutral" political justification).

34. Cf. Michael W. McConnell, "Political and Religious Disestablishment," 1986 Brigham Young U. L. Rev. 405, 413: "Religious differences in this country have never generated the civil discord experienced in political conflicts over such issues as the Vietnam War, racial segregation, the Red Scare, unionization, or slavery."

35. Cf. Koppelman, "Secular Purpose," at 112 (hypothesizing a law that "makes it a felony to operate machinery on the Sabbath, to drive a car, to turn on an electric appliance, or to make a telephone call … ").

36. See Perry, *We the People*, at 131–50.

37. See note 19.

38. Again, if political choices disfavoring conduct on the basis of religiously grounded moral belief do not violate the nonestablishment norm, it is difficult to see how political choices that do not disfavor conduct, if based on religiously grounded moral belief, violate the nonestablishment norm.

My argument in this chapter is certainly not meant to deny that the free exercise norm forbids government to discriminate against religion, including religious conduct. The free exercise norm is, whatever else it is, an antidiscrimination norm. See Perry, "Freedom of Religion in the United States," at 297–302.

CHAPTER 3

1. See Michael J. Perry, *The Idea of Human Rights: Four Inquiries* (New York: Oxford University Press, 1998), at 11–41.

2. Samuel Brittan, "Making Common Cause: How Liberals Differ, and What They Ought To Agree On," *Times Literary Supplement*, Sept. 20, 1996, at 3, 4. Cf. Charles Larmore, "The Moral Basis of Political Liberalism," 96 J. Philosophy 599, 624–25 (1999) (arguing that "our commitment to [liberal] democracy…

cannot be understood except by appeal to a higher moral authority, which is the obligation to respect one another as persons").

3. Larmore, "The Moral Basis of Political Liberalism," at 621.

4. The conference – a Calvin College Seminar in Christian Scholarship – took place on May 27–29, 1999, at Calvin College, Grand Rapids, Michigan. Nicholas Wolterstorff, the Noah Porter Professor of Philosophical Theology at Yale University, organized and hosted the conference.

5. What about judges? Are they a special case? See Michael J. Perry, *Religion in Politics: Constitutional and Moral Perspectives* (New York: Oxford University Press, 1997), at 102–04. "Religion and the Judicial Process: Legal, Ethical, and Empirical Dimensions," 81 Marquette L. Rev. 177–567 (1998).

6. See Perry, *Religion in Politics*, at 32–33. Cf. *McDaniel v. Paty*, 435 U.S. 618, 640–41 (1978) (Brennan, J. concurring in judgment):

    That public debate of religious ideas, like any other, may arouse emotion, may incite, may foment religious divisiveness and strife does not rob it of constitutional protection.... The mere fact that a purpose of the Establishment Clause is to reduce or eliminate religious divisiveness or strife, does not place religious discussion, association, or political participation in a status less preferred than rights of discussion, association and political participation generally.... The State's goal of preventing sectarian bickering and strife may not be accomplished by regulating religious speech and political association.... Government may not as a goal promote "safe thinking" with respect to religion.... The Establishment Clause, properly understood, ... may not be used as a sword to justify repression of religion or its adherents from any aspect of public life.

7. Mark Tushnet, "The Limits of the Involvement of Religion in the Body Politic," in James E. Wood, Jr., and Derek Davis, eds., *The Role of Religion in the Making of Public Policy* (Waco, Tex.: J. M. Dawson Institute of Church-State Studies, Baylor University, 1991), at 191, 213.

8. Richard Rorty, "Religion as Conversation-Stopper," in Richard Rorty, *Philosophy and Social Hope* (New York: Penguin, 1999), at 168, 169.

9. Jeffrey Siker, a Christian ethicist and ordained minister of the Presbyterian Church (USA), has persuasively criticized the effort to analogize homosexuality to alcoholism. See Jeffrey S. Siker, "Homosexual Christians, the Bible, and Gentile Inclusion: Confessions of a Repenting Heterosexist," in Jeffrey S. Siker, ed., *Homosexuality in the Church: Both Sides of the Debate* (Louisville, Ky.: Westminster/J. Knox Press, 1994), at 178, 181–83.

10. Luke Timothy Johnson, "Religious Rights and Christian Texts," in John Witte, Jr., and Johan David van der Vyver, eds., *Religious Human Rights in Global Perspective: Religious Perspectives* (The Hague: Martinus Nijhoff Publishers, 1996), at 65, 72–73.

11. Indeed, American history does not suggest that debates about religious (theological) issues are invariably more divisive than debates about political issues. To the contrary: "Religious differences in this country have never generated the civil discord experienced in political conflicts over such issues

as the Vietnam War, racial segregation, the Red Scare, unionization, or slavery." Michael W. McConnell, "Political and Religious Disestablishment," 1986 Brigham Young U. L. Rev. 405, 413.

12. One might be tempted to claim that even if relying on religiously grounded moral argument, in public debate about whether to disfavor conduct, will usually *not* be more divisive than relying only on secularly grounded moral belief, the fact remains that the totality of the good consequences minus the totality of the bad consequences of relying only on secularly grounded moral belief is a number that is greater than the number reached by subtracting the totality of the bad consequences from the totality of the good consequences of relying on religiously grounded moral belief. But that would be a difficult claim to sustain. As Chris Eberle has explained, in an e-mail message to me:

1. The argument to which you are objecting is a *consequentialist* argument: it mandates restraint regarding religion in virtue of the undesirable consequences of refusing to privatize religion. The undesirable consequences are, of course, the division, alienation, frustration, resentment, etc., religious believers cause when they bring their religious convictions into the public square.

2. I take your objection to the argument from divisiveness to be a point about consistency: religious discourse is no *more* divisive than secular discourse, so it is *arbitrary* to mandate restraint regarding the former but not the latter on grounds of divisiveness.

3. Regarding many formulations of the argument from divisiveness, I take your objection to be utterly compelling.

4. But I think that the version of the argument mentioned in 1 can't (or shouldn't) be the argument its proponents have in mind (in spite of the fact that they very often formulate it in the very terms you attack!). The reason why has to do with the nature of consequentialist arguments. As I understand them, a consequentialist argument requires a fair amount of "higher math": the proponent must identify *all* of the relevant alternatives, identify *all* of the relevant consequences of each alternative, "add" up all the positive consequences of each alternative, "subtract" the negative consequences from the sum just arrived at. The alternative that generates the highest net total of beneficial consequences, or at least the lowest negative total, is the morally preferable alternative.

5. So as I see it, the two relevant alternatives are: to privatize religion or not to privatize religion. Otherwise put, the two relevant alternatives are: public discourse that is only secular or public discourse that is both secular and religious.

6. The next step is to identify the likely consequences of those alternatives, add, subtract, and compare.

7. One immediate consequence of this point about the nature of the argument from divisiveness: that argument can succeed even if you are correct that secular discourse is just as divisive as religious discourse.

Indeed, it can succeed even if secular discourse is *more* divisive than religious discourse. The reason is, as I see it, as follows: even though secular discourse might generate a larger amount of division than religious discourse, it is counterbalanced by a large quantity of positive consequences that far "outweighs" the bad consequences of secular discourse (including divisiveness). And this seems right: the value of public deliberation regarding political policies is a very weighty good; public deliberation in at least secular terms is essential to healthy public deliberation; consequently, the deficits of secular discourse are far outweighed by the benefits of secular discourse.

8. Another implication of this point about the consequentialist nature of the argument from divisiveness. If it is going to work, and if it is going to avoid the kind of consistency objection you level against it, its proponents will have to make good on the following claim: that the consequences of privatizing religion are more beneficial, all things considered, than are the consequences of refusing to privatize religion. That is, the relevant difference between religious and secular discourse is that the negative consequences of the former are *not* outweighed by the positive consequences of the former but the negative consequences of the latter *are* outweighed by the positive consequences of the latter. (Or something like that.)

9. If this is correct, then it seems obvious that the argument from divisiveness is going to be a *lot* more complicated and difficult to pull off than its proponents often imagine. Regarding the formulations I am aware of, they almost always fail to recognize the implications of the fact that they are presenting a consequentialist argument and thus satisfy themselves with the observation that refusing to privatize religious commitments is very divisive. But that's nowhere nearly sufficient to make their case. They must also determine whether those divisive consequences are outweighed by the positive consequences. That's a *monumental* task and no one I know of has come even close to doing it.

10. This might seem to be a small point, but, personally, I take it to be essential. If those who advocate restraint want to appeal to the consequences of refusing to privatize religion, then they have to do more than just selectively identify some of the negative consequences of refusing to privatize religion. (Which is what typically happens.) And once they have to make that more complicated case, I think that it is plausible to suppose (and argue in my manuscript) that the argument from divisiveness fails. (E-mail message from Christopher J. Eberle ⟨eberle@usna.edu⟩ to Michael J. Perry ⟨mperry@law.wfu.edu⟩, July 21, 2000.)

The manuscript to which Eberle refers in his final sentence has now been published: Christopher J. Eberle, *Religious Conviction in Liberal Politics* (New York: Cambridge University Press, 2002).

13. John A. Coleman, SJ, *An American Strategic Theology* (New York: Paulist Press, 1982), at 192–95. Coleman adds: "I am further strongly convinced that the

Enlightenment desire for an unmediated universal fraternity and language (resting as it did on unreflected allegiance to *very particular* communities and language, conditioned by time and culture) was destructive of the lesser, real 'fraternities' – in [Wilson Carey] McWilliams' sense – in American life." Ibid. at 194.

14. See Daniel O. Conkle, "Different Religions, Different Politics: Evaluating the Role of Competing Religious Traditions in American Politics and Law," 10 J. L. & Religion 1 (1993–94).

15. David Tracy speaks for many of us religious believers when he writes:

> For believers to be unable to learn from secular feminists on the patriarchal nature of most religions or to be unwilling to be challenged by Feuerbach, Darwin, Marx, Freud, or Nietzsche is to refuse to take seriously the religion's own suspicions on the existence of those fundamental distortions named sin, ignorance, or illusion. The interpretations of believers will, of course, be grounded in some fundamental trust in, and loyalty to, the Ultimate Reality both disclosed and concealed in one's own religious tradition. But fundamental trust, as any experience of friendship can teach, is not immune to either criticism or suspicion. A religious person will ordinarily fashion some hermeneutics of trust, even one of friendship and love, for the religious classics of her or his tradition. But, as any genuine understanding of friendship shows, friendship often demands both critique and suspicion. A belief in a pure and innocent love is one of the less happy inventions of the romantics. A friendship that never includes critique and even, when appropriate, suspicion is a friendship barely removed from the polite and wary communication of strangers. As Buber showed, in every I-Thou encounter, however transient, we encounter some new dimension of reality. But if that encounter is to prove more than transitory, the difficult ways of friendship need a trust powerful enough to risk itself in critique and suspicion. To claim that this may be true of all our other loves but not true of our love for, and trust in, our religious tradition makes very little sense either hermeneutically or religiously. (David Tracy, *Plurality and Ambiguity: Hermeneutics, Religion, Hope* [San Francisco: Harper and Row, 1987], at 84–85, 86, 97–98, 112).

To his credit, Richard Rorty insists that there is "hypocrisy . . . in saying that believers somehow have no right to base their political views on their religious faith, whereas we atheists have every right to base ours on Enlightenment philosophy. The claim that in doing so we are appealing to reason, whereas the religious are being irrational, is hokum." Rorty, "Religion as Conversation-stopper," at 172.

16. As David Tracy has written, religion is "the single subject about which many intellectuals can feel free to be ignorant. Often abetted by the churches, they need not study religion, for 'everybody' already knows what religion is: It is a private consumer product that some people seem to need. Its former social role was poisonous. Its present privatization is harmless enough to wish it well from a civilized distance. Religion seems to be the sort of thing one likes

'if that's the sort of thing one likes.' " David Tracy, *The Analogical Imagination* (New York: Crossroad, 1981), at 13. See also Kent Greenawalt, *Religious Convictions and Political Choice* (New York: Oxford University Press, 1988), at 6: "A good many professors and other intellectuals display a hostility or skeptical indifference to religion that amounts to a thinly disguised contempt for belief in any reality beyond that discoverable by scientific inquiry and ordinary human experience."

17. See Greenawalt, *Religious Convictions and Political Choice*, at 159: "[I]f the worry is openmindedness and sensitivity to publicly accessible reasons, drawing a sharp distinction between religious convictions and [secular] personal bases [of judgment] would be an extremely crude tool."

David Tracy has lamented that "[f]or however often the word is bandied about, dialogue remains a rare phenomenon in anyone's experience. Dialogue demands the intellectual, moral, and, at the limit, religious ability to struggle to hear another and to respond. To respond critically, and even suspiciously when necessary, but to respond only in dialogical relationship to a real, not a projected other." David Tracy, *Dialogue with the Other* (Louvain: Peeters Press; Grand Rapids, Mich.: W. B. Eerdmans, 1990), at 4. Steven Smith, commenting wryly that " 'dialogue' seems to have become the all-purpose elixir of our time," has suggested that "[t]he hard question is not whether people should talk, but rather what they should say and what (among the various ideas communicated) they should believe." Steven D. Smith, "The Pursuit of Pragmatism," 100 Yale L. J. 409, 434–35 (1990). As Tracy's observation suggests, however, there is yet another "hard" question, which Smith's suggestion tends to obscure. It is not *whether* but *how* people should talk – what qualities of character and mind they should bring, or try to bring, to the task.

18. David Hollenbach, SJ, "Civil Society: Beyond the Public-Private Dichotomy," *The Responsive Community*, Winter 1994/95, at 15, 22. One of the religious communities to which Hollenbach refers is the Catholic community. See David Hollenbach, SJ, "Contexts of the Political Role of Religion: Civil Society and Culture," 30 San Diego L. Rev. 877, 891 (1993):

> For example, the Catholic tradition provides some noteworthy evidence that discourse across the boundaries of diverse communities is both possible and potentially fruitful when it is pursued seriously. This tradition, in its better moments, has experienced considerable success in efforts to bridge the divisions that have separated it from other communities with other understandings of the good life. In the first and second centuries, the early Christian community moved from being a small Palestinian sect to active encounter with the Hellenistic and Roman worlds. In the fourth century, Augustine brought biblical faith into dialogue with Stoic and Neoplatonic thought. His efforts profoundly transformed both Christian and Graeco-Roman thought and practice. In the thirteenth century Thomas Aquinas once again transformed Western Christianity by appropriating ideas from Aristotle that he had learned from Arab Muslims and from Jews. In the process he also transformed Aristotelian

ways of thinking in fundamental ways. Not the least important of these transformations was his insistence that the political life of a people is not the highest realization of the good of which they are capable – an insight that lies at the root of constitutional theories of limited government. And though the Church resisted the liberal discovery of modern freedoms through much of the modern period, liberalism has been transforming Catholicism once again through the last half of our own century. The memory of these events in social and intellectual history as well as the experience of the Catholic Church since the Second Vatican Council leads me to hope that communities holding different visions of the good life can get somewhere if they are willing to risk conversation and argument about these visions. Injecting such hope back into the public life of the United States would be a signal achievement. Today, it appears to be not only desirable but necessary.

See also ibid. at 892–96.

19. See Hollenbach, "Civil Society: Beyond the Public-Private Dichotomy," at 22: Conversation and argument about the common good [including religious conversation and argument] will not occur initially in the legislature or in the political sphere (narrowly conceived as the domain in which conflict of interest and power are adjudicated). Rather it will develop freely in those components of civil society that are the primary bearers of cultural meaning and value – universities, religious communities, the world of the arts, and serious journalism. It can occur wherever thoughtful men and women bring their beliefs on the meaning of the good life into intelligent and critical encounter with understandings of this good held by other peoples with other traditions. In short, it occurs wherever education about and serious inquiry into the meaning of the good life takes place.

20. Hollenbach, "Contexts of the Political Role of Religion," at 900. Cf. Kent Greenawalt, "Religious Convictions and Political Choice: Some Further Thoughts," 39 DePaul L. Rev. 1019, 1034 (1990) (expressing skepticism about "the promise of religious perspectives being transformed in what is primarily political debate").

21. Hollenbach, "Contexts of the Political Role of Religion," at 900.

22. See Chapter 2, note 25.

23. Paul G. Stern, "A Pluralistic Reading of the First Amendment and Its Relation to Public Discourse," 99 Yale L. J. 925, 934 (1990).

24. No one suggests that presenting religiously grounded moral belief in *nonpublic* political argument – political argument around the kitchen table, for example, or at a meeting of the local parish's Peace and Justice Committee – is illegitimate. A practical problem with the position that presenting religiously grounded moral belief in public political argument is somehow illegitimate is that it might sometimes be difficult to say when "nonpublic" political argument has crossed the line and become "public." Moreover, it is no more possible to maintain "an airtight barrier" between the religiously grounded moral discourse that takes place in nonpublic political argument

and that which takes place in public political argument than it is to maintain an airtight barrier between the religiously grounded moral discourse that takes place in "universities, religious communities, the world of the arts, and serious journalism" and that which takes place in "the domains of government and policy-formation." Why not, then, just welcome the presentation of religiously grounded moral belief in public as well as in relatively nonpublic political argument?

25. Michael J. Perry, *Morality, Politics, and Law* (New York: Oxford University Press, 1988), at 183. The point is not that we must be open to the possibility of religious conversion, least of all conversion to a fundamentalist faith. What is the point, then? Jeremy Waldron articulates it well:

> Even if people are exposed in argument to ideas over which they are bound to disagree – and how could *any* doctrine of public deliberation preclude *that?* – it does not follow that such exposure is pointless or oppressive. For one thing, it is important for people to be acquainted with the views that others hold. Even more important, however, is the possibility that my own view may be improved, in its subtlety and depth, by exposure to a religion or a metaphysics that I am initially inclined to reject.... I mean ... to draw attention to an experience we all have at one time or another, of having argued with someone whose world view was quite at odds with our own, and of having come away thinking, "I'm sure he's wrong, and I can't follow much of it, but, still, it makes you think ..." The prospect of losing that sort of effect in public discourse is, frankly, frightening – terrifying, even, if we are to imagine it being replaced by a kind of "deliberation" that, in the name of "fairness" or "reasonableness" (or worse still, "balance") consists of bland appeals to harmless nostrums that are accepted without question on all sides. This is to imagine open-ended public debate reduced to the formal trivia of American televisions networks.... [This] might apply to *any* religious or other philosophically contentious intervention. We do not have (and we should not have) so secure a notion of public consensus, or such stringent requirements of fairness in debate, as to exclude any view from having its effect in the marketplace of ideas. (Jeremy Waldron, "Religious Contributions in Public Deliberation," 30 San Diego L. Rev. 817, 841–42 [1993].)

See also Michael J. Sandel, "Political Liberalism," 107 Harvard L. Rev. 1765, 1794 (1994): "It is always possible that learning more about a moral or religious doctrine will lead us to like it less. But the respect of deliberation and engagement affords a more spacious public reason than liberalism allows. It is also a more suitable ideal for a pluralist society. To the extent that our moral and religious disagreements reflect the ultimate plurality of human goods, a deliberative mode of respect will better enable us to appreciate the distinctive goods our different lives express."

Kent Greenawalt and John Rawls have each defended a position (though not the same position) less congenial to the airing of religiously grounded moral belief in public political argument than the position I have defended here. I have explained elsewhere why I disagree both with Greenawalt's position and with Rawls's. See Perry, *Religion in Politics*, at 49–61.

26. See note 8.

27. See Michael J. Perry, "Freedom of Religion in the United States: Fin de Siècle Sketches," 75 Indiana L. J. 295, 327–29 (2000).

28. I therefore disagree with John Rawls (and others, such as Robert Audi) on this important point, as I have explained elsewhere. See Perry, *Religion in Politics*, at 54–61.

29. Nicholas Wolterstorff, "Audi on Religion, Politics, and Liberal Democracy," in Robert Audi and Nicholas Wolterstorff, *Religion in the Public Square* (Lanham, Md.: Rowman and Littlefield, 1997), at 145, 147. See also Douglas Laycock, "Freedom of Speech That Is Both Religious and Political," 29 U. California, Davis L. Rev. 793 (1996); Michael W. McConnell, "Correspondence: Getting Along," *First Things*, June-July 1996, at 2. Cf. Sanford Levinson, "Religious Language and the Public Square," 105 Harvard L. Rev. 2061, 2077 (1992) (suggesting that "liberal democracy give[s] everyone an equal chance, without engaging in any version of epistemic abstinence, to make his or her arguments, subject, obviously, to the prerogative of listeners to reject the arguments should they be unpersuasive").

30. See note 3.

31. See John Rawls, *Political Liberalism* (New York: Columbia University Press, 1993), at 217.

32. Stephen Macedo, "Transformative Constitutionalism and the Case of Religion: Defending the Moderate Hegemony of Liberalism," 26 Political Theory 56, 71 (1998).

33. William A. Galston, *Liberal Purposes* (New York: Cambridge University Press, 1991), at 108–09.

34. Michael J. Perry, "Religious Morality and Political Choice: Further Thoughts – and Second Thoughts – on *Love and Power*," 30 San Diego L. Rev. 703, 711 n. 23 (1993) (quoting Larmore).

35. Larmore, "The Moral Basis of Political Liberalism," at 611 (emphasis added).

36. I have oversimplified. Eberle develops and defends this important position with great care in his excellent *Religious Conviction in Liberal Politics*.

37. See, e.g., Robert Audi, *Religious Commitment and Secular Reason* (New York: Cambridge University Press, 2000), at 197.

38. Robert Audi, "The Place of Religious Argument in a Free and Democratic Society," 30 San Diego L. Rev. 677, 701 (1993). I wonder what it might mean for one to be "fully rational" – and also what "concepts we share as rational beings."

39. Gerald R. Dworkin, "Equal Respect and the Enforcement of Morality," 7 Social Philosophy & Policy 180, 193 (1990) (criticizing Ronald Dworkin). See also John M. Finnis, *Natural Law and Natural Rights* (Oxford: Clarendon Press, 1980), at 221–22. (criticizing Ronald Dworkin). I concur in Nicholas Wolterstorff's critique of Audi's position on this point. See

Wolterstorff, "Audi on Religion, Politics, and Liberal Democracy," at 159–
61. It seems to me that in his recent essay on "the moral basis of political liberalism," Larmore fails to close the gap to which Gerald Dworkin
refers. See Larmore, "The Moral Basis of Political Liberalism," at 608 and
n. 13.

40. Put another way, it is altogether obscure why one does not show her compa-
triots the respect that is their due if she adheres to what Chris Eberle's calls
"the ideal of conscientious engagement." See Eberle, *Religious Conviction in
Liberal Politics*, at 104–08.

41. The argument from divisiveness, unlike the argument from respect, is a consequentialist argument. One might be tempted to mount a more complicated version of the argument, according to which even if basing a political choice on a controversial moral belief will *not* usually be more divisive
if there is only a religious ground for the belief than if there is a secular
ground, the fact remains that the totality of the good consequences minus
the totality of the bad consequences of basing a political choice on a controversial moral belief that has a secular ground is a number that is greater
than the number reached by subtracting the totality of the bad consequences
from the totality of the good consequences of basing a political choice on
a controversial moral belief that has only a religious ground. But so far as
I know, no one has tried to make an argument in support of *that* claim –
a claim that in any event would be difficult to sustain. See note 12 to this
chapter.

42. Lawrence B. Solum, "Faith and Justice," 39 DePaul U. L. Rev. 1083, 1096
(1990). Solum is stating the argument, not making it. Indeed, Solum is wary
of the argument. See ibid. at 1096–97. Solum cites, as an instance of the
argument, Stephen L. Carter, "The Religiously Devout Judge," 64 Notre Dame
L. Rev. 932, 939 (1989). For another instance, see Maimon Schwarzschild,
"Religion and Public Debate in a Liberal Society: Always Oil and Water or
Sometimes More Like Rum and Coca-Cola?," 30 San Diego L. Rev. 903 (1993).

43. John Courtney Murray, *We Hold These Truths* (Kansas City. Mo.: Sheed and
Ward, 1960), at 23–24.

44. Kent Greenawalt, *Private Consciences and Public Reasons* (New York: Oxford
University Press, 1991), at 130.

45. A third argument – call it the argument from alienation – bears mention:
Reliance on religiously grounded moral belief as a basis of political decision making makes many persons feel politically marginalized or alienated –
namely, persons who do not subscribe to the supporting religious premise or
premises. For Kent Greenawalt's version of the argument, see ibid. at 156–
58. I have explained elsewhere why, in my judgment, the argument from
alienation is implausible. See Perry, *Religion in Politics*, at 50–52 (criticizing
Greenawalt's argument). Cf. Mark V. Tushnet, "The Constitution of Religion," 18 Connecticut L. Rev. 701, 712 (1986) ("nonadherents who believe
that they are excluded from the political community are merely expressing
the disappointment felt by everyone who has lost a fair fight in the arena of
politics"); Steven D. Smith, *Foreordained Failure: The Quest for a Constitutional*

Principle of Religious Freedom (New York: Oxford University Press, 1995), at 164–65 n. 66:

> [T]he very concept of "alienation," or symbolic exclusion, is difficult to grasp. How, if at all, does "alienation" differ from "anger," "annoyance," "frustration," or "disappointment" that every person who finds himself in a political minority is likely to feel? "Alienation" might refer to nothing more than an awareness by an individual that she belongs to a religious minority, accompanied by a realization that at least on some issues she is unlikely to be able to prevail in the political process. . . . That awareness may be discomforting. But is it the sort of phenomenon for which constitutional law can provide an efficacious remedy? Constitutional doctrine that stifles the message will not likely alter the reality – or a minority's awareness of that reality.

46. See Michael J. Perry, "What Is 'Morality' Anyway?" 45 Villanova L. Rev. 69 (2000) (the 1999 Donald M. Giannella Memorial Lecture).
47. See note 2 and accompanying text.
48. See Michael J. Perry, "The Putative Inviolability of 'The Other': A Nonreligious Ground?" (forthcoming). See also Perry, "What Is 'Morality' Anyway?," at 81–88; Perry, *The Idea of Human Rights*, at 11–41.
49. This is the relevant part of the *Oxford English Dictionary*'s definition of "inviolable." See 8 Oxford English Dictionary 51 (2d ed., 1989).
50. In an otherwise laudatory review of a book by Frances Kamm, Jeff McMahon writes:

> The burden of the third and final part of the volume is to explain why it is generally not permissible for one to engage in killing even when, by doing so, one could prevent a greater number of killings from occurring. Here, Kamm's central contention is that people must be regarded as inviolable, as ends-in-themselves. . . . [Kamm's] arguments often raise difficult questions that the book fails to address. A conspicuous instance of this is Kamm's failure to identify the basis of our moral inviolability. Understanding the basis of our alleged inviolability is crucial both for determining whether it is plausible to regard ourselves as inviolable, and for fixing the boundaries of the class of inviolable beings. (Jeff McMahon, "When Not to Kill or Be Killed," *Times Literary Supplement*, Aug. 7, 1998, at 31 [reviewing Frances Kamm, *Morality, Mortality*, Volume 2: *Rights, Duties, and Status* (1997)].)

It is revealing that Kamm, one of the principal neo-Kantian moral philosophers among the younger generation of secular moral theorists, "conspicuously" fails in her otherwise rigorously argued book to tell her audience why – in virtue of what – persons are inviolable.

51. In the United States, liberal democracy's commitment to the true and full humanity of every person (without regard to race, etc.) is a constitutional commitment. See Perry, *We the People*, at 48–87. For government to make any political choice even partly on the ground that some persons are not inviolable, that some are not subjects of justice, is to violate the Fourteenth Amendment.

CHAPTER 4

1. Letter to Madame Christina of Lorraine, grand duchess of Tuscany (1615), in *Discoveries and Opinions of Galileo*, trans. Stillman Drake (Garden City, N.Y.: Doubleday, 1957), at 175, 181. See Ernan McMullin, "Galileo on Science and Scripture," in Peter Machamer, ed., *The Cambridge Companion to Galileo* (New York: Cambridge University Press, 1998), at 271.

2. In this chapter, I use the term same-sex "union" rather than same-sex "marriage" to avoid the dispute, which seems to me secondary, about whether the law should bestow the label "marriage" on a same-sex union. I am interested here in the question of whether the law should grant legal recognition to same-sex unions, whether or not the law calls these unions "marriages."

3. See, e.g., the editorial "Separate but Equal?," *New Republic*, Jan. 10, 2000, at 9. "As civil marriage is currently conceived and practiced in America, it contains no requirements and holds out no aspirations that homosexuals cannot achieve as easily as heterosexuals."

4. The state of Vermont is an exception. See note 7 and accompanying text.

5. David Matzko McCarthy, "Homosexuality and the Practices of Marriage," 13 Modern Theology 371, 372 (1997).

6. See Michael J. Perry, *We the People: The Fourteenth Amendment and the Supreme Court* (New York: Oxford University Press, 1999), at 131–50.

7. *Baker v. State* [Vermont], 744 A.2d 864, 867 (Vt. 1999).

> We hold that the State is constitutionally required to extend to same-sex couples the common benefits and protections that flow from marriage under Vermont law. Whether this ultimately takes the form of inclusion within the marriage laws themselves or a parallel "domestic partnership" system or some equivalent statutory alternative, rests with the Legislature. Whatever system is chosen, however, must conform with the constitutional imperative to afford all Vermonters the common benefit, protection, and security of the law. (Ibid.)

   In April 2000, in response to the Vermont Supreme Court's ruling, "the Vermont General Assembly passed 'An Act Relating to Civil Unions' ..., which affords same-sex couples many of the rights and responsibilities of marriage." "Domestic Relations – Same-Sex Couples – Vermont Creates System of Civil Unions. – Act Relating to Civil Unions, No. 91, Vt. Adv. Legis. Serv. 68 (LEXIS)," 114 Harvard L. Rev. 1421 (2001).

8. See Michael J. Perry, "What Is 'Morality' Anyway?" 45 Villanova L. Rev. 69 (2000) (the 1999 Donald M. Giannella Memorial Lecture).

9. See Michael J. Perry, *Love and Power: The Role of Religion and Morality in American Politics* (New York: Oxford University Press, 1991), at 132–38.

10. According to the 1998 edition of the *Statistical Abstract of the United States* (at p. 72), 84 percent of the "civilian noninstitutional population, 18 years old and over," identify themselves as Christian; 58 percent identify themselves as Protestant, 26 percent as Catholic.

11. Cf. Peter Cicchino, letter to Michael Perry, Sept. 2, 1998: "Consider the question of whether God's commands are intrinsically related to the flourishing

of human life. If God's commands are only accidentally related to human flourishing, then God is a capricious tyrant. If God's commands inhibit or prevent human flourishing, then God is a sadistic tyrant. If God's commands are intrinsically related to human flourishing, then presumably we have a reason for obeying those commands independent of whether God commands them: namely, our own good. . . ."

12. Letter to Michael Perry, Aug. 7, 1995.

13. Bernard Williams, *Ethics and the Limits of Philosophy* (Cambridge, Mass.: Harvard University Press, 1985), at 96.

14. Richard B. Hays, "Awaiting the Redemption of Our Bodies: The Witness of Scripture Concerning Homosexuality," in Jeffrey S. Siker, ed., *Homosexuality in the Church: Both Sides of the Debate* (Louisville, Ky.: Westminster / J. Knox Press, 1994), at 3, 7.

15. In addition to the pieces I am about to mention, see the pieces in the following collection: David L. Balch, ed., *Homosexuality, Science, and the "Plain Sense" of Scripture* (Grand Rapids, Mich.: W. B. Eerdmans, 2000). For a review of the most recent literature, see Deirdre Good, "The New Testament and Homosexuality: Are We Getting Anywhere?," 26 Religious Studies Rev. 307 (2000).

16. In Choon-Leong Seow, ed., *Homosexuality and Christian Community* (Louisville, Ky.: Westminster / J. Knox Press, 1996), at 86.

17. In Siker, ed., *Homosexuality in the Church*, at 3.

18. In Seow, ed., *Homosexuality and Christian Community*, at 39.

19. In John Corvino, ed., *In Same Sex: Debating the Ethics, Science, and Culture of Homosexuality* (Lanham, Md.: Rowman and Littlefield, 1997), at 93.

20. In Seow, ed., *Homosexuality and Christian Community*, at 28.

21. In Siker, ed., *Homosexuality in the Church*, at 18.

22. In Corvino, ed., *In Same Sex*, at 81.

23. In Patricia Beattie Jung and Ralph F. Smith, *Heterosexism: An Ethical Challenge* (Albany: State University of New York Press, 1993), at 61.

24. In Patricia Beattie Jung with Joseph Andrew Coray, eds., *Sexual Diversity and Catholicism: Toward the Development of Moral Theology* (Collegeville, Minn.: Liturgical Press, 2001), at 150.

25. In Seow, ed., *Homosexuality and Christian Community*, at 14.

26. In Siker, ed., *Homosexuality in the Church*, at 178.

27. For an important recent collection, see Jung with Coray, eds., *Sexual Diversity and Catholicism*.

28. See Gustav Niebuhr, "Laws Aside, Some in Clergy Quietly Bless Gay 'Marriage'," *New York Times*, Apr. 17, 1998, at A1.

29. Gustav Niebuhr, "Presbyterian Church Upholds Ban on Ordaining Homosexuals," *New York Times*, June 26, 1999, at A26.

30. Laurie Goldstein, "Presbyterian Court Upholds Holy Unions for Same-Sex Couples," *New York Times*, May 25, 2000, at A16.

31. Associated Press, "Presbyterians Reject Ban on Same-Sex Marriages," March 14, 2001.

32. For several informative essays by Christian ethicists about the role of scripture in moral discernment and argument, see Lisa Sowle Cahill and James F. Childress, eds., *Christian Ethics: Problems and Prospects* (Cleveland: Pilgrim Press, 1996).

33. John Mahoney, SJ, *The Making of Moral Theology: A Study of the Roman Catholic Tradition* (Oxford: Clarendon Press, 1987), at 327 (emphasis added).

34. John T. Noonan, Jr., "Development in Moral Doctrine," 54 Theological Studies 662, 676–77 (1993).

35. Margaret A. Farley, "An Ethic for Same-Sex Relations", in Robert Nugent, ed., *A Challenge to Love: Gay and Lesbian Catholics in the Church* (New York: Crossroad, 1983), at 93, 99–100.

36. Robin W. Lovin, "Empiricism and Christian Social Thought," *Annual of Society of Christian Ethics* 25, 41 (1982).

37. Margaret A. Farley, "The Role of Experience in Moral Discernment," in Cahill and Childress, *Christian Ethics*, at 134, 148.

38. Noonan, "Development in Moral Discourse," at 674 (emphasis added).

39. Margaret A. Farley, "Response to James Hanigan and Charles Curran," in Saul M. Olyan and Martha C. Nussbaum, eds., *Sexual Orientation and Human Rights in American Religious Discourse* (New York: Oxford University Press, 1998), at 101, 106.

40. Ibid.

41. Farley, "The Role of Experience in Moral Discernment," at 144–45.

42. Farley, "An Ethic for Same-Sex Relations," at 100.

43. Mahoney, *The Making of Moral Theology*, at 106, 107, 108. Mahoney then adds: "[B]ut such human thinking is not always or invariably at its best." (109) See also ibid. at 105–06: "['In principle', because t]he participation by man in God's eternal law through knowledge ... can be corrupted and depraved in such a way that the natural knowledge of good is darkened by passions and the habits of sin. For Aquinas, then, not all the conclusions of natural law are universally known, and the more one descends from the general to the particular, the more possible it is for reason to be unduly influenced by the emotions, or by customs, or by fallen nature."

    The American philosopher Robert Audi (who identifies himself as a Christian) seems to me naive about the vulnerability of "secular" argument relative to religious argument in suggesting that

    > good secular arguments for moral principles may be *better* reasons to believe those principles to be divinely enjoined than theological arguments for the principles, based on scripture or tradition. For the latter arguments seem (even) more subject than the former to cultural influences that may distort scripture or tradition or both; more vulnerable to misinterpretation of religious or other texts or to their sheer corruption across time and translation; and more liable to bias stemming from political or other non-religious aims. Granting, then, that theology and religious inspiration can be sources of ethical insight, we can also reverse this traditional idea: one may sometimes be better off trying to understand God through ethics than ethics through theology.

(Robert Audi, "Liberal Democracy and the Place of Religion in Politics," in Robert Audi and Nicholas Wolterstorff, *Religion in the Public Square* [Lanham, Md.: Rowman and Littlefield, 1997], at 1, 20–21.) Secular moral argument can be no less vulnerable to distorting "cultural influences" than religious argument. See Paul F. Campos, "Secular Fundamentalism," 94 Columbia L. Rev. 1814 (1994).

44. Basil Mitchell, "Should Law Be Christian?," *Law & Justice*, no. 96/97 (1988), at 12, 21.

45. Discussing usury, marriage, slavery, and religious freedom, John Noonan has demonstrated that:

> Wide shifts in the teaching of moral duties, once presented as part of Christian doctrine by the magisterium, have occurred. In each case one can see the displacement of a principle or principles that had been taken as dispositive – in the case of usury, that a loan confers no right to profit; in the case of marriage, that all marriages are indissoluble; in the case of slavery, that war gives a right to enslave and that ownership of a slave gives title to the slave's offspring; in the case of religious liberty, that error has no rights and that fidelity to the Christian faith may be physically enforced.... In the course of this displacement of one set of principles, what was forbidden became lawful (the cases of usury and marriage); what was permissible became unlawful (the case of slavery); and what was required became forbidden (the persecution of heretics).
> (Noonan, "Development in Moral Discourse," at 669.)

See also Seán Fagan, SM, "Interpreting the Catechism," 44 Doctrine & Life 412, 416–17 (1994):

> A catechism is supposed to "explain," but this one does not say why Catholics have to take such a rigid, absolutist stand against artificial contraception because it is papal teaching, but there is no reference to the explicit centuries-long papal teaching that Jews and heretics go to hell unless they convert to the Catholic faith, or to Pope Leo X, who declared that the burning of heretics is in accord with the will of the Holy Spirit. Six different popes justified and authorised the use of slavery. Pius XI, in an encyclical at least as important as *Humanae Vitae*, insisted that co-education is erroneous and pernicious, indeed against nature. The Catechism's presentation of natural law gives the impression that specific moral precepts can be read off from physical human nature, without any awareness of the fact that our very understanding of "nature" and what is "natural" can be coloured by our culture.

46. Richard John Neuhaus, "Reason Public and Private: The Pannenberg Project," *First Things*, March 1992, at 55, 57. Listen, too, to J. Bryan Hehir, who, as the principal drafter of the U.S. Catholic bishops' 1983 letter on nuclear deterrence (National Conference of Catholic Bishops, *Challenge of Peace: God's Promise and Our Response* [Washington, D.C.: United States Catholic Conference, 1983]), has some experience in the matter:

> [R]eligiously based insights, values and arguments at some point must be rendered persuasive to the wider civil public. There is legitimacy

to proposing a sectarian argument within the confines of a religious community, but it does violence to the fabric of pluralism to expect acceptance of such an argument in the wider public arena. When a religious moral claim will affect the wider public, it should be proposed in a fashion which that public can evaluate, accept or reject on its own terms. The [point] ... is not to banish religious insight and argument from public life[, but only to] establish[] a test for the religious communities to meet: to probe our commitments deeply and broadly enough that we can translate their best insights to others. (Bryan Hehir, "Responsibilities and Temptations of Power: A Catholic View," unpublished ms. [1988].)

The Dutch theologian Edward Schillebeeckx, who is Catholic, has written: "Even when their fundamental inspiration comes from a religious belief in God, ethical norms ... must be rationally grounded. None of the participants in [religiously grounded moral discourse] can hide behind an 'I can see what you don't see' and then require [the] others to accept this norm straight out." Edward Schillebeeckx, *The Schillebeeckx Reader*, ed. Robert Schreiter (New York: Crossroad, 1984). Even if we assume for the sake of argument that Schillebeeckx's principle should not govern moral discourse in *all* contexts – for example, in the context of a small, monistic, charismatic religious community – the principle should certainly govern moral discourse in *some* contexts, especially in the context of a large, pluralistic, democratic political community such as the United States.

47. *The Williamsburg Charter: A National Celebration and Reaffirmation of the First Amendment Religious Liberty Clauses* (Williamsburg, Va., 1988), at 22. Richard John Neuhaus, who was a principal drafter of the Williamsburg Charter, has cautioned that "publicly assertive religious forces will have to learn that the remedy for the naked public square is not naked religion in public. They will have to develop a mediating language by which ultimate truths can be related to the penultimate and prepenultimate questions of political and legal contest." Richard John Neuhaus, "Nihilism without the Abyss: Law, Rights, and Transcendent Good," 5 J. L. & Religion 53, 62 (1987). In commenting on this passage, Stanley Hauerwas has said that "[r]ather than condemning the Moral Majority, Neuhaus seeks to help them enter the public debate by basing their appeals on principles that are accessible to the public." Stanley Hauerwas, "A Christian Critique of Christian America," in J. Roland Pennock and John W. Chapman, eds., *Religion, Morality, and the Law* (New York: New York University Press, 1988), at 110, 118.

48. Siker, "Homosexual Christians, the Bible, and Gentile Inclusion," at 184. For Siker's criticism of such interpretations, see ibid. at 184–91.

49. I have discussed the value of ecumenical political dialogue elsewhere. See Perry, *Love and Power*, Chapter 6. See also David Lochhead, *The Dialogical Imperative: A Christian Reflection on Interfaith Encounter* (Maryknoll, N.Y.: Orbis Books, 1988), at 79. "In more biblical terms, the choice between monologue and dialogue is the choice between death and life. If to be human is to live in community with fellow human beings, then to alienate ourselves from

community, in monologue, is to cut ourselves off from our own humanity. To choose monologue is to choose death. Dialogue is its own justification."

50. Robin W. Lovin, "Why the Church Needs the World: Faith, Realism, and the Public Life," unpublished ms. (the 1988 Sorenson Lecture, Yale Divinity School).

51. Joseph Cardinal Bernardin, "The Consistent Ethic of Life After *Webster*," 19 Origins 741, 748 (1990) (emphasis added).

52. See, e.g., Corvino, ed., *In Same Sex*; David M. Estlund and Martha C. Nussbaum, eds., *Sex, Preference, and Family: Essays on Law and Nature* (New York: Oxford University Press, 1997); "Forum: Sexual Morality and the Possibility of 'Same-Sex Marriage'," 1997 American J. Jurisprudence 51–157; Olyan and Nussbaum, eds., *Sexual Orientation and Human Rights*; Siker, ed., *Homosexualty in the Church*; Andrew Sullivan, ed., *Same-Sex Marriage: Pro and Con* (New York: Vintage, 1997); Christopher Wolfe, ed., *Homosexuality and American Public Life* (Dallas: Spence Publishing, 1999).

53. In a letter to the editor, Francis Cardinal George, archbishop of Chicago, wrote: "No Catholic ministry to sexually active homosexuals can deliberately choose, out of a false sense of pity or spurious solidarity, not to call them from a lifestyle that is always spiritually and often physically destructive." *The Tablet* [London], Aug. 5, 2000, at 1049.

54. This collection of essays was published after I had finished drafting this chapter: Jung with Coray, eds., *Sexual Diversity and Catholicism*.

55. For a laudatory review of Kelly's book, see James F. Keenan, SJ, *The Tablet* [London], July 6, 1998, at 878–79.

56. 59 Theological Studies 60 (1998). Compare Janet E. Smith, "Thomas Aquinas on Homosexuality," in Wolfe, ed., *Homosexuality and American Public Life*, at 129.

57. In Nugent, ed., *A Challenge to Love*. See also Farley, "The Role of Experience in Moral Discernment"; Farley, "Response to James Hanigan and Charles Curran."

58. Fuller presented this paper at the fifty-fifth annual meeting of the Catholic Theological Society of America, June 2000, San Jose, California.

59. *Commonweal*, Jan. 26, 2001.

60. 13 Modern Theology 371 (1997). Cf. David Matzko McCarthy, "Sexual Utterances and Common Life," 16 Modern Theology 443 (2000).

61. In Estlund and Nussbaum, eds., *Sex, Preference, and Family*, at 227.

62. See Richard Westley, *Morality and Its Beyond* (Mystic, Ct.: Twenty-Third Publications, 1984), at 169–98.

63. The first essay (re)appears at 9 Notre Dame J. L., Ethics & Public Policy 11 (1995); the second appears at 1997 American J. Jurisprudence 97. I have commented critically on the first essay. See Michael J. Perry, *Religion in Politics: Constitutional and Moral Perspectives* (New York: Oxford University Press, 1997), at 85–96.

64. In Olyan and Nussbaum, eds., *Sexual Orientation and Human Rights*, at 63. See also James P. Hanigan, *Homosexuality: The Test Case for Christian Sexual Ethics* (New York: Paulist Press, 1988); James P. Hanigan, "Unity and Procreative

Meaning: The Inseparable Link," in Jung with Coray, eds., *Sexual Diversity and Catholicism*, at 22.

65. 1997 American J. Jurisprudence 135.
66. See note 44.
67. John M. Finnis, "Law, Morality, and 'Sexual Orientation'," 9 Notre Dame J. L., Ethics & Public Policy 11, 16 (1995).
68. W. Sibley Towner, "The Renewed Authority of Old Testament Wisdom for Contemporary Faith," in G. W. Coats and B. O. Long, eds., *Canon and Authority: Essays in Old Testament Religion and Authority* (Philadelphia: Fortress Press, 1977), at 146 (quoted in Seow, "A Heterotextual Perspective," at 21–22).
69. Not that there aren't many non-Catholic thinkers defending the morality of same-sex unions. For a sampling of the literature, see John Corvino, "Why Shouldn't Tommy and Jim Have Sex? A Defense of Homosexuality," in Corvino, ed., *In Same Sex*, at 3; Andrew Koppelman, "Is Marriage Inherently Heterosexual?" 1997 American J. Jurisprudence 51; Stephen Macedo, "Against the Old Sexual Morality of the New Natural Law," in Robert P. George, ed., *Natural Law, Liberalism, and Morality* (Oxford: Clarendon Press, 1996), at 27; Siker, "Homosexual Christians, the Bible, and Gentile Inclusion." Both Macedo and Koppelman address the arguments of the "new natural lawyers": John Finnis, Robert George, and others.
70. *Baker v. State* [Vermont], 744 A.2d 864, 889 (Vt. 1999).
71. See notes 33 and 34.
72. See note 10.
73. David Hollenbach, SJ, "Contexts of the Political Role of Religion: Civil Society and Culture," 30 San Diego L. Rev. 877, 894 (1993).
74. Ibid. at 894–95.
75. See notes 35 and 42 and accompanying text.
76. Farley, "The Role of Experience in Moral Discernment," at 148.
77. Not all morally conservative Christians reject or even marginalize "human reason" as a source of moral understanding. Many Catholics, for example, defend morally conservative positions on issues such as contraception and homosexuality not by rejecting "human reason" but by exercising it. John Finnis is a prominent example. See, e.g., Finnis, "Law, Morality, and 'Sexual Orientation'," at 16.
78. However, "[e]arly-nineteenth-century evangelicals . . . saw no radical disjunction between reason and revelation." John G. West, Jr., *The Politics of Revelation and Reason: Religion and Civic Life in the New Nation* (Lawrence: University Press of Kansas, 1996), at 121. "Most American evangelicals were more than willing to find an agreement between reason and revelation in the realm of morality." Ibid. at 120. See ibid. at 119–26.
79. David M. Smolin, "The Enforcement of Natural Law by the State: A Response to Professor Calhoun," 16 U. Dayton L. Rev. 318, 391–92 (1991).
80. Ibid.
81. Glenn Tinder, "Can We Be Good Without God?" *Atlantic Monthly*, December 1989, at 69, 83.
82. Ibid. at 83–84.

83. Mark Noll, *The Scandal of the Evangelical Mind* (Grand Rapids, Mich.: W. B. Eerdmans, 1994), at 207–08.
84. George Marsden, "Common Sense and the Spiritual Vision of History," in C. T. McIntire and Ronald A. Wells, eds., *History and Historical Understanding* (Grand Rapids, Mich.: W. B. Eerdmans, 1984), at 55, 59.
85. Quoted in Thomas Merton, ed., *The Wisdom of the Desert* (New York: New Directions, 1960), at 62.
86. Seow, "A Heterotextual Perspective," at 22.
87. Ibid. See ibid. at 14–27.
88. Michael J. Perry, *Morality, Politics, and Law* (New York: Oxford University Press, 1988), at 181–82. See also Perry, *Love and Power*, at 4.
89. See note 45.
90. John 13:34.
91. Robert N. Bellah, Foreword to Richard L. Smith, *AIDS, Gays and the American Catholic Church* (Cleveland: Pilgrim Press, 1994), at xii–xiii.
92. Of course, many Christians will and do conclude that the reflective yield of human experience, including contemporary human experience, does *not* put that traditional Christian belief into serious question. But the number of such Christians is diminishing sharply over time, and there is little if any reason to doubt that in the United States and kindred societies, that process will continue.
93. See note 1.

CHAPTER 5

1. Bernard Hoose, "Authority in the Church," 63 Theological Studies 107 (2002). See also Bernard Hoose, *Authority in Roman Catholicism* (Essex, England: Matthew James Publishing, 2002); Bernard Hoose, ed., *Authority in the Roman Catholic Church* (Aldershot, England, and Burlington, Vt.: Ashgate, 2002).
2. John T. McGreevy, "A Case of Doctrinal Development: John T. Noonan – Jurist, Historian, Author, Sage," *Commonweal*, Nov. 12, 2000, at 12, 17. See also Thomas P. Rausch, SJ, *Reconciling Faith and Reason* (Collegeville, Minn.: Liturgical Press, 2000), at 45–46: "A presentation of the Catholic tradition able to acknowledge not just development, but also change in the doctrinal tradition is a more honest one." Cf. Robert McClory, *Faithful Dissenters: Stories of Men and Women Who Loved and Changed the Church* (Maryknoll, N.Y.: Orbis Books, 2000).
3. The "magisterium" is the "teaching office and authority of the Catholic Church; also the hierarchy as holding this office." *The HarperCollins Encyclopedia of Catholicism*, ed. Richard P. McBrien et al. (New York: HarperCollins, 1995), at 805. "The whole episcopal college is the bearer of supreme magisterium, which it exercises both when dispersed throughout the world and when gathered in an ecumenical council. The pope, as head of the episcopal college, can exercise the supreme teaching authority that resides in this college." Ibid. "At the present time the term 'magisterium' refers, for all practical

purposes, to the hierarchical magisterium alone, especially that of the pope."
Ibid. at 807. For a fuller discussion, see ibid. at 805–08. See also Francis A.
Sullivan, "The Magisterium in the New Millennium," *America*, Aug. 27, 2001,
at 12; Hoose, *Authority in Roman Catholicism.*

4. Patricia Beattie Jung, "Introduction," in Patricia Beattie Jung with Joseph
Andrew Coray, eds., *Sexual Diversity and Catholicism: Toward the Development of
Moral Theology* (Collegeville, Minn.: Liturgical Press, 2001), at x, xxix n. 31.

5. Lindy Boggs was married to the the late Hale Boggs, a U.S. Representative from Louisiana, and is the mother of the journalist Cokie
Roberts.

6. "John Paul II on the American Experiment," *First Things*, April 1998, at 36,
37.

7. Is all this "seeming" an illusion? Well, if it is, then so much the better; I would
be relieved. But I don't think it is an illusion. See, e.g., Bishop James McHugh,
"Political Responsibility and 'Living the Gospel of Life,'" 29 Origins 190, 292
(1999):

> [A] bishop may establish a policy that protects people from being mis-
> led. Such a policy could contain the following elements for Catholic
> [public] officials who persist in their actions and statements contrary to
> the Gospel of Life.
>
> Such persons would not be invited:
> * To leadership positions in the diocese, parish, or other church agen-
>   cies or organizations.
> * To receive any type of honor or public recognition by church agen-
>   cies or organizations.
> * To serve as a chairperson or committee member of major church
>   celebrations or events, including fund-raising programs.
> * To exercise any liturgical ministry or public role in the celebration
>   of Mass or the sacraments.
> * To be speakers at graduation ceremonies, celebrated lectures or
>   other public events where the speaker is given positive recognition
>   or approval.

In October 2000, on the eve of the presidential election, Bishop McHugh repeated his position. See Bishop James McHugh, "Letters to Pastors: Building
a Culture of Life," 30 Origins 300 (2000). Bishop McHugh does not stand
alone. See, e.g., George F. Will, "Being 'Most Mentioned,'" *Newsweek*, June
12, 2000, at 84 (referrring to Erie, Pennsylvania, Bishop Donald Trautman's
decree that "public officials whose policies are opposed to church teachings
will not be featured participants at church events"). Consider, too, that in
a recent "working draft" of "recommended principles to guide policies and
programs affecting student life at Catholic colleges and universities," the
Cardinal Newman Society for the Preservation of Catholic Higher Education
stated:

> It is essential that no university funds, facilities, or other support en-
> able campus activities that present philosophies, causes, or organiza-
> tions which are not consistent with the teaching of the Catholic Church.

This would include the invitation of campus speakers, the collection of signatures for petitions, the posting of publicity, or other promotion of individuals or businesses. (Cardinal Newman Society for the Preservation of Catholic Higher Education, "Student Life Guidelines for the Catholic Campus: Recommended Principles to Guide Policies and Programs Affecting Student Life at Catholic Colleges and Universities," 7 [working draft, 11/10/00].)

8. See note 2. For a illustrative statement of the position that "faithful" Catholics owe "religious assent" to the teaching of the magisterium, see Gerard V. Bradley, "Grounds for Assent," *Commonweal,* Sept. 9, 1994, at 29 (letter to the editor). Compare Garry Wills, *Papal Sin* (New York: Doubleday, 2000), at 6:

> The priests [cannot] keep a straight face or an honest heart – to be truly concerned for those they serve – if they echo what Rome is saying about women or the priesthood, marriage or natural law. Their own integrity rebels, against the calculus of personal gain or the pressures of careerism. The arguments for much of what passes as current church doctrine are so intellectually contemptible that mere self-respect forbids a man to voice them as his own.

9. The list of examples could go on for quite some time: nuclear deterrence, economic justice, immigration, etc.
10. Hoose, "Authority in the Church," at 110.
11. These passages are from a brief excerpt of the bishops' 101-page text – an excerpt translated into English – that appears on pages 1–3 of the Winter 2000 issue of the Canadian journal *The Ecumenist.*
12. Catechism of the Catholic Church, par. 2357. Francis Cardinal George, archbishop of Chicago, has written that "[n]o Catholic ministry to sexually active homosexuals can deliberately choose, out of a false sense of pity or spurious solidarity, not to call them from a lifestyle that is always spiritually and often physically destructive." *The Tablet* [London], Aug. 5, 2000, at 1049.
13. John T. Noonan, Jr., "Development in Moral Doctrine," 54 Theological Studies 662, 674 (1993) (emphasis added).
14. Joseph Cardinal Bernardin, "The Consistent Ethic of Life After *Webster,*" 19 Origins 741, 748 (1990) (emphasis added).
15. With respect to the "how to persuade" question, such Catholics might concur in the judgment of the Williamsburg Charter: "Arguments for public policy should be more than private convictions shouted out loud. For persuasion to be principled, private convictions should be translated into publicly accessible claims. Such public claims should be made publicly accessible . . . because they must engage those who do not share the same private convictions. . . ." *The Williamsburg Charter: A National Celebration and Reaffirmation of the First Amendment Religious Liberty Clauses* (Williamsburg, Va., 1988), at 22. They might also concur in the judgment of Richard John Neuhaus, who was a principal drafter of the Williamsburg Charter: "[P]ublicly assertive religious forces will have to learn that the remedy for the naked public square is not naked religion in public. They will have to develop a mediating language by

which ultimate truths can be related to the penultimate and prepenultimate questions of political and legal contest." Richard John Neuhaus, "Nihilism without the Abyss: Law, Rights, and Transcendent Good," 5 J. L. & Religion 53, 62 (1987). In commenting on this passage, Stanley Hauerwas has said that "[r]ather than condemning the Moral Majority, Neuhaus seeks to help them enter the public debate by basing their appeals on principles that are accessible to the public." Stanley Hauerwas, "A Christian Critique of Christian America," in J. Roland Pennock and John W. Chapman, eds., *Religion, Morality, and the Law* (New York: New York University Press, 1988), at 110, 118.

16. 29 Origins 625 (2000). The "preliminary note" to the document states:
    The study of the topic "The Church and the Faults of the Past" was proposed to the International Theological Commission by its president, Joseph Cardinal Ratzinger, in view of the celebration of the jubilee year 2000. A subcommission was prepared to prepare this study. . . . The general discussion of this theme took place in numerous meetings of the subcommission and during the plenary session of the International Theological Commission held in Rome from 1998 to 1999. By written vote, the present text was approved in *forma specifica* by the commission and was then submitted to the president, Cardinal Ratzinger, prefect of the Congregation for the Doctrine of the Faith, who gave his approval for its publication.

17. Ibid. at 629.

18. Ibid.

19. Ibid. at 635.

20. Francis A. Sullivan, SJ, "The Papal Apology," *America*, April 8, 2000, at 17, 19, 22.

21. See Garry Wills, "The Vatican Regrets," *New York Review of Books*, May 25, 2000, at 19. "This constant distinction between 'the Church' and its children, or members, or erring sons and daughters, goes against the [Second] Vatican Council's definition of the Church as the whole 'people of God'." Ibid. See also Gregory Baum, "The Church We Love: A Conversation with Miroslav Volf," *The Ecumenist*, Winter 2000, at 13, 15:
    I still remember my excitement when reading – in the fifties! – Hans Urs von Balthasar's long essay, "*Casta Meretrix*" (in English: "The Chaste Whore"). In this essay, von Balthasar argues that church fathers and mediaeval theologians often spoke of the Church in paradoxical language; they saw the Church as at once holy and sinful, ever faithful and ever in need of conversion, as both *virgo* (virgin) and *meretrix* (whore). These authors recognized contradictory dimensions in the history of the believing community. On the one hand, there is the indefectible divine presence in the Church, while on the other hand there are the Church's alliance with the powerful, its subservience to the rich, and its unwillingness to be led by the Spirit. Again, these failures are met by the divine gifts, the gospel message and the sacraments, ever summoning and enabling the Church to repent and renew its fidelity. After

the Reformation, this paradoxical discourse was no longer used in the Catholic Church.

Volf's critique of Zizioulas' and Ratzinger's ecclesiology is well taken. According to both of these theologians, Christ's identification with the Church is so complete that the Church must be seen as his earthly body, a sacred subject, the bride of Christ "without spot or wrinkle," standing over and above the historical gathering of the faithful. Since the Reformation, the Catholic Church, relying upon this ecclesiology, has been increasingly unable to acknowledge its faults and failures. In this view, the Church *qua* Church cannot sin. The members of the Church are sinners, and some of them sin in the name of the Church. However, the Church remains holy, ever free of sin. Today Pope John Paul II wants the Catholic Church in various parts of the world to confess its infidelities. Nonetheless, he continues to insist that these betrayals were committed by the sons and daughters of the Church and not by the Church itself, which remains immaculate, as sacred subject. If the Church's approval of slavery, its blessing on colonialism, its identification with the powerful, its teaching of contempt for Jews and other outsiders and its opposition to religious liberty and human rights are simply failings of the Church's sons and daughters, and do not involve the Church as such, then the Church is no longer a visible, historical entity. Instead, it follows the Lutheran proposal and becomes an invisible church.

22. Noonan, "Development in Moral Doctrine," at 669.
23. Seán Fagan, SM, "Interpreting the Catechism," 44 Doctrine & Life 412, 416–17 (1994)
24. Noonan, "Development in Moral Doctrine," at 669.
25. Fagan, "Interpreting the Catechism," at 416.
26. Ibid. Seán Fagan's entire paragraph bears quotation here:

A catechism is supposed to "explain," but this one does not say why Catholics have to take such a rigid, absolutist stand against artificial contraception because it is papal teaching, but there is no reference to the explicit centuries-long papal teaching that Jews and heretics go to hell unless they convert to the Catholic faith, or to Pope Leo X, who declared that the burning of heretics is in accord with the will of the Holy Spirit. Six different popes justified and authorised the use of slavery. Pius XI, in an encyclical at least as important as *Humanae Vitae*, insisted that co-education is erroneous and pernicious, indeed against nature. The Catechism's presentation of natural law gives the impression that specific moral precepts can be read off from physical human nature, without any awareness of the fact that our very understanding of "nature" and what is "natural" can be coloured by our culture. (Ibid. at 416–17.)

27. Robert N. Bellah, "Foreword" to *Richard L. Smith, AIDS, Gays and the American Catholic Church* (Cleveland: Pilgrim Press, 1994), at xii–xiii.
28. David Hollenbach, SJ, "Contexts of the Political Role of Religion: Civil Society and Culture," 30 San Diego L. Rev. 877, 894–95 (1993).

29. Margaret A. Farley, "An Ethic for Same-Sex Relations," in Robert Nugent, ed., *A Challenge to Love: Gay and Lesbian Catholics in the Church* (New York: Crossroad, 1983), at 93, 100.
30. Margaret A. Farley, "The Role of Experience in Moral Discernment," in Lisa Sowle Cahill and James F. Childress, eds., *Christian Ethics: Problems and Prospects* (Cleveland: Pilgrim Press, 1996), at 134, 148.
31. See note 8 (Bradley).
32. John Mahoney, SJ, *The Making of Moral Theology: A Study of the Roman Catholic Tradition* (Oxford: Clarendon Press, 1987), at 327.
33. See note 1 and accompanying text.
34. Margaret O'Brien Steinfels, "Dissent and Communion," *Commonweal*, Nov. 18, 1994, reprinted in Patrick Jordan and Paul Baumann, eds., *Commonweal Confronts the Century: Liberal Convictions, Catholic Tradition* (New York: Simon and Schuster, 1999), at 324, 326–31.
35. Ibid. at 326–27. (Steinfels adds: "But I do want to argue ... that in the practical, everyday life of the church, the question of distinguishing between responsible and irresponsible dissent, between dissent in the service of communion and dissent destructive of it, is less than we often suppose a matter of intellectual propositions, and more often a matter of conduct, of attitude, of affection, and of heart." Ibid.) Cf. Wills, *Papal Sin*, at 6:

    Who am I – or who is anyone except the Pope – to decide what a Catholic may or may not accept as binding doctrine? That is a serious question, not just the growling of authoritarians who feel they have some of the Pope's excommunicating power themselves. But the question is based on an assumption that is not only challengeable but extremely unhealthy. It assumes that the whole test of Catholicism, the essence of the faith, is submission to the Pope. During long periods of the church's history, that was not the rule – Saint Augustine, for one, would have flunked such a test. And today it is a test that would decimate the ranks of current churchgoers. It is not a position that has a solid body of theology behind it, no matter how common it is as a popular notion (*vulgaris opinio*).

36. The disputed question of "infallibility" rears its troublesome head here. (See Hans Küng, "Waiting for Vatican III," *The Tablet* [London], Dec. 16, 1995, at 1616. See also Wills, *Papal Sin*, at 233–74. What is the relationship between the ITC's *Memory and Reconciliation: The Church and the Faults of the Past* and the doctrine of infallibility? For one view, see Wills, "The Vatican Regrets," at 19.) This is not the place – and, in any event, I am certainly not the person – to address the question. Two points bear emphasis, however. The first point was stated by Richard McCormick in an entry he wrote for the *Encyclopedia of Catholicism*. (The entry: "magisterium and morality.")

    [According to the Dogmatic Constitution on the Church (*Lumen Gentium*) promulgated by the Second Vatican Council (1962–65),] the charism of infallibility is coextensive with the "deposit of divine revelation" (n. 25). This would seem to exclude from infallibility those moral positions that are not revealed. If that is the case, the magisterium can be competent in concrete moral questions without being infallibly competent.

This question remains a disputed one, but it is hardly very practical since, in the view of most theologians, the magisterium has never taught infallibly on the level of concrete morals, nor would such authority be required for the Church to fulfill its mandate to provide moral guidance. (*The HarperCollins Encyclopedia of Catholicism*, at 808.)

The second point was stated by Nicholas Lash in a recent essay in *The Tablet*: The teaching that the Church is incapable of ordaining women has "not been 'received' by the faithful of the Church as expressive of their Catholic belief." So we read in the report commissioned by the Australian bishops, *Women and man: one in Jesus Christ*, on the participation of women in the Catholic Church in Australia. Yet the Pope and the Congregation for the Doctrine of the Faith have asserted the contrary. What are we to make of this?

The First Vatican Council taught that there are – however unusually and exceptionally – certain circumstances in which we may trust that a papal utterance shares in "that infallibility with which the divine Redeemer wished to endow his Church." The reference is to the whole Church: it is because the Church is kept in truth that, in certain circumstances, we may trust that what its chief bishop says is true. But the articulation of doctrine needs normally to be recognised or "received" by the Church at large. *This is an important criterion by which a dogmatic statement may be recognised as such.* It is the discriminating exercise of Christian faith. In recent years, however, there has been an increasing tendency for the Roman congregations to behave as if faith were only exercised through indiscriminate obedience. (Nicholas Lash, "Waiting for the Echo," *The Tablet* [London], March 4, 2000, at 309 [emphasis added].)

See also Richard Westley, "We Are Makers of Love," *Praying*, May-June 1994, at 28, 31: "Forgotten is the old theological dictum that the 'teaching' church can only teach what the 'believing' church believes. Having it the wrong way around skews everything; it discounts the religious experience of all us believers and allows the church to be a curator of all truth, so that no more truth can get into the enterprise." For further discussion of the point that "[t]he Holy Spirit works not just in the hierarchy [but] is present in the entire Church," see Rausch, *Reconciling Faith and Reason*, at 62ff.

37. This is not to deny that some religious believers too would like to marginalize the role of religion in politics.

38. Richard Rorty, "Religion as Conversation-stopper," in Richard Rorty, *Philosophy and Social Hope* (New York: Penguin, 1999), at 168, 169.

39. See note 11. "Bishop Roger Ébacher of the Gatineau-Hull diocese, one of two bishops who served as lead authors of the document, said that modern culture's democratic ethos can help the church recover forgotten aspects of its own tradition. 'We must rediscover the truth that the church is the people of God, it's the community,' he said.... Ébacher noted that synods, collegiality and subsidiarity were Catholic ideas that helped form the basis for

modern democracy." John L. Allen, Jr., "Quebec Bishops Praise Autonomy, Democracy," *National Catholic Reporter*, Apr. 21, 2000, at 5.

40. David O'Brien, *Public Catholicism* (New York: Macmillan, 1989), at 7.
41. USCC Administrative Board, "Faithful Citizenship: Civic Responsibility for a New Millennium," 29 Origins 309, 317 n. 1 (1999).
42. Ibid. at 317.
43. Kenneth Himes, OFM, "Catholic Political Responsibility in This Time and Place," 29 Origins 614, 616 (2000).

CHAPTER 6

1. *Reinhold Niebuhr, Theologian of Public Life*, ed. Larry Rasmussen (Minneapolis, Minn.: Fortress Press, 1989), at 126–27.
2. Carey Goldberg with Janet Elder, "Public Still Backs Abortion, but Wants Limits, Poll Says," *New York Times*, Jan. 16, 1998, at A1.
3. See generally Elizabeth Mensch and Alan Freeman, *The Politics of Virtue: Is Abortion Debatable?* (Durham, N.C.: Duke University Press, 1993).
4. This question is prior to the question of whether the law should punish the woman who has an abortion or just those, or some of those, who assist her in having an abortion. Cf. M. Cathleen Kaveny, "Toward a Thomistic Perspective on Abortion and the Law in Contemporary America," 55 The Thomist 343, 393 (1991): "[C]riminal sanctions . . . should be directed primarily at physicians rather than women, who are likely to be obtaining even the most morally dubious abortions under conditions of duress."
5. 410 U.S. 113, 163.
6. Sheryl Gay Stolberg, "Shifting Certainties in the Abortion War," *New York Times*, Jan. 11, 1998, §4, at 3.
7. 410 U.S. at 164.
8. See the editorials "*Roe*: Twenty-Five Years Later," *First Things*, January 1998, at 9, and "Dead Reckoning," *National Review*, Jan. 26, 1998. Cf. Carey Goldberg with Janet Elder, "Public Still Backs Abortion": "[T]he country remains irreconcilably riven over what many consider to be the most divisive American issue since slavery, with half the population considering abortion murder, the poll found. Despite a quarter-century of lobbying, debating and protesting by the camps that call themselves 'pro-choice' and 'pro-life,' that schism has remained virtually unaltered."
9. I also explained why the Court's ruling in *Planned Parenthood of Southeastern Pennsylvania v. Casey*, 505 U.S. 833 (1992), was mistaken, too. See note 10.
10. See Michael J. Perry, *We the People: The Fourteenth Amendment and the Supreme Court* (New York: Oxford University Press, 1999), at 151–68, 177–79.
11. Connecticut's law, for example, provides that no abortion can be performed after viability unless necessary to preserve the women's life or health. Connecticut General Statutes, §19a–602(b). Only ten states are *without* such laws: Alaska, Colorado, Hawaii, Mississippi, New Hampshire, New Jersey, New Mexico, Oregon, Vermont, and West Virginia.

178

12. See Michael J. Perry, "What Is 'Morality' Anyway?" 45 Villanova L. Rev. 69 (2000) (the 1999 Donald M. Giannella Memorial Lecture).
13. Even orthodox Catholic teaching allows that it is not immoral to take action that results in the death of the fetus in order to save the life of the mother. See, e.g., Norman Ford, SDB, "Letter: Morality after Rape," *The Tablet* [London], June 19, 1999, at 846: "[T]he Catholic Church rightly opposes direct abortion, i.e. one willed as an end or as a means, since it is the deliberate killing of an innocent human being. But a procedure performed with the purpose of saving a women's life by removing a life threatening ectopic pregnancy would not be a direct abortion, even if it is foreseen that the death of the fetus would result as a side-effect." But cf. Leslie C. Griffin, "*Evangelium Vitae*: Abortion," in Kevin Wm. Wildes, SJ, and Alan C. Mitchell, eds., *Choosing Life: A Dialogue on Evangelium Vitae* (Washington, D.C.: Georgetown University Press, 1997), at 159:

    > The direct/indirect distinction has faced extensive criticism [within the Catholic Church] as an inadequate formulation of the Church's theological tradition. "No direct killing of the innocent" has been described as a rule, not a principle, and so subject to exceptions. On the subject of abortion, the direct/indirect distinction has been criticized for its excess physicalism. The principle allows, for example, the excision of the cancerous uterus and the ectopic pregnancy, but not other measures calculated to save the life of the mother. Moreover, in these two situations it requires that the mother's fertility not be spared.

14. A fertilized ovum, or zygote, becomes a human embryo after two weeks and a human fetus after eight weeks.
15. 8 Oxford English Dictionary 51 (2d ed., 1989).
16. Robert F. George, book review, 88 American Political Science Rev. 445, 445–46 (1994) (reviewing Ronald Dworkin, *Life's Dominion: An Argument About Abortion, Euthaniasia, and Individual Freedom* [1993]).
17. Ibid. at 446.
18. See Patrick Lee, *Abortion and Unborn Human Life* (Washington, D.C.: Catholic University of America Press, 1996).
19. See, e.g., Germain Grisez. "When Do People Begin?," *Proceedings of the American Catholic Philosophical Association* 64: 27 (1990).
20. See, e.g., John Finnis, "Abortion and Health Care Ethics," in Ranaan Gillon, ed., *Principles of Health Care Ethics* (New York: Wiley, 1994), at 547.
21. See, e.g., Robert P. George, "Public Reason and Political Conflict: Abortion and Homosexuality," 106 Yale L. J. 2475 (1997).
22. Moreover, there is skepticism in some quarters about the extent to which the "Catholic" argument is "compatible with Catholic tradition." See Daniel A. Dombrowski and Robert Deltete, *A Brief, Liberal, Catholic Defense of Abortion* (Urbana: University of Illinois Press, 2000). See also Jean Porter, "Is the Embryo a Person? Arguing with the Catholic Traditions," *Commonweal*, Feb. 8, 2002, at 8.
23. For the reader interested in exploring both (1) the moral position of the Catholic Church in the abortion controversy and (2) the Church's political

role in the controversy (i.e., its political role in the United States), see R. Randall Rainey, SJ, and Gerard Magill, eds., *Abortion and Public Policy: An Interdisciplinary Investigation within the Catholic Tradition* (Omaha, Neb.: Creighton University Press, 1996).

24. See Richard A. McCormick, "double effect, principle of," in Richard P. McBrien, ed., *The HarperCollins Encyclopedia of Catholicism* (New York: HarperCollins, 1995), at 432.

25. See George, "Public Reason and Political Conflict," at 2491–95.

26. For a different argument that most abortions are immoral, see Don Marquis, "Why Most Abortions Are Wrong," 5 Advances in Bioethics 215 (1999). For critical commentary on Marquis's argument, see Bonnie Steinbock, "Why Most Abortions Are Not Wrong," 5 Advances in Bioethics 245 (1999); see also Walter Sinnott-Armstrong, "You Can't Lose What You Ain't Never Had: A Reply to Marquis on Abortion," 96 Philosophical Studies 59 (1997); Earl Conee, "Metaphysics and the Morality of Abortion," 108 Mind 619, 638–44 (1999); Jeff McMahan, *The Ethics of Killing: Problems at the Margins of Life* (New York: Oxford University Press, 2002), at 270–71.

27. Laurence H. Tribe, "Will the Abortion Fight Ever End?: A Nation Held Hostage," *New York Times*, July 2, 1990, at A13.

28. See, e.g., Mary Warnock, *An Intelligent Person's Guide to Ethics* (London: Duckworth, 1998), at 43–49. (reporting and defending the position of the Committee of Enquiry concerning the Embryology Bill, which the British Parliament, following the committee's recommendation, enacted into law in 1990):

> Before fourteen days from fertilisation, . . . the embryo is not really one thing, but a loose collection of cells that have not yet differentiated (often referred to as the pre-embryo). Any one of these cells may take on any role when the embryo forms, or may become part of the placenta, rather than of the embryo itself. The cells are totipotent. Moreover for up to fourteen days it is possible that twinning will take place, and that there will, if normal development occurs, be two individuals who are born, rather than one. It is therefore difficult for me, or anyone else, to trace my origin as an individual back beyond the fourteen day stage to the stage when I might have been two. Who, which of the two, would "I" be? At about fourteen days, however, what is known as the "primitive streak" appears, which is a piling up of cells, as they reproduce themselves, at the caudal end of the embryonic disc; and this is the first beginning of what will become the spinal cord and central nervous system of the embryo. From this moment on, the embryo as a whole grows and develops extremely rapidly, and the cells are differentiated into their future functions. . . . [There is] a morally significant difference between the pre-and post-fourteen-day cells, in that only after fourteen days can the human individual properly be said to exist. . . .
>
> It is sometimes argued against this that the individual human must exist before the appearance of the primitive streak, because all of the genome, the complete set of the hereditary factors of the embryo, is

already in place from fertilisation onwards. But this argument suggests that an individual human is nothing except his genome. This cannot be true. For one thing, the whole genetic make-up of a person can be discovered from a small bit of tissue, or a drop of saliva; yet we do not think of these as *being* the person. Moreover it is his whole developing body and brain which distinguishes him from other individuals. Even identical twins, whose genome is shared, develop differently from one another at the level of the functioning and thus the development of their brains. It is perfectly consistent, therefore, to hold that though the genetic factors in an individual's development may be given at the zygote stage (that is the one-cell stage immediately following fertilisation of egg and sperm), the individual himself has not yet come into being.

...

It would ... be much clearer and less misleading if people asked [not when human life begins, but] at what stage an embryo becomes morally significant; or at what stage we ought to start to treat a human embryo as we treat other human beings. It would then be clear that no further scientific knowledge would settle the question. It is a matter of ethical decision, a decision that society had to make in the period of consultation before the Embryology Act was passed, and Parliament had to make during the passage of the Bill. During the passage of the Bill there was no party whip involved. Each member of both Houses voted freely according to conscience. For what is at issue, as I have said, is the moral status to be accorded to the very early embryo in the laboratory. There are no analogies to help us here, and it is of no use to scan Holy Writ for an answer. Until a few years earlier there had been no such entities as separate four- or sixteen-cell embryos, existing outside the body. The question was new. Of course the science of embryonic development had a bearing on the moral decision that had to be taken; no one can make a sound moral judgement without knowledge of the facts about which they are to judge. And a close scrutiny of the facts may seem almost necessarily to dictate a moral judgement. Thus, in my own case, and that of a majority in both Houses, the very fact of the development of the primitive streak, the true emergence of one single individual, on however physically tiny a scale, seemed to dictate the judgement that one could treat the collection of cells before this stage differently from its treatment thereafter, and that, given the immense benefits that will come from research using these very early embryos, or pre-embryos, it was right that they should be used.

... [T]he embryo develops gradually from the beginning of the process of fertilisation, and it is for us to value the emerging life as we think right, according to its development. The then Archbishop of York, John Habgood, put this very clearly, in defending the fourteen-day cut-off point for the use of embryos for research (*Hansard*, 7th December 1989): "Scientists in general and biologists in particular deal mostly in continuities and in gradual changes from one state to another. This is

true of evolution, in which the transition from the pre-human to the human took place over countless generations. There was never a precise moment when it could have been said, 'Here is a hominid and here is a man.' But this is not to deny that as a result of the process there emerged a profound and indeed crucial set of differences between hominids and men. The same is true of individual lives . . . It seems strange to a biologist that all the weight of moral argument should be placed on one definable moment at the beginning. What matters is the process." And he went on to say, to the alarm of some, "Christians are no more required to believe that humanness is created in an instant than we are required to believe in the historical existence of Adam and Eve." (This led at a later stage of the debate, when someone remarked that no Christian could countenance research using early embryos, and it was pointed out that the Archbishop had argued in favor of it, to the reply that it was well known that the Archbishop was not a Christian.)
. . .
. . . The central question, What status should be accorded to the early embryo?, had to be settled by different means. And the only means available was the degree to which people felt that the early embryo was in fact, to all intents and purposes, a child. For, as I have suggested, no one would countenance the use of children for research, still less their subsequent destruction. As it turned out, a majority felt that the early embryo, before it had formed itself into a single individual and (having as yet no central nervous system) before it was capable of even rudimentary sensation or perception, was not sufficiently like a child to be accorded the status of a child. Therefore research was permitted. Utilitarian considerations came in, insofar as the benefits to the infertile and to society at large were cited in justification of research. The consequences to the embryos were discounted.

29. For a learned, thoughtful discussion of the difficult but important question of "personhood," see Stanley Rudman, *Concepts of Person and Christian Ethics* (Cambridge: Cambridge University Press, 1997). For a recent collection of writings by Christian thinkers, see "Personhood: Beginnings and Endings," 6 *Christian Bioethics* 3–122 (2000).

30. Daniel Callahan, *Abortion, Law, Choice and Morality* (New York: Macmillan, 1970), at 497–98 (emphasis added).

31. See, e.g., Joseph Fletcher, "Indicators of Humanhood: A Tentative Profile," *Hastings Center Report* 2 (1972); Mary Ann Warren, "On the Moral and Legal Status of Abortion," in James A. Sterba, ed., *Morality in Practice* (Belmont, Calif.: Wadsworth, 1980), at 144–45; James Rachels, *The End of Life* (New York: Oxford University Press, 1986), at 5; Joan C. Callahan, "The Fetus and Fundamental Rights," in Patricia Beattie Jung and Thomas A. Shannon, eds., *Abortion & Catholicism: The American Debate* (New York: Crossroad, 1988), at 217; Carol A. Tauer, "Abortion: Embodiment and Prenatal Development," in Lisa Sowle Cahill and Margaret A. Farley, eds., *Embodiment, Morality, and Medicine* (Dortrecht: Kluwer, 1995), at 75; Dombrowski and Deltete, *A Brief,*

Liberal, Catholic Defense of Abortion. For a recent example (which criticizes some earlier examples), see Jeffrey H. Reiman, *Critical Moral Liberalism: Theory and Practice* (Lanham, Md.: Rowman and Littlefield, 1997), at 189–210. In Chapter 8 ("Abortion, Infanticide, and the Asymmetric Value of Human Life"), Reiman argues that human fetuses (and indeed human infants) lack a property that a human being must have if we are to adjudge him or her inviolable: "the *subjective* awareness that one is already alive and counting on staying alive.... The loss to an aware individual of the life whose continuation she is counting on, is a loss that can only exist once an aware individual exists." Two years later, Reiman provided a more elaborate version of his argument. See Jeffrey Reiman, *Abortion and the Ways We Value Human Life* (Lanham, Md.: Rowman and Littlefield, 1999), at 10–11.

32. Lee, *Abortion and Unborn Human Life*, at 2–3.
33. Peter Steinfels, "The Search for an Alternative," *Commonweal*, Nov. 20, 1981, reprinted in Patrick Jordan and Paul Baumann, eds., *Commonweal Confronts the Century: Liberal Convictions, Catholic Tradition* (New York: Simon and Schuster, 1999), at 204, 209–11. Cf. Porter, "Is the Enbryo a Person?," at 8: "[We Catholics] have not convinced our fellow citizens that embryonic stem cell research is morally wrong because we have not convinced them that the embryo, from the first moment of its existence, is a human person in the fullest sense, with the same right to life as anyone else." Steinfels went on, in his essay, to recommend

> the protection of unborn life not from conception but from that point when not one but a whole series of arguments and indicators have converged to support the "humanness" of the unborn.
>
> The goal, in sum, should be the prohibition of abortion after eight weeks of development. At this point, when the embryo is now termed a fetus, all organs are present that will later be developed fully, the heart has been pumping for a month; the unborn individual has a distinctively human appearance, responds to stimulation of its nose or mouth, and is over an inch in size. Electrical activity in its brain is now discernible.... [A]t this point "with a good magnifier the fingerprints could be detected. Every document is available for a national identity card."
>
> The argument is not that this is the "magic moment" when "human life" begins. The argument is rather that this is one moment when an accumulation of evidence should compel a majority, even in a pluralist society and despite whatever obscurities about early life continue to be debated, to agree that the unborn individual now deserves legal protection. After this point, abortion should be permitted only for the most serious reasons: endangerment of the mother's life or risk of her incapacitation.... (Steinfels, "The Search for an Alternative," at 211–12.)

34. Ibid. at 204.
35. Of course, the claim that a human being is not inviolable (or not a "person" and so not inviolable) unless and until he or she possesses the proposed property is controversial among moral philosophers – as is the claim that a sufficient condition of an entity's being inviolable is that the entity be a

human being. All who defend the former claim necessarily challenge the latter claim. For responses to such challenges by those who defend the latter claim – that is, for critiques of instances of the former claim – see, e.g., Lee, *Abortion and Unborn Human Life*, at 7–68; Robert E. Joyce, "Personhood and the Conception Event," 52 New Scholasticism 97 (1978) (at p. 100, Joyce comments critically on Daniel Callahan's argument [see note 30]); Diane Nutwell Irving, "Scientific and Philosophical Expertise: An Evaluation of the Arguments on 'Personhood'," *Linacre Quarterly*, February 1993, at 18.

36. Garry Wills, *Papal Sin* (New York: Doubleday, 2000), at 229.

37. Ibid.

38. Jeff McMahan, "When Not to Kill or Be Killed," *Times Literary Supplement*, Aug. 7, 1998, at 31 (reviewing Frances Kamm, *Morality, Mortality*, Volume 2: *Rights, Duties, and Status* [1997]).

39. Ibid.

40. See David Smith, MSC, "What Is Christian Teaching on Abortion?," 42 Doctrine & Life 305, 316 (1992) (focusing on Britain and Ireland):

> As can be observed from this brief survey of certain Christian Churches, all agree that the human embryo has "value" and must be respected. The disagreement concerns what precisely is the "value" of the human embryo. One view, represented explicitly by the Roman Catholic Church, states that it has exactly the same value as any other human being. Another view, represented by a strong body of opinion in the Church of England, asserts that its value, prior to individuation (consciousness), is less than that of a human being in the proper sense of the word. A third view, represented by the Methodist Conference, would argue that its value depends on its stage of development: thus a progressively increasing value. The Baptist Union seems to favour a similar position, as does the Church in Wales and the Free Churches.

41. See Michael J. Perry, "The Putative Inviolability of 'The Other': A Nonreligious Ground?" (forthcoming). See also Perry, "What Is 'Morality' Anyway?," at 81–88; Perry, *The Idea of Human Rights*, at 11–41.

42. Kevin Wm. Wildes, SJ, "In the Service of Life: *Evangelium Vitae* and Medical Research," in Wildes and Mitchell, eds., *Choosing Life*, at 186, 190.

43. This is Robert Joyce's view. See Joyce, "Personhood and the Conception Event," at 100.

44. Steinfels, "The Search for an Alternative," at 209 (emphasis deleted).

45. Cf. Tauer, "Abortion," at 89–90 (suggesting that, and why, "the view that there is an objective point at which each human life begins, independent of the perspectives and conceptual frameworks of moral agents and communities, is properly questioned by the modern or postmodern thinker ... ").

46. See note 41 and accompanying text.

47. J. M. Winter and D. M. Joslin, eds., *R. H. Tawney's Commonplace Book* (Cambridge: Cambridge University Press, 1972), at 67. Tawney wrote the quoted passage in his diary on Aug. 13, 1913. Three days earlier, on Aug. 10, he had quoted in his diary T. W. Price, Midland secretary of the Workers' Educational Association and lecturer at Birmingham University: "Unless a

man believes in spiritual things – in God – altruism is absurd. What is the sense of it? Why shld [sic] a man recognize any obligation to his neighbor, unless he believes that he has been put in the world for a special purpose and has a special work to perform in it? A man's relations to his neighbors become meaningless unless there is some higher power above them both." Ibid. Cf. Dennis Prager, "Can We Be Good without God?," 9 Ultimate Issues 3, 4 (1993): "If there is no God, you and I are purely the culmination of chance, pure random chance. And whether I kick your face in, or support you charitably, the universe is as indifferent to that as whether a star in another galaxy blows up tonight."

48. Jeffrie Murphy, "Afterword: Constitutionalism, Moral Skepticism, and Religious Belief," in Alan S. Rosenbaum, ed., *Constitutionalism: The Philosophical Dimension* (New York: Greenwood Press, 1988), at 239, 248. See also Czeslaw Milosz, "The Religious Imagination at 2000," *New Perspectives Quarterly*, Fall 1997, at 32:

> What has been surprising in the post-Cold War period are those beautiful and deeply moving words pronounced with veneration in places like Prague and Warsaw, words which pertain to the old repertory of the rights of man and the dignity of the person.
>
> I wonder at this phenomenon because maybe underneath there is an abyss. After all, those ideas had their foundation in religion, and I am not over-optimistic as to the survival of religion in a scientific-technological civilization. Notions that seemed buried forever have suddenly been resurrected. But how long can they stay afloat if the bottom is taken out?

Cf. Richard Rorty, "Human Rights, Rationality, and Sentimentality," in Stephen Shute and Susan Hurley, eds., *On Human Rights: The Oxford Amnesty Lectures* (New York: Basic Books, 1993), at 111, 124–25: "Kant's account of the respect due to rational agents tells you that you should extend the respect you feel for people like yourself to all featherless bipeds. That is an excellent suggestion, a good formula for secularizing the Christian doctrine of the brotherhood of man. But it has never been backed up by an argument based on neutral premises, and it never will be."

49. Finnis has applied these terms to his argument about the (im)morality of homosexual sexual conduct. See John M. Finnis, "Law, Morality, and 'Sexual Orientation'," 9 Notre Dame J. L., Ethics & Public Policy 11, 16 (1995). But there is no doubt that Lee, Finnis, and George all mean their argument about the (im)morality of abortion to be, and all believe that it is, similarly "reflective, critical, publicly intelligible, and rational."

50. James K. Fitzpatrick, "A Pro-Life Loss of Nerve?" *First Things*, December 2000, at 35, 38.

51. The polling data that I'm about to present makes this clear.

52. See Margaret O'Brien Steinfels, "On Catholics and Democrats," *Dissent*, Winter 2000, at 86, 88:

> My own church can be described as virtually absolutist on this question, believing as it does that an individual human life is present and

to be protected from the moment of conception. That many Catholics do not share that exact understanding does not mean that we do not think that there are better and worse reasons in the decision to seek an abortion, and that some of those decisions will fail the test of moral seriousness. And they often fail, in the minds of many people, Catholics and others, precisely because they seem to be wholly dismissive of the value of the human fetus. How is it at a time that we are becoming more sensitive, and rightly so, to the protection of animal life and endangered species, we can treat the life that comes from our own bodies so indifferently?

53. *New Republic*, Oct. 16, 1995, at 26.
54. Carey Goldberg with Janet Elder, "Public Still Backs Abortion." "The survey, which was the first New York Times/CBS News Poll devoted to abortion since 1989, was based on telephone interviews conducted Jan. 10 to Jan. 12 [1998] with 1,101 people around the country and had a margin of sampling error of plus or minus three percentage points." Ibid. For other relevant, but less recent, polling data, see Elizabeth Adell Cook, Ted G. Jelen, and Clyde Wilcox, *Between Two Absolutes: Public Opinion and the Politics of Abortion* (Boulder, Colo.: Westview, 1992). See also Roger Rosenblatt, *Life Itself: Abortion in the American Mind* (New York: Random House, 1992).
55. Goldberg with Elder, "Public Still Backs Abortion."
56. Ibid.
57. Further relevant data: A Gallup poll conducted in 1999 revealed that a majority of American Catholics – 53 percent – believes that one can be a "good Catholic . . . without obeying the church hierarchy's teaching regarding abortion." See *National Catholic Reporter*, Oct. 29, 1999, at 12 (Table 2). (Twelve years earlier, in 1987, the figure was 39 percent. Ibid.) For American Catholics who identified themselves as parish members, the figure was 50 percent; for non-parish members, the figure was 61 percent. Ibid. at 14 (Table 7).
58. Goldberg with Elder, "Public Still Backs Abortion."
59. Ibid.
60. This statement was made by Carol Crossed, one of the liberal activists quoted in Pamela Schaeffer's article "Liberal Activists Oppose Abortion as Part of 'Seamless' Package," *National Catholic Reporter*, Jan. 21, 2000, at 3. Compare Gregg Easterbrook, "Abortion and Brain Waves: What Neither Side Wants You to Know," *New Republic*, Jan. 31, 2000, at 21, 25: "Senator Diane Feinstein of California, *in what was surely one of the all-time lows for American liberalism*, brought to the Senate floor a bill intended to affirm a women's right to terminate a healthy, viable late-term fetus" (emphasis added).
61. Kenneth D. Wald, *Religion and Politics in the United States* (Washington, D.C.: CQ Press, 1997), at 212. To say that the Bible does not provide explicit guidance, however, is not to say that it provides no guidance. "Religious arguments about abortion must thus search the [biblical] text for clues about its principles regarding life, motherhood, and the dignity of persons." Ibid. For a debate about how much, and what, guidance the Bible provides, compare Paul D. Simmons, "Biblical Authority and the Not-So Strange Silence

of Scripture about Abortion," 2 Christian Bioethics 66 (1996), to Michael J. Gorman, "Scripture, History, and Authority in a Christian View of Abortion: A Response to Paul Simmons," 2 Christian Bioethics 83 (1996). Whatever guidance the Bible provides substantially underdetermines the claim that a human zygote, a human embryo, and a human fetus at an early stage of development are all no less inviolable than a born human being. See, e.g., Mark Olson, "Back to the Bible," *Church & Society*, March/April 1981, at 54. But cf. Griffin, "*Evangelium Vitae*: Abortion," at 161–62 (reporting on John Paul II's encyclical *Evangelium Vitae*):

> In the encyclical's second lengthy section on abortion, the Pope's emphasis remains scriptural and theological. A verse from Psalm 139, "For you formed my inmost being," provides the section heading. It is from Scripture that we learn that the ban on abortion extends to every fetus from conception. The Pope concedes that "there are no direct and explicit calls to protect human life at its very beginning" in Scripture. Nonetheless the Old and New Testaments provide a normative argument against all abortion: "Denying life in these circumstances in completely foreign to the religious and cultural way of thinking of the people of God." The Pope's review of the relevant Old Testament text demands, "How can anyone think that even a single moment of this marvelous process of the unfolding of life could be separated from the wise and loving work of the Creator?" Then the New Testament "confirms the indisputable recognition of the value of life from its very beginning." A passage in chapter 3 [of the encyclical] reiterates this argument: "The texts of Sacred Scripture never address the question of deliberate abortion and so do not directly and specifically condemn it. But they show such great respect for the human being in the mother's womb that they *require as a logical consequence* that God's commandment 'you shall not kill' be extended to the unborn child as well."

62. Kaveny, "Toward a Thomistic Perspective on Abortion and the Law in Contemporary America," at 345, 374. For further, later argument by Kaveny in support of her suggestion "that stringent criminal penalties for abortion" may not be "the best way for [the law] to express its concern," see M. Cathleen Kaveny, "The Limits of Ordinary Virtue: The Limits of the Criminal Law in Implementing *Evangelium Vitae*," in Wildes and Mitchell, eds., *Choosing Life*, at 132.

63. Kaveny, "Toward a Thomistic Perspective on Abortion and the Law in Contemporary America," at 361.

64. Ibid. at 392–96.

65. Restrictions on abortion vary by state and territory in Australia. I am referring not to each and every state and territory in Australia, but to the general state of affairs in Australia.

66. See Republic of Ireland, *Green Paper on Abortion* (Dublin: Government of Ireland Stationery Office, 1999), Appendix 3 ("The Law Relating to Abortion in Selected Other Jurisdictions"); Reuters, "Switzerland Votes to Relax Strict Abortion Laws," *New York Times*, June 2, 2002.

67. See James Kingston, Anthony Whelan, and Ivana Bacik, *Abortion and the Law* (Dublin: Round Hall Sweet and Maxwell, 1997); Gerard Hogan and G. F. Whyte, *J. M. Kelly's The Irish Constitution*, 3rd ed. (Dublin: Butterworths, 1994), at 790–810.

68. According to a recent estimate, "about 9 percent of Irish pregnancies end in abortion." Sarah Lyall, "Increasingly, Irish Turn to Britain for Abortions," *New York Times*, Dec. 24, 2001. For a sketch by the Irish government of various options for legal reform, see Republic of Ireland, *Green Paper on Abortion*.

69. See Chapter 2, note 25.

70. "Human life must be respected and protected absolutely from the moment of conception. From the first moment of his existence, a human being must be recognized as having the rights of a person – among which is the inviolable right of every innocent being to life." Catechism of the Catholic Church, par. 2270. "Since the first century the Church has affirmed the moral evil of every procured abortion. This teaching has not changed and remains unchangeable. Direct abortion, that is to say, abortion willed either as an end or as a means, is gravely contrary to the moral law. . . . " Ibid., par. 2271.

71. Kevin Wm. Wildes, SJ, "The Stem Cell Report," *America*, Oct. 16, 1999, at 12, 13, 14.

72. Ibid. at 14.

73. Ibid. Wildes explains: "Such a view has the potential to support a view that sees the human person as programmed by his or her genes. This view loses the mystery of biology, freedom and morality that have been important for Roman Catholic thought. It represents a type of materialism that Christianity has consistently challenged." Ibid. For another, earlier statement in support of a developmental view – another statement by a Jesuit ethicist – see Joseph F. Donceel, SJ, "Immediate Animation and Delayed Homonization," 31 Theological Studies 76 (1970); Joseph F. Donceel, SJ, "A Liberal Catholic's View," in Robert Hall, ed., *Abortion in a Changing World* (New York: Columbia University Press, 1970), at 39. Other contemporary Catholic ethicists who support a "delayed hominization" position include Jean Porter, of Notre Dame, and Thomas Shannon, of the Worcester Polytechnic Institute. See Porter, "Is the Embryo a Person?," at 10 ("I myself find Aquinas's view [i.e., delayed hominization] to be convincing . . . "); Thomas A. Shannon, "Human Embryonic Stem Cell Therapy," 62 Theological Studies 811, 814–21 (2001).

74. These are the terms used by John Paul II is his encyclical *Evangelium Vitae*. For varied commentary on the encyclical, see Wildes and Mitchell, eds., *Choosing Life*.

75. See Chapter 5, note 7.

76. Porter, "Is the Embryo a Person?," at 8.

77. Of course, not every party to a religious controversy is a religious believer. Atheists are not religious believers, but they are parties to what is perhaps the most fundamental religious controversy of all: Does God exist?

78. Porter, "Is the Embryo a Person?," at 9.

79. Wildes, "In the Service of Life: *Evangelium Vitae* and Medical Research," at 192, 193. For Wildes's illustration of the point that "one of the central

arguments of the letter is rooted in the Christian experience of God and is articulated in very particular, theological categories," see ibid. at 191. See also the passage from Leslie Griffin's essay quoted in note 61.

80. Robert Audi, *Religious Commitment and Secular Reason* (Cambridge: Cambridge University Press, 2000), at 197. Audi adds: "It may also be an example of an issue for which there simply is no determinate answer in terms of purely rational considerations (roughly, those accessible to any rational person)." Ibid.

81. Wildes, "In the Service of Life: *Evangelium Vitae* and Medical Research," at 192.

82. See note 62 and accompanying text. Given the essentially religious/theological character of the Pope's argument against abortion in *Evangelium Vitae* (see note 61).

> *Evangelium Vitae* imposes on [Catholic legislators a] difficult dilemma of conscience. *Evangelium Vitae* ... asks [them] to enact a theological teaching into law.... [It asks them] to impose the Church's teaching on non-Catholics. For pragmatic reasons, Catholics may vote for less restrictive abortion laws when their absolute ban on abortion cannot be passed. Catholics may vote only to restrict abortion rights or to ban abortions altogether. Their goal must be for Catholicism's teaching on abortion to become law for all citizens of the United States, so that no [immoral] abortion is permitted. Moral error has no rights. (Griffin, "*Evangelium vitae*: Abortion," at 171).

83. Joan Callahan, "The Fetus and Fundamental Rights," at 229.

CONCLUSION

1. Richard Pérez-Peña, "Lieberman Seeks Greater Role for Religion in Public Life," *New York Times*, Aug. 28, 2000, at A1.
2. Ibid.
3. Richard Rorty, "Religion as Conversation-stopper," in Richard Rorty, *Philosophy and Social Hope* (New York: Penguin, 1999), at 168, 169.
4. "John Paul II on the American Experiment," *First Things*, April 1998, at 36–37 (quoting John Paul's speech, which was delivered in Rome on Dec. 17, 1997).
5. I have heard it said that whereas before the Civil War the phrase "the United States of America" was spoken with the emphasis on "States," since the Civil War the phrase has been spoken with the emphasis on "United."
6. This statement by Neibuhr is drawn from the passage that is the epigraph to Chapter 6.
7. For a history of the Pledge of Allegiance, which makes its first appearance in 1892, see John W. Baer, *The Pledge of Allegiance: A Centennial History, 1892–1992* (Annapolis, Md.: J. W. Baer, 1992).
8. For the interesting history of this development, which involves both the Knights of Columbus (a Roman Catholic organization) and post–World War II anticommunism, see ibid. at 62–63. "These religious sentiments were

common in this period. In 1954 Congress requested that all U.S. coins and paper currency bear the slogan, 'In God We Trust.' On July 11, 1955, President
Eisenhower made this slogan mandatory on all currency. In 1956 the national
motto was changed from 'E Pluribus Unum' to 'In God We Trust.'" Ibid. at
63.

9. See note 8.

10. To open a legislative session with a prayer is one thing; to hire a chaplain to
open it with a prayer is another thing altogether. The Supreme Court's ruling
in *Marsh v. Chambers*, 463 U.S. 783 (1983), upholding the constitutionality of
the chaplaincy at issue there, is extremely problematic: Public funds were
used to pay the chaplain. See ibid. at 784–85: "The Nebraska Legislature
begins each of its sessions with a prayer offered by a chaplain who is chosen
biennially by the Executive Board of the Legislative Council and paid out of
public funds. Robert E, Palmer, a Presbyterian minister, has served as chaplain
since 1965 at a salary of $319.75 per month for each month the legislature
is in session." I have criticized the Court's ruling elsewhere. See Michael J.
Perry, "Freedom of Religion in the United States: *Fin de Siècle* Sketches," 75
Indiana L. J. 295, 317 n. 71 (2000).

11. See *Marsh v. Chambers*, 463 U.S. 783, 786 (1983): "In the very courtrooms in
which the United States District Judge and later three Circuit Judges heard
and decided this case, the proceedings opened with an announcement that
concluded, 'God save the United States and this Honorable Court.' The same
invocation occurs at all sessions of this Court."

12. See Perry, "Freedom of Religion in the United States," at 308ff.

13. Consider, for example, the overwhelmingly negative response to the court's
decision in *Newdow v. U.S. Congress*, 292 F. 3d 597 (9th Cir. 2002). See Evelyn
Nieves, "Judges Ban Pledge of Allegiance from Schools, Citing 'Under God',"
New York Times, June 27, 2002; Howard Fineman, "One Nation, Under . . .
Who?," *Newsweek*, July 8, 2002, at 20.

14. Justice William Brennan once suggested that routine public recital of the
Pledge of Allegiance no longer retained "any true religious significance."
In his dissenting opinion in *Marsh v. Chambers*, Justice Brennan, joined by
Justice Thurgood Marshall, wrote: "I frankly do not know what should be
the proper disposition of features of our public life such as 'God save the
United States and this Honorable Court,' 'In God We Trust,' 'One Nation,
Under God,' and the like. I might well adhere to the view . . . that such
mottos are consistent with the Establishment Clause . . . because they have lost
any true religious significance." 463 U.S. 783, 818 (1983). Following Justice
Brennan's lead, an exclusionist might be tempted to reply that the reason that
the practices mentioned in the paragraph accompanying this note are not
unconstitutional is that they are not *really* religious practices; they are, instead,
merely ceremonial practices devoid of serious, authentic religious content.
There are, no doubt, some citizens, even many, for whom the practices are
merely ceremonial and religiously empty, but there is no warrant – I have
seen none, I am aware of none – for believing that for *most* citizens of the
United States the practices are religiously empty.

15. Jeffery L. Sheler, "Faith in America," *U.S. News*, May 6, 2002, at 40, 42.
16. Bob Abernethy, "Special Report: Exploring Religious America," *Religion & Ethics Newsweekly*, Apr. 26, 2002 ⟨www.pbs.org/wnet/religionandethics/week534/cover.html⟩.
17. Sheler, "Faith in America," at 42.
18. Michael Hout and Claude S. Fischer, "Why More Americans Have No Religious Preference: Politics and Generations," 67 American Sociological Rev. 165 (2002).
19. Ibid. at 188. Hout and Fischer argue that the increase in those claiming no religious preference from 7 percent to 14 percent "was *not* connected to a loss of religious piety, and that it *was* connected to politics. In the 1990s many people who had weak attachments to religion and either moderate or liberal political views found themselves at odds with the conservative political agenda of the Christian Right and reacted by renouncing their weak attachment to organized religion." Ibid. at 165–66.
20. For a discussion of this point, see Christopher J. Eberle, *Religious Conviction in Liberal Politics* (New York: Cambridge University Press, 2002), at 23–47.
21. This is the claim of Diana Eck, a professor of comparative religion at Harvard Divinity School. See Diana Eck, *A New Religious America: How a "Christian Country" Has Become the World's Most Religiously Diverse Nation* (San Francisco: HarperSanFranciso, 2001).
22. Sheler, "Faith in America," at 42. Christians remain the overwhelming majority in America (80 percent); only about 6.5 percent of the population identifies itself as belonging to a non-Christian religion. Ibid.
23. See Michael J. Perry, *Love and Power: The Role of Religion and Morality in American Politics* (New York: Oxford University Press, 1991).
24. Joseph Cardinal Bernardin, "The Consistent Ethic of Life After *Webster*," 19 Origins 741, 748 (1990) (emphasis added). See David Lochhead, *The Dialogical Imperative: A Christian Reflection on Interfaith Encounter* (Maryknoll, N.Y.: Orbis Books, 1988), at 93.

> All that I [as a Christian] need to believe for genuine dialogue [with, for example, a Buddhist] to begin, is that Buddhists are not out of touch with reality. Once the fundamental sanity of Buddhists is granted, it follows that there is some point to dialogue, to understanding how the world looks through Buddhist eyes.... [T]he Buddhist critique of theism will inevitably cause me to examine and reexamine my own theistic assumptions. As a result of coming to understand reality as seen by Buddhists, my own doctrine of God will be transformed.

25. There are different ways of specifying the ideal of ecumenical politics. I understand Chris Eberle's "ideal of conscientious engagement" to be one way – a very attractive way, in my judgment – of specifying the ideal. See Eberle, *Religious Conviction in Liberal Politics*, at 104–08.
26. Max Horkheimer and Theodor Adorno, quoted in Hans Küng, *Does God Exist?* (Garden City, N.Y.: Doubleday, 1978), at 490.
27. See Sheler, "Faith in America," See also Alan Wolfe, "Civil Religion Revisited: Quiet Faith in Middle Class America," in Nancy L. Rosenblum, ed., *Obligations*

of Citizenship and Demands of Faith: Religious Accommodation in Pluralist Democracies (Princeton, N. J.: Princeton University Press, 2000), at 32.

28. John Courtney Murray, *We Hold These Truths* (Kansas City, Mo.: Sheed and Ward, 1960), at 23–24.
29. For discussion of the point, see Eberle, *Religious Conviction in Liberal Politics,* at 152–86.

Index